RECONCILIATION IN PRACTICE

A Cross-Cultural Perspective

EDITED BY RANJAN DATTA

FERNWOOD PUBLISHING
HALIFAX & WINNIPEG

Editing: Kaitlin Littlechild
Cover design: Jess Koroscil
Printed and bound in Canada

Published by Fernwood Publishing
32 Oceanvista Lane, Black Point, Nova Scotia, B0J 1B0
and 748 Broadway Avenue, Winnipeg, Manitoba, R3G 0X3
www.fernwoodpublishing.ca

Fernwood Publishing Company Limited gratefully acknowledges the financial
support of the Government of Canada, the Canada Council for the Arts, the
Manitoba Department of Culture, Heritage and Tourism under the Manitoba
Publishers Marketing Assistance Program and the Province of Manitoba,
through the Book Publishing Tax Credit, for our publishing program. We are
pleased to work in partnership with the Province of Nova Scotia to develop
and promote our creative industries for the benefit of all Nova Scotians.

Library and Archives Canada Cataloguing in Publication

Title: Reconciliation in practice: a cross-cultural perspective / Ranjan Datta (editor)
Names: Datta, Ranjan, 1977- editor.
Description: Includes bibliographical references and index.
Identifiers: Canadiana (print) 20190148985 | Canadiana (ebook)
20190149078 ISBN 9781773631707 (softcover) | ISBN
9781773631714 (EPUB) | ISBN 9781773631721 (Kindle)
Subjects: LCSH: Canada—Race relations. | LCSH: Canada—Ethnic
relations. | LCSH: Reconciliation. | LCSH: Immigrants—Canada. | LCSH:
Indigenous peoples—Canada. | LCSH: Colonists—Canada. | LCSH: Social
justice—Canada. | LCSH: Colonization—Social aspects—Canada. | LCSH:
Decolonization—Social aspects—Canada. | CSH: Native peoples—Canada.
Classification: LCC FC104 .R43 2019 | DDC 305.800971—dc23

CONTENTS

ACKNOWLEDGEMENTS

First and foremost I want to thank Drs. Alex Wilson, Linda Smith, Marie Battise, Manulani Meyer, Shawn Wilson, and Verna St. Denis for their continuous motivation, encouragement, and enlightenment for unlearning and relearning who I am and who I need to be. I am also grateful to the Indigenous Peoples in Canada, particularly Indigenous Elders, Knowledge Keepers, leaders, and youth who so warmly welcomed my family to their land and community and provided opportunities to learn the meanings of land and sustainability stories. I also thank my friends (too many to list here but you know who you are!) for providing the support and friendship that I needed. I am sincerely grateful to Mel Sysing with whom I initially started the conversation for this project. Finally, I owe a lot to Candida Hadley (Acquisitions and Development Editor, Fernwood Publishing) for being supportive throughout her time here and for helping me with the editing of this book.

ABOUT CONTRIBUTORS

Ali Abukar is a refugee and new immigrant in Canada. He has a bachelor of arts (BA) and a master of social work. He is currently the executive director of Saskatoon Open Door Society, an organization that provides settlement and integration services to newcomers to Canada. Previously, he worked with immigrants and refugees in Egypt and Uganda. Ali has more than ten years of experience in the sector of settlement and integration of immigrants and refugees. He is a trained social worker, community builder, and advocate for immigrant and refugee rights. Ali considers himself a global citizen and wants to see the impact of his work across the globe.

Chris Scribe is Nakoda/Cree from the Kinosao Sipi Cree Nation and Nakota Oyate Assiniboine Nation. Since obtaining his bachelor of education degree from the Indian Teacher Education Program (ITEP) in 2005, Chris has taught every grade in the K–12 system. Upon completing his master of education (MEd) in educational administration, Chris went on to become a principal and administrator for the Mosquito First Nation School. In 2014, Chris began work at the University of Saskatchewan as the director of the ITEP. Chris is also in the process of completing his PhD in educational administration at the University of Saskatchewan. Throughout his professional and academic career, Chris has always been an advocate for Indigenous knowledge and values above all else.

Colleen J. Charles is Woodland Cree from the Lac La Ronge Indian Band in northern Saskatchewan. She is a single mother of three children and has a granddaughter. She is a certified anti-racism education facilitator. Colleen has her MEd from the University of Saskatchewan. She has a BA and an Aboriginal Human Justice diploma from the First Nations University of Canada. Also, she has a recreation and leisure management diploma from Saskatchewan Polytechnic. She credits her mother for her strong qualities. Colleen has been presenting her art workshop, Colonialism on Canvas, for the past two years.

Farzana Ali is a new immigrant and international doctoral researcher in Canada. Being a pharmacist by training, her goal is to become a community-engaged scholar by facilitating and supporting the conversion of existing and new health research into measurable improvements for patients of diverse backgrounds. Her research interests include the following: patient-centred care, Indigenous health and OCAP principles (ownership, control, access, and possession), immigrant and refugee health, social determinants of health, and community-based participatory research. She is currently coordinating community-based HIV research to reduce barriers and build capacity by harnessing rich experiences, perspectives, and recommendations from both Indigenous and non-Indigenous Peoples living with HIV.

Irja Seurujärvi-Kari has a PhD in Sámi and Finno-Ugric studies. She is a researcher of Indigenous Studies and a retired Sámi lecturer of Sámi studies at the University of Helsinki. Her dissertation *Ale jaskkot eatnigiella* (Meaning of Indigenous movement and language to Sámi identity), which deals with the Indigenous movement and the role of language in it, was published in 2012. She has co-edited several anthologies of the Sámi people and their culture. *The Saami: A Cultural Encyclopedia* was awarded the State Prize Award by the Ministry of Education in 2005. In addition to her academic work, she has been the chairman and a board member of the Sámi Parliament, the Sámi Council, and the World Council of Indigenous Peoples, as well as several other Indigenous organizations since the 1980s.

Janet McVittie is a faculty member in the Department of Educational Foundations, College of Education, University of Saskatchewan. Her current research areas are place- and land-based learning and the role of more natural areas for promoting healthy, holistic human growth and learning. This involves recognizing differences in the concepts of land ownership and the inherent value of land, as well as working toward greater social equity among people. She has been fortunate to work with Indigenous colleagues, which means learning again and again of the privileges she carries due to the colour of her skin.

Jebunnessa Chapola is a Bangladeshi–Canadian feminist, researcher, singer, cultural performer, community radio host, social justice activist, and community volunteer. Currently, she is a PhD candidate in the Department of

Women's and Gender Studies at the University of Saskatchewan. She attended postsecondary institutions in Bangladesh, Sweden, and Norway.

Khodi Dill is a Bahamian-Canadian spoken word artist, emcee, and educator who lives and works in Saskatoon, Saskatchewan. Combining literary and hip hop elements in his writing, he's best known for his riveting stage performances and biting social justice themes. Khodi received his master's degree in the area of anti-oppressive education from the University of Saskatchewan in 2013. His award-winning thesis, titled "'The Safest Place': Anti-Oppression in Spoken Word Poetry" can be read online. His debut hip hop mixtape, *New Technology*, is available on iTunes, and much of his spoken word poetry can be seen on YouTube. Khodi is married to Saskatoon artist and educator Carly Brown.

Pirjo Kristiina Virtanen is an assistant professor of Indigenous Studies at the University of Helsinki. She has a PhD in Latin American Studies and her research interests include human-environment collectives and epistemological plurality, as well as decolonizing research methods. Recently, she has also addressed the questions of evidence in state politics. Since 2003, she has collaborated with Indigenous groups in the Purus River region, Brazilian Amazonia. She has written about nonhuman agencies' central role in the construction of heritage in Amazonian Indigenous communities. Her publications include *Creating Dialogues: Indigenous Perceptions and Forms of Leadership in Amazonia* and *Indigenous Youth in Brazilian Amazonia*; articles on mobility, shamanism, Indigenous politics, and ethnohistory; as well as Indigenous ontologies and epistemologies. In addition to her research interests, she has co-authored various Indigenous school materials.

Ranjan Datta is a Banting Postdoctoral Fellow in the Johnson Shoyama Graduate School of Public Policy at the University of Regina. Dr. Datta's research interests include advocating for Indigenous environmental sustainability, decolonization, Indigenous reconciliation, community-based research, and cross-cultural community empowerment. As an Indigenous scholar, he has developed a strong understanding of relational research frameworks from his fifteen years of working with various Indigenous and cross-cultural communities in Canada, the United States, Norway, India, and Bangladesh. He has a total of twenty-six peer-reviewed publications on Indigenous and minority justice issues, including his recent book *Land-Water Management and Sustainability in Bangladesh: Indigenous Practices in the Chittagong Hill Tracts.*

Valerie Onyinyechi Umaefulam is a PhD candidate at the Department of Community Health and Epidemiology at the University of Saskatchewan. She is an optometrist and a public health professional. Valerie's areas of interest are community eye health and health technology, with emphasis on mobile, electronic, and Telehealth for health promotion, education, and health care. Valerie is interested in utilizing health education to empower individuals and communities to make healthy choices. In addition, Valerie is keen on community engagement and mobilization; working with remote and hard-to-reach communities, people with special needs, and women in various communities.

PART ONE

UNDERSTANDING RECONCILIATION

Chapter One

POSSIBILITIES AND CHALLENGES IN RECONCILIATION

RANJAN DATTA

This edited collection, *Reconciliation in Practice: A Cross-Cultural Perspective*, is a response to the Truth and Reconciliation Commission (TRC) of Canada's assertion that meaningful engagement between Indigenous Peoples and non-Indigenous Canadians will be key in advancing reconciliation. The contributions to this book showcase various cross-cultural, community-oriented activities that represent serious attempts to understand and take responsibility for the meaningful implications of reconciliation. Through these essays, personal reflections, and poems we begin to identify areas of opportunity, as well as current obstacles, to progress toward reconciliation.

The book initiates a transdisciplinary discussion that challenges not only traditional science and social science mindsets but enlarges the concept of reconciliation to include building respectful relationships with Indigenous Peoples, respecting Indigenous treaties, taking action to decolonize our ways of knowing and acting, understanding the role of colonized education processes, protecting our land and environment, creating food security, ensuring nutritious food, creating an intercultural space for social interactions, and developing transnational empowerment.

Inspired by the work of Indigenous scholars Drs. Marie Battiste (2017, 2013, 2000), Eve Tuck and Wayne Yang (2012), Shawn Wilson (2011, 2008), Verna St Denis (2007), and Margaret Kovach (2010) about decolonizing our ways of knowing, thinking, and acting, this book encourages a fundamental shift to thinking of reconciliation as a continuous process that belongs to everyone. As such, it has huge implications and possibilities for reimagining our relationships with both Indigenous and non-Indigenous Peoples. This book hopes to support all of us (i.e., Indigenous, settlers, old immigrants, new immigrants, and refugees) as we envision how Indigenous histories, perspectives, worldviews, and approaches to learning can thoughtfully and respectfully be made part of the work we do in our everyday practice.

Approaching the topic of reconciliation from an interdisciplinary perspective, the contributors employ a variety of participatory research engagement methods. As a result, the scholarship that comes out of this research varies in form and content and speaks to a wide and diverse audience. Bringing together community engagement, activism, research, and scholarship to advocate for socio-environmental justice, the book provides the learning support for researchers, teachers, students, and community members who want to develop their capacity to engage with Indigenous communities based on intercultural understanding, empathy, and respect.

Reconciliation in Practice invites non-Indigenous Canadians, particularly new immigrants and refugees, to learn about Indigenous history, culture, values, and goals, to join in solidarity with Indigenous communities, and to engage in the process of determining what reconciliation in practice means to them and to their collective communities. The book is an invitation for all of us to work together as Indigenists, to build relational networks for the important task of intercultural bridging, to move beyond cultural awareness and inclusion, and to challenge racist ideology as we rethink and re-imagine our relationships with one another in a sharing place — a motherland (Battiste 2013; Wilson 2013). Our target is to build bridges between Indigenous Peoples, settlers, refugees, and new immigrants that can lead us to rethink and redo the work that we do in classrooms, organizations, communities, and in our everyday lives in ways that are thoughtful, respectful, and responsible.

This book is designed to engage us in a discussion on the responsibilities between Indigenous and non-Indigenous Peoples as part of the process of developing our personal and collective understandings and practices. In the process of reflecting on our responsibilities, we demonstrate how Indigenous guidance on reconciliation can assist us in further contextualizing our roles and responsibilities. From a responsibility perspective, we realize that reconciliation is not an abstract entity that exists in a vacuum waiting for the enlightened among us to bring them into practice. Rather, the meanings of reconciliation are varied, dynamic, and forever transforming.

Here, we offer a critical gaze that brings together community engagement, activism, research, and scholarship to advocate for socio-environmental justice and trans-systematic reconciliation of cross-cultural knowledge. Contributors are from various disciplines, including science, social science, arts, and interdisciplinary. We used our disciplinary, interdisciplinary, and transdisciplinary expert eyes in a type of social entrepreneurship model— working on sustainable, critical, anti-racist learning, responsible learning, and community building.

While significant emphasis has been placed on the process of reconciliation, there have been misunderstandings, a lack of trust and respect, and negligence from and within both settler and new Canadian (i.e., immigrant and refugee) communities regarding its meaningful interpretation (Clark, de Costa, and Maddison 2017; Egan 2011; Morgan 2018). This book addresses several unanswered questions in current practices of reconciliation, including: *Is reconciliation an end goal to be achieved or is it a process? Is it a collective or individual responsibility? Why am I responsible for the meaningful implementation of reconciliation? How am I benefiting from Indigenous perspectives on reconciliation?* To begin to address these questions, we must first understand what reconciliation is and the challenges and possibilities it holds. What does reconciliation mean? How do we follow the Truth and Reconciliation Commission's (TRC) calls to action and work together to change our practice?

WHAT DOES RECONCILIATION MEAN?

Reconciliation is a complex process with a variety of definitions (Battiste 2013; Morgan 2018; Wilson 2018). Reconciliation involves remembering and acknowledging the wrongs that have been done, which include residential schools, the reserve system, cultural genocide, and systemic racism in Canada (McCrossan and Ladner 2016). It is important that all Canadians are educated about these wrongs, including the false narrative of Canadian history that fails to mention Indigenous Peoples (McCrossan and Ladner 2016). Through reconciliation, the colonial structures that have affected Indigenous Peoples for centuries must be removed and traditional ways of life must be restored.

Reconciliation takes on different meanings for different individuals and groups (Palmater 2014). It is a complex process with little agreement on how to define it or even go about defining it. There is no single meaning, program, or policy that can address reconciliation, and much remains to be done to achieve a social awareness of the historical and contemporary contexts that have contributed to the current socioeconomic reality of Indigenous Peoples. Any narrow, static definition of reconciliation is problematic. For instance, according to the Cambridge Dictionary, the word reconciliation defines a situation in which two people or groups of people become friendly again after they have argued. This narrow definition has been misinterpreted and applied incorrectly in many communities (James 2012; Wildcat, McDonald, Irbacher-Fox, and Coulthard 2014; Wilson 2018), causing misunderstanding and problems for Indigenous lives, culture, and land. It focuses on the past and on individual apologies and interpersonal forgiveness rather than the reshaping of collective relationships or redress for broader structural and systemic harms (James 2012). A narrow definition also implies that Indigenous cultures are fixed and unchanging (Morgan 2018). To avoid the problems connected with a narrow interpretation of reconciliation, it is important to understand ongoing processes prior to addressing the actual meaning of reconciliation.

Many Canadians, particularly members of immigrant and refugee communities, do not have adequate opportunities to learn the meaning of reconciliation (Abu-Laban 2018, 2014; Clark, de Costa, and Maddison 2017; Egan 2011; Morgan 2018; Simpson 2014), which may lead to numerous misconceptions about Indigenous Peoples and Indigenous expectations of reconciliation (Abu-Laban 2018, 2014; Clark, de Costa, and Maddison 2017; Tully 2000). Yasmeen Abu-Laban, an immigrant scholar in Canada (2018, 2014), argues that, based on his eight-year study with various new and old immigrant communities in Canada, the lack of knowledge/education on Indigenous communities can create many misconceptions not only of Indigenous Peoples but also of the process of reconciliation itself. In addition, other Indigenous and non-Indigenous studies suggest that we need to not only understand the complexity of reconciliation from various perspectives, but we must also take responsibility for practising it in our everyday lives (Clark, de Costa, and Maddison 2017; Egan 2011). For many Indigenous communities in Canada and other parts of the world, reconciliation is not a static process. Its meaning is complex, relational, and deeply rooted in the Indigenous history of colonization, land rights, self-governance, cultural heritage, socio-ecological justice, and environmental well-being (Barkaskas and Buhler 2017; Morgan 2018). Indigenous scholars, Elders, and Knowledge Keepers also suggest that reconciliation is primarily a settler responsibility and decolonization must be led by Indigenous Peoples (CBC 2018, 2017, 2016). In order to understand the varied and complex dynamics of reconciliation, I discuss the related possibilities and challenges through the frames of decolonization, land-based education, settler colonialism/colonial legacy, relational accountabilities, and Indigenous worldview.

Decolonization

Decolonization is a central aspect of reconciliation. It is another ambiguous concept, but one that essentially demands the "repatriation of Indigenous land and life" (Tuck and Yang 2012: 1). Decolonization is not a metaphor, Eve Tuck and Ken Yang (2012) remind us; in its simplest form, it is something that aims to unsettle and dismantle settler colonialism. Many Indigenous scholars see reconciliation as a decolonial process (Battiste 2013). Reconciliation as decolonization "exposes places where dominant structures must be re-made to embrace other than dominant ways of knowing and doing" (Sasakamoose and Pete 2015: 4). Indigenous scholars Marie Battiste (2013) and Tuck and Yang (2012) explicitly argue that there can be no reconciliation without decolonization as the two processes are interconnected. Anishinaabe comedian and writer Ryan McMahon (2016: 10) says, "I would argue that before reconciliation, we really need to look at decolonization." He explains how we can begin to practise decolonization: "Decolonization starts with land. It starts with the question of land. Do Indigenous people have the ability to live freely on and with relationship to the land, as we did prior to confederation? And the answer right now is no" (2016: 12). Reconciliation as a decolonial process supports a resurgence in Indigenous culture, politics, knowledge, and on-the-land skills. The clear articulation of reconciliation as a decolonial process is an important step in realizing our responsibility. Decolonization can only be achieved by removing the effects of colonialism and encouraging self-determination for Indigenous Peoples. Understanding reconciliation in this context means envisioning a place for everyone to build this vital future, it is just one way forward in a larger struggle for justice, coexistence, and a better world for everyone.

Indigenous scholars define decolonization as an ongoing process of deconstructing colonial ideologies of the superiority and privilege of Western thought and approaches (Battiste 2017; Simpson 2014; Tuck and Yang 2012; Wilson 2017). They suggest that decolonization has dual meanings. On the one hand, decolonization involves dismantling structures that perpetuate the status quo, problematizing dominant discourses, and addressing unbalanced power dynamics. On the other hand, decolonization involves valuing and revitalizing Indigenous knowledge and approaches and weeding out settler biases or assumptions that have impacted Indigenous ways of being. Linda Smith (1999: 39) notes that "decolonization is about centering our concerns and worldviews and then coming to know and understand theory from our own perspectives and for our own purposes." Smith reveals that Indigenous perspectives and worldviews are paramount in a decolonization project. Similarly, Indigenous scholar Marie Battiste (2013, 2008, 2000) suggests that decolonization necessitates shifting our frames of reference with regard to the knowledge we hold; examining how we have arrived at such knowledge; and considering what we need to do to change misconceptions, prejudice, and assumptions about Indigenous Peoples.

Decolonization as a means to reconciliation is important for everyone, including newcomers in Canada (Battiste 2017). Battiste discussed the meaning of reconciliation from the perspective of decolonization on a CFCR 90.5 (Saskatchewan) radio program with me and radio host Jebunnessa Chapola in 2017. According to Battiste, decolonization has two pillars. First, we (immigrants, refugees, and settlers) need to understand that "our system of education is deeply colonial," and decolonization is a means to "help people to understand where colonialism came from ... and unpack these histories from our own perspectives." She suggests that reconciliation "education needs to not just be a colonial experience ... but it has to be a way to help people to understand their situation where they are and how they are in an inequitable situation." Second, decolonization in reconciliation is "recovery from colonial impact, restoration of Indigenous Peoples' identities, Indigenous Peoples' languages, Indigenous Peoples' experiences, and all things that we [Indigenous Peoples] need for restoring us in this country [Canada] which builds in treaties that have been signed, ignored, marginalized for many, many years in Canada."

Battiste explained that decolonization education can empower all of us. For her, reconciliation is a lifelong unlearning and relearning process. It can inspire us to ask questions: "How are we related to the colonization, oppressions? Who are the people who belong to the colonial culture? Who are the people benefiting from the oppressive systems? Who is privileged by oppressing others?" (n.p.). However, Battiste and Henderson (2000) warn that there is not just one Indigenous way of knowing or understanding. Thus, as we work to decolonize, we must be sensitized to the histories, cultures, knowledge, ways of knowing, and governance systems of various Indigenous Peoples and cultures. Discovering the traditions of different Indigenous groups can be difficult because, throughout our long history of colonization, Indigenous Peoples were not allowed to practise their traditions and as a result, many of those traditions are now lost. Therefore, Indigenous scholars (see for example Battiste 2013; Simpson 2014; Tuck and Yang 2012; Wilson 2017) argue that decolonization is an important component of reconciliation because it challenges the dominance of Western thought and brings Indigenous thought to the forefront.

Taiaiake Alfred, Elder, scholar, and writer from Kahnawá:ke in the Mohawk Nation, agrees that reconciliation is not possible without decolonization:

> When we talk about colonization, we tend to think of brutally stolen land, racism, broken treaties, and residential schools. Those are things that happened. Those well-known things shaped the relationship between Indigenous people and the settler society on this continent. But what was the deeper and lasting impact of those things on nations of Indigenous people? Alienation, separation, disconnection. To decolonize, we need to reclaim the sacred spaces of our traditional territories. Rename those spaces to sever the emotional and intellectual ties of colonially imposed names and restore the full histories and ancient significances embedded in Indigenous languages. Resurgence builds on the idea of resistance and deepens the understanding of decolonization. It is a way of thinking and being and practicing politics that roots resistance in the spirit, knowledge, and laws of our ancestors. It links pushing back against oppression to cultural restoration and healing practices at the individual, social, and national levels. (Alfred 2018: 8)

Elder Alfred emphasizes that through decolonization non-Indigenous people can play a role in Indigenous resurgence, and that, in fact, "decolonization starts inside of you" (12). He argues that we all need decolonization, Indigenous and settler alike. Decolonization is self-questioning and embraces the commitment to listen to the voices of Indigenous ancestors channelled through the young people of Indigenous nations, learn from Indigenous culture how to walk differently and love the land as best we can.

Many Indigenous scholars see the lack of decolonization as one of the most significant challenges to understanding and practising reconciliation (Battiste 2013; Smith 2008). Reconciliation as decolonization "exposes places where dominant structures must be re-made to embrace other than dominant ways of knowing and doing" (Sasakamoose and Pete 2015: 4). There is, for example, a consensus that globally, and particularly in Canada, universities have not decolonized; the curriculum is predominantly Eurocentric, "rooted in colonial, apartheid and Western worldviews and epistemological traditions" and, therefore, "continues to reinforce white and Western dominance and privilege" (Heleta 2016: 1). Linda Tuhaiwai Smith (2008) also argues that universities are places of colonialism, a legacy that has not completely ended. Decolonizing education systems involves rethinking the way schooling is delivered, including the curriculum, methodologies, and relationships with communities (TD Economics 2012), Many Elders and Knowledge Keepers suggest that decolonizing the education system has the potential to re-engage Indigenous and non-Indigenous youth in learning and empower them to achieve greater success (Morgan 2018; Simpson 2014).

Focusing on decolonization, a Cree Elder explains that reconciliation means not only respectful relationships but also doing the work together to make sure that Indigenous Peoples can fully exercise and enjoy their rights (Gray 2016). Therefore, according to Indigenous Elders and Knowledge Keepers, decolonization means restoring culture and presence on the land — revitalizing Indigenous ways of being on the land — and using the strength that comes from that to confront the forces that seek to oppress and harm Indigenous Peoples.

Reconciliation as a lifelong decolonial process has an impact on Indigenous youth, and Indigenous youth activists have suggested that they want to focus on decolonization prior to discussing the process of reconciliation. Jeremy Garcia and Valerie Shirley (2012) suggest that for youth, decolonization offers ways to address issues specific to their needs and aspirations within education settings. Indigenous youth have shared in-depth accounts of the holistic benefits that can result from participation in the decolonization process. For instance, a Dene youth explains, "In decolonization, we have our own nations. We have our own political practices. We have rights to land, to establish our own economies, our own ways of life" (Saskatoon Star Phoenix 2018). First Nations youth activist and blogger Andrea Landry (2018: n.p.), from Treaty Six Territory in Poundmaker Cree Nation, says, "The only reconciliation that exists for us, as Indigenous nations, is the reconciliation we need to find within ourselves and our communities, for agreeing and complying to this madness for so long." She continues, "I want our children to learn about our own liberation, rather than the colonizer's reconciliation ... And I want our children to know that Indigenous liberation will always overthrow colonial reconciliation." The decolonization of education is a powerful tool for both Indigenous and non-Indigenous youths, wherein processes of decolonizing and historical consciousness are deeply linked (Donald 2012). It is a learning opportunity in service to both historical truth-telling and reconciliation. For youth, decolonization education encourages and facilitates learning experiences that explore difficult histories and contemporary challenges and mobilizes Indigenous and non-Indigenous youth to stand alongside each other in understanding, respect, solidarity, and resilience (Donald 2012; McGregor 2018).

Land-Based Education

Aimed at reclaiming Indigenous Land Rights, land-based education is another important aspect of meaningful reconciliation (Simpson 2014; Wilson 2018). For instance, John George Hansen and Rose Antsanen (2017: 16) observe that "Indigenous lives and communities can be improved by connecting to traditional teachings, practices and spiritual ceremonies." Smith (1999: 142) reminds us that Indigenous education involves a decolonizing movement that seeks to restore the cultural ideas and practices from a history of colonial oppression, and that "cultural survival, self-determination, healing, restoration and social justice are engaging Indigenous researchers and Indigenous communities in a diverse array of projects." Thus, Indigenous Land-based education is a fundamental part of reconciliation because it promotes an Indigenous model of education in a culturally appropriate way; it is more than a set of beliefs, it has developed into a finely tuned model of Indigenous ways of knowing (Ermine 1995; Hansen and Antsanen 2017). Michael Chandler and Christopher Lalonde (1998: 191) have found that restoring the teachings within Indigenous education has produced some incredible results in Indigenous communities and that those that "have taken active steps to preserve and rehabilitate their own cultures are shown to be those in which youth suicide rates are dramatically lower."

Land-based education plays an active role in Indigenous ways of knowing and being and provides students with an explicit critique of how colonial processes impacted the reciprocal relationship Indigenous Peoples traditionally had with the land (Datta 2018). Students are given the tools to imagine an alternative environmental paradigm informed by Indigenous ways of knowing that subverts anthropocentric ways of relating to the Earth (Bang et al. 2014; Paperson 2014; Tuck, McKenzie, and McCoy 2014).

Many Indigenous Elders and Knowledge Keepers agree that land-based education is one of the most important parts of reconciliation (Datta 2018). For instance, at a traditional Knowledge Keepers' forum in Winnipeg in 2014, Mary Deleary, an Anishinaabe Elder, expressed very clearly that the work of reconciliation must continue in ways that honour Indigenous ancestors, respect the land, and rebalance relationships. Integrating Indigenous ways of knowing and being into the content and process of land rights and land-based education can create a sense of belonging for our students — Indigenous, immigrants, new immigrants, refugees, and settlers — thereby improving educational engagement and attainment. Focusing on Indigenous Land Rights also has the potential to shift the human relationship with the natural world, fostering an environmental paradigm protective of land-based practices (Anuik, Battiste, and George 2010; Battiste 2013; Simpson 2014).

Land-based education understands that Indigenous Land Rights and the process of reconciliation are interconnected and cannot be separated (Datta 2018). Traditional Powwow dancer and artist Shady Hafez challenges the Western process of reconciliation:

> The project of reconciliation, as it is currently framed, is a project I have little faith in. The reasoning is simple: The root of historical and current conflicts between Indigenous nations and the Canadian state is land, more specifically the occupation of Indigenous lands and the dispossession of Indigenous bodies from our lands. Therefore, if reconciliation is a goal that the Canadian state and the Canadian populace are fully committed to achieving, then why are we not resolving the primary issue of contention between our nations — that being land title and the ability of Indigenous nations to have autonomous control over our lands and affairs? If Canada is serious about reconciliation and implementing a nation-to-nation relationship with indigenous peoples, the process must begin by returning unused Crown lands to their respective Indigenous nations or providing restitution for lands that cannot be returned. Following which Canada should abolish the Indian Act and allow for full Indigenous autonomy over our lands. Canadians need to understand that part of reconciliation is appreciating the reality that we may not want to be part of the Canadian state. (Postmedia 2017: n.p.)

Conflicts about land and control over natural resources have often prompted extensive efforts to resolve differences through negotiation and dialogue. In instances where these processes have failed to result in a settlement, Indigenous communities have tried to protect their land through litigation or direct action, for example, the Idle No More movement, protests, occupations, and blockades. Many Indigenous scholars, community Elders, and Knowledge Keepers suggest that the Canadian government's current reconciliation initiatives are not enough to create Indigenous sovereignty and self-governance, presenting an additional hurdle to meaningful reconciliation (Antaki and Kirkby 2009). The rights of Indigenous Peoples need to be reconciled with the proclaimed sovereignty of non-Indigenous people in Canada. In many cases, reconciliation speaks to the need for non-Indigenous people in Canada to acknowledge the unfairness of the colonial assertion of sovereignty, assimilation policies, and denial of self-governance in order to develop harmonious and just relations with Indigenous Peoples.

Recognizing the Historical Colonial Legacy

Recognizing, learning, and challenging the historical colonial legacy is another important part of reconciliation. Battiste (2017: n.p.) emphasizes the importance of not only "understanding and/or unpacking whiteness, colonization, and oppression that belongs with the kinds of language," but also suggests that we need to understand our own relationships to that. According to Battiste, decolonization is "beginning to understanding that 'I got it.' Once we get it, we will not go back to the colonial process in our research." When conducting research with Indigenous communities, Elizabeth Moje (2000: 25) says that "researchers should engage in research not only to produce knowledge but also to make positive change in the lives of those who participate in research, change that the participants desire and articulate for themselves." Battiste (2017) suggests that once we can recognize the historical colonial legacy of oppression, colonial culture, and colonial impact on our practice, we will be able to appreciate our relationship as researchers with that legacy. Once we understand the processes of colonization and our relationships with them, we can find out who we are as immigrants, refugees, and settlers and what we should do for the meaningful implementation of reconciliation. Recognizing the historical colonial legacy in reconciliation learning includes an in-depth understanding of settler colonialism, refusal of Indigenous Land Rights and self-governance, and ongoing racism.

One way of learning this important history is through critical anti-racist education, which helps to recognize the historical colonial legacy (St. Denis 2007). It is also useful for the understanding that the refusal to recognize Indigenous Rights to their land and natural resources is a significant concern for many Indigenous communities, particularly in Canada (Datta 2018 2017; Wildcat, McDonald, Irbacher-Fox, and Coulthard 2014). The lack of critical anti-racist education is a major challenge for meaningful action on reconciliation in Canada (Cannon and Sunseri 2011; St. Denis 2011a, 2011b, 2012, 2007) as it offers an in-depth understanding of the colonial history of Canada and facilitates action against ongoing colonial practices (St. Denis 2012). In proposing anti-racist education, Indigenous scholar St. Denis (2012) argues that the legitimating ideology of colonialism is rampant and is a daily reality for Indigenous Peoples. Verna St. Denis argues that the education system in Canada is challenging for many Indigenous communities. For instance, the residential school system is one of the darkest examples of Canada's colonial policies to eradicate Indigenous Peoples from settler society. Lasting for over a hundred years, with the last school closing in the mid-1990s, the extensive government- and church-run school system was "characterized by forced removal of families; systemic physical and sexual assault; spiritual, psychological and emotional abuse; and malnutrition, inhumane living conditions, death, and murder" (Cannon and Sunseri 2011: 278). Through colonization, the Canadian state attempted to assimilate Indigenous Peoples into the settlers' European ways of living. Settler policies and attitudes meant that Indigenous Peoples were cut off from their traditional cultures, languages, spiritualities, economies, systems of governance, and other important parts of their identity (St. Denis 2012, 2007; Steckley and Cummins 2008). Critical anti-racist education shows that understanding Canada's colonial history and debunking the racist myths that run through Canadian society is an important part of the truth and reconciliation process (TD Economics 2012). It also demonstrates how the legacy of colonization has affected and continues to affect many settler, immigrant, and refugee communities across many generations in Canada.

The legacy of the past is daunting but anti-racist education can show us the way forward by creating many possibilities for reconciliation in relationship-shifting restorative practices. It is an important tool for reconciliation because it is grounded in intergenerational Indigenous knowledge systems and the worldviews and cultures of the individual, family, or community being served; it is framed within an awareness of and engagement with colonial history; it is strength-based and holistic rather than punitive and isolated; and it leads to measurable positive change for the individual, family, or community being served. Critical anti-racist learning in land-based practices and approaches provides a concrete means to address colonial history while recognizing the complexity of intergenerational issues and working toward the mutual understanding and respect that truth and reconciliation require.

Settler Colonialism

The challenges to reconciliation in settler-colonial societies are complex. Settler colonialism, as various studies emphasize (Barker 2012; Barker and Lowman 2015; Wolfe 1999), operates with its own particular logic, at the core of which is the elimination of the Indigenous, who must be displaced or destroyed to make space for settlement. This logic is "an organizing principle of settler-colonial society rather than a one-off (and superseded) occurrence," because in settler-colonial societies "invasion is a structure not an event" (Wolfe 2006: 388). Indigenous difference (presence, culture, identity, memory, history) is thus always threatening because it challenges the legitimacy of the settler state. Assimilation, read this way, is the logic of elimination in another form, for it seeks to eliminate the threatening and radical difference of the Indigenous other. The transformation of the colonial relationship is particularly challenging, not least because its psycho-affective structures mean that Indigenous Peoples have internalized their own domination, thus complicating the politics of recognition as it is typically conceived.

In the Canadian context, settler colonialism is about land, resources, sovereignty, and self-determination (Tuck and Yang 2012); as such, it involves the creation of a new social order. It is a mutual undertaking involving the colonizer and the colonized (Wildcat, McDonald, Irbacher-Fox, and Coulthard 2014). Settler colonialism is used in this chapter to describe white settlers and the associated white settler privileges. It recognizes the connecting processes of racial and colonial power inherent within the settler-colonial context of Canada and elsewhere.

Despite the importance of race to the dynamics of settler colonialism, discussions around racism have been overlooked in current reconciliation policies and practice, and anti-racist education and initiatives are extremely limited (Gebhard 2017). It is critical to address racism using the languages of racism and anti-racism — this acknowledges the presence of racism and, in doing so, overcomes denial. Deeply rooted racist attitudes and stereotypes surface when Canadians question why Indigenous Peoples cannot simply "get over it," show a lack of understanding of the intergenerational impact of colonization, and fail to commit to truth and reconciliation as a national priority. Chief Justice of the Supreme Court of Canada Beverley McLachlin has labelled Canada's failure to denounce racism as "cultural genocide" against Indigenous Peoples. Anti-racist educator and scholar St. Denis (2007: 1087) argues that Indigenous Peoples are not and have never been a homogenous population although they do share "a common experience with colonization and racialization." The concept of racialization "brings attention to how race has been used and is continually used to justify inequality and oppression of Aboriginal peoples" (1071). Alex Wilson, a professor at the University of Saskatchewan, a member of the Opaskwayak Cree Nation and an organizer of Idle No More, says, "In our view the education system has failed us. It's not just failed us, it's failed everybody" (CBC 2018: n.p.). Similarly, Verna St. Denis, a professor at the University of Saskatchewan who is Cree and Métis and who has been teaching about anti-racism for thirty-five years, argues that "we're taking responsibility in that and saying we have a responsibility as educational institutions to teach about racism and anti-racism and that's not really happening" (CBC 2018: n.p.). Therefore, to truly understand the process of reconciliation, Indigenous scholars, Elders, and activists believe we need to understand settler colonialism, how it gives control of resources to some people and economically marginalizes others, and how it enables some to negotiate pathways to educational success and discourages others from even participating (Battiste and Herderson 2000). It is through this system of settler colonialism that the settler state committed what is today considered cultural genocide against Indigenous Peoples (Tasker 2015). Landry (2018: n.p.) says that the current form of reconciliation "is for the Colonizer." She argues that "this settler-colonial reconciliation branded by the government is artificially sweetened with handshake photo-ops and small pockets of money buying our silence on real issues." According to Landry, "This type of reconciliation is a distraction ... This reconciliation is not our reconciliation. And we need to leave this conversation." Indigenous Elders and Knowledge Keepers argue that accounts of settler colonization are not included in current education and citizenship programs and this lack of education has resulted in the proliferation of various myths about Indigenous Peoples. Some of the commonly held racist myths include that Indigenous Peoples do not pay taxes, do not have to pay for postsecondary education, almost all live on reserves and in rural areas, are falling further behind in the job market, very few Indigenous Peoples start their own business, and so on (TD Economics 2012). The perpetuation of myths and negative stereotypes like these make reconciliation very difficult. In order to begin on the path to reconciliation, we must challenge these myths, the historical colonial legacy, and the system of settler colonialism that has damaged Indigenous ways of life and our collective relationships.

Reconciliation as Relational Responsibility

Reconciliation is a relational responsibility for all of us — Indigenous Peoples, settlers, and immigrants (Wilson 2018). Alison Norman, a research adviser in the Ontario Ministry of Indigenous Relations and Reconciliation and a researcher at Trent University, explains that reconciliation is also a personal issue. She says, "We have to ask, 'How am I benefiting by living on this land that is a traditional territory of Indigenous people?'" (CBC 2017: n.p.). This statement is a reminder to all of us that being accountable for our relationships with Indigenous Peoples and the land involves not only learning about colonization and its impact but also building solidarity for Indigenous Land and Cultural Rights in Canada and beyond.

Cree Indigenous Elder Florence Highway from Saskatchewan believes that we should educate people about the trials and triumphs of Indigenous Peoples, especially since, in some ways, Indigenous Peoples are still coming to terms with their own history. Concepts like treaties, the Indian Act, and the residential school system are not necessarily common knowledge to new immigrants (CBC 2017). Similarly, settler scholar Dr. Ken Coates, who works with various Indigenous and non-Indigenous communities, suggests that "all Canadians, including new Canadians, need to understand the collective responsibility for dealing with issues of the past" (CBC 2017: n.p.). Coates' research focuses on new immigrants and their interaction with Indigenous Peoples and their history. He believes that we are "much overdue and thinks First Nations people — and all Canadians — also have something to learn from newcomers" (CBC 2017: n.p.).

Dr. Jean-Paul Restoule (2015: 1), an associate professor of Aboriginal Education at the Ontario Institute for Studies in Education at the University of Toronto and a member of the Dokis First Nation (Anishinaabe), explains that "reconciliation between Aboriginal and non-Aboriginal peoples in Canada is a responsibility we all share. We can't wait for our governments or our administrative heads to make a change." His call for reconciliation is a process of relationship building and recognizing that we have responsibilities toward each other. Similarly, North American Indigenous scholar Dorothy Christian (2011) believes that Indigenous Peoples in Canada have the right to lead the process of reconciliation and that reconciliation is all our responsibility. Christian suggests that new immigrants and refugees are a significant part of Canada; therefore, they also need to accept responsibility for understanding the process of reconciliation. Learning about reconciliation not only creates belongingness for immigrants and refugees in Canada, but also benefits them by giving them self-awareness of their own rights. She goes on to describe accepting responsibility as a healing process. Once the silence is broken and each party has taken responsibility for their part in the relationship, they can begin relating to each other as dignified, autonomous human beings and a new relationship can begin.

Collective and individual responsibilities play a significant role in reconciliation; Indigenous Elders and Knowledge Keepers suggest that each of us (as a collective and as individuals) is responsible for building trustful reconciliation (Morgan 2018). Further, individual and collective responsibility are fluid. Responsibilities in reconciliation can involve participating in ceremonies, personal actions, nature walks to experience the power of place, critical learning, anti-racist activities, acting against injustice, creative arts, hands-on application of theory, individual reflection, and group activities. According to Indigenous Elders and Knowledge Keepers, there are a number of actions we can be responsible for, including the following: understanding the United Nations Declaration on the Rights of Indigenous Peoples and the Truth and Reconciliation Commission's (TRC) process and calls to action; building relationships with Indigenous communities; advancing relations with Indigenous Peoples; communicating through deep listening; creating partnership opportunities with Indigenous Peoples; sharing Indigenous ways of knowing; developing curiosity; practising relational leadership; empowering individuals to take action on reconciliation in their own lives; and increasing respect, understanding, and meaningful connections between citizens (Morgan 2018). Accepting responsibility also includes relearning the colonial history of Canada (Morgan 2018) and debunking the racist myths that run through Canadian society (TD Economics 2012). Through this relearning, we bring truth and reconciliation into our everyday practice, education, and discussion, and provide a concrete means to address colonial history. Reconciliation as relational responsibility also includes the responsibility for honouring and respecting treaties and healing.

Responsibility for Honouring and Respecting Treaties

Many Indigenous youth think that honouring and respecting treaties is a significant aspect of reconciliation (Morgan 2018). According to Ivana Yellowback, Nehinaw from Manto Sipi Cree Nation, student, and youth worker with the child welfare system:

> Being an Indigenous person in Canada, reconciliation is the treaties, honouring and acknowledging our treaties. The reason I say 'our' is because it's all of ours. Our communities are sovereign, distinct nations. Our nations made an agreement with Canada on a nation-to-nation basis. These were peace and friendship treaties. In these treaties, we did not cede our lands. These are still our territories, these are still our lands. (CBC 2016)

Ivana explains that talking about reconciliation will require learning about each of the different territorial treaties.

Responsibility for honouring and respecting treaties is also a healing process (Simpson 2014) and a virtue that involves making creation a better place to live. Healing is an important part of reconciliation for many Indigenous youth. For instance, Maya Nabigon, Anishinaabe from Sagkeeng First Nation, thinks reconciliation "is the healing of two nations coming together to find common ground and to move forward on any difficulties they have had" (CBC 2016: n.p.). Therefore, she says, "We need to educate ourselves and be ready." Another immigrant young person, Rehana Tejpar, says:

> Regardless of who we are, whether we have benefited from, or been a victim of colonization, perpetrator or survivor, we all have been wounded by colonization of people and the Earth and we all must heal from this wound in order to bring forth a more just and sustainable world. Healing intergenerational trauma collectively strengthens our capacity to do the work of radical adult education and community organizing and we recognize it as a valid part of the process of righting relations. (Tejpar 2018: 2)

The outcome of this process of reconciliation is healing. By working together, Indigenous and non-Indigenous Peoples can heal a country, heal our institutions and relationships, and heal the people.

Indigenous Worldview

From the Indigenous perspective, reconciliation is a process, and non-Indigenous people have important roles and responsibilities in following Indigenous guidelines for meaningful reconciliation. For instance, Dr. Malcolm Saulis, an Elder from Tobique First Nation, Indigenous scholar, and educator in the Faculty of Social Work at Wilfrid Laurier University in Waterloo, Ontario, explains that in the Indigenous worldview, the focus of reconciliation is on "building a relationship between people that doesn't have any differences attached to it" (Postmedia 2017: 2). People would have a common vision of the world in which they want to live. Saulis lists three complex but interconnected components in this ongoing process. First, reconciliation includes sharing responsibility for creation, that "the first thing that we share as people is that we have a responsibility to make Creation a healthy, livable place" (4). We have a responsibility to future generations and what we do now will have an impact. Second, reconciliation is a human process. That is, it is a process of building relationships that reflect reconciliation, such as the mutual acknowledgement that we are working together for the good of future generations. For explaining reconciliation Saulis uses ceremonies. Through ceremonies, Saulis asks: "What are you doing for reconciliation?" (4). He notes that "the usual response is 'I don't know what reconciliation is,' thus leaving it up to Indigenous people in the civil service to be responsible for it. But this is not reconciliation" (5). He reminds us that reconciliation is not only the responsibility of Indigenous Peoples but is the responsibility of all of us. Third, for Saulis, reconciliation is about respecting Indigenous ways of knowing and doing. Indigenous Peoples and their knowledge systems can guide all of us to the true meanings of reconciliation. While Indigenous Peoples can lead the way and help us define reconciliation, according to Saulis respect for Indigenous traditional ways of knowing will lead all of us to embrace our responsibilities for reconciliation.

Jaime Koebel is Michif/Nehiyaw from Lac La Biche, Alberta, and is the founder of Indigenous Walks, a series of guided walking tours that explore Ottawa's monuments, architecture, landscape, and art through an Indigenous perspective. Koebel (2017: 5) explains reconciliation from a philosophical perspective: "I think reconciliation can happen on a local scale and a large scale." For him, it is about starting to learn about the territory we are in. "It's one of the reasons why I started Indigenous Walks. Do you own land? What's your relationship to the place where you are, your house, the place you work? Who is a local Elder? Can you smudge in your building? Who were the people who lived here? What was their language, their basic cultural protocols?" (6). With this message, Koebel suggests that we should raise our children to be aware of both local and large-scale perspectives and that these perspectives should be connected with relationships with Indigenous Land, languages, and culture. Understanding the Indigenous worldview also allows us to see reconciliation through Indigenous eyes. North American Indigenous scholars Jim Dumont (1997) and Brian Rice (2005) suggest that seeing the world with Indigenous eyes opens four significant doors for both Indigenous and non-Indigenous Peoples. The first is the seeing path, also known as the Eastern door. It includes cosmology, visions, sounds, beliefs, and values that evolve from the spiritual world. The second is ways of relating. This Southern door is about cycles of life, time, mathematics, relationships between people, the Earth spirit, and Sky Worlds. The third is coming to knowing, also known as the Western door. It includes Elders, the learning path, and Indigenous knowledge. The fourth is ways of doing. This is the Northern door and it includes ethical and moral issues, ceremonies, healing, prayers, and lifeways. Within the Indigenous world-view, the four sacred directions provide a window for understanding patterns of thought; concepts of time, sacredness, and the natural world; development and role of consciousness, perception, language, dance and song; understandings of relationships (metaphorical and literal); morality and ethics; the environment; knowledge, wisdom stories and creation stories; and many other aspects of Indigenous Traditional Knowledge. This work provides a bridge between Traditional Knowledge and Western knowledge; it explores some connections of understandings from the different ways of knowing, including the perspectives of Indigenous cultures from other continents.

The term *reconciliation*, in the Indigenous worldview, has neither a fixed meaning nor an ending point. For instance, while Leanne Simpson (2014: 22) supports the broad approach to reconciliation as discussed by the TRC, she cautions that a focus on residential schools alone permits Canadians to assume that "the historical 'wrong' has now been 'righted,'" effectively discounting "the broader set of relationships that generated policies, legislation, and practices aimed at assimilation and political genocide." From a broader perspective, if reconciliation is to be meaningful for Indigenous Peoples, it must be grounded in cultural regeneration and political resurgence while requiring Canada to "engage in a decolonization project and a re-education project that would enable its government and its citizens to engage with Indigenous Peoples in a just and honourable way in the future" (Simpson 2014: 23). Similarly, Indigenous scholar Shawn Wilson (2018) argues that reconciliation is a process that seeks honour, respect, and accountability for our relationships with the land. These relationships seek truth, justice, accountability, and healing. It is about co-existing, cooperating, and sharing with the goal of a better life for all.

THE TRUTH AND RECONCILIATION COMMISSION'S PERSPECTIVES ON RECONCILIATION

The meaning of reconciliation cannot be understood without discussing Canada's Truth and Reconciliation Commission (TRC) (Barkaskas and Buhler 2017; Battiste 2017; Morgan 2018). Over the past few years, the TRC has emerged as an important catalyst for renewed dialogue and debate about the importance of reconciliation between Indigenous and non-Indigenous Peoples in Canada. While the TRC (2015) affirmed a broad and inclusive definition of reconciliation with both individual and collective dimensions, its mandate was specifically linked to the historic harm and the ongoing effects of Indian residential schools (IRS). The goals of the TRC (2015) included the following:

A. Acknowledge residential school experiences, impacts and consequences;

B. Provide a holistic, culturally appropriate, and safe setting for former students, their families, and communities as they come forward to the Commission;

C. Witness, support, promote, and facilitate truth and reconciliation events at both the national and community levels;

D. Promote awareness and public education of Canadians about the IRS system and its impacts;

E. Identify sources and create as complete a historical record as possible of the IRS system and its legacy. The record shall be preserved and made accessible to the public for future study and use;

F. Produce and submit to the Parties of the Agreement a report including recommendations to the Government of Canada concerning the IRS system and experience including the history, purpose, operation, and supervision of the IRS system; the effect and consequences of IRS (including systemic harms, intergenerational consequences, and the impact on human dignity); and the ongoing legacy of the residential schools;

G. Support commemoration of former IRS students and their families.

The TRC believed that for all of us in Canada to flourish in the twenty-first century, reconciliation between non-Indigenous and Indigenous Peoples in Canada must be based on ten principles. *Ricochet* (2015) reported the ten TRC principles, and numbers 1, 5, and 6 directly address non-Indigenous communities' collective responsibility for meaningful reconciliation:

- The *United Nations Declaration on the Rights of Indigenous Peoples* is the framework for reconciliation at all levels and across all sectors of Canadian society.
- Reconciliation must create a more equitable and inclusive society by closing the gaps in social, health, and economic outcomes that exist between Aboriginal and non-Aboriginal Canadians.
- All Canadians, as Treaty peoples, share responsibility for establishing and maintaining mutually respectful relationships.

The TRC emphasized collective learning processes and the need to do more than just talk about reconciliation: we must learn how to take responsibility for reconciliation in our everyday lives — within ourselves and our families, in our communities, in our education, and in our workplaces. In response to the TRC's calls to action, immigrant and refugee communities need to take responsibility for creating space to better understand the truth of Canada's shared history with Indigenous Peoples. This includes fostering a dialogue between Indigenous and non-Indigenous Peoples and asking each of us to enter a respectful relationship with one another as we work toward shared purposes. Responsibilities include developing a deeper understanding of our shared history, the meaning of reconciliation, and the role all Canadians can play in improving our relationships — including sharing existing reconciliation practices and inviting Canadians to integrate reconciliation into their lives, communities, and organizations.

Clearly, reconciliation is a lifelong unlearning and relearning process. Reconciliation learning must inspire Indigenous and non-Indigenous Peoples to transform Canadian society so that our children and grandchildren can live together in dignity, peace, and prosperity on the lands we now share. In addition, the TRC (2015) recognizes that part of reconciliation is to support Indigenous Peoples as they heal from the destructive legacies of colonization.

The Truth and Reconciliation Commission (2015: 3) states that "reconciliation is about establishing and maintaining a mutually respectful relationship between Aboriginal and non-Aboriginal peoples in this country. In order for that to happen, there has to be awareness of the past, an acknowledgement of the harm that has been inflicted, atonement for the causes, and action to change behaviour." According to the TRC, all of us (Indigenous, settlers, immigrants, new immigrants, and refugees) have a responsibility for the successful implementation of reconciliation in our everyday practice. The renowned Mi'kmaw scholar, Knowledge Keeper, and educator from Nova Scotia's Potlotek First Nation, Dr. Marie Battiste, notes that Indigenous knowledge "does not come from within a book and does not come from Eurocentric research. It comes from Indigenous Peoples, from their continued living on the land and their continued relationships with each other" (Shewaga 2019: 1). Maintaining our relational responsibilities to each other and ensuring the continuation of Indigenous cultures, languages, and heritages are key to reconciliation; everybody has a role to play in making these things possible (Shewaga 2019).

Reconciliation is the restoration of an equal relationship between Indigenous Peoples and non-Indigenous peoples in Canada (Sinclair 2016). As the TRC notes, reconciliation has a variety of meanings for individuals, communities, institutions, and organizations. It is an ongoing "individual and collective process, and will require commitment from all those affected including First Nations, Inuit and Métis former Indian residential school (IRS) students, their families, communities, religious entities, former school employees, government and the people of Canada" (Knight 2019: 1). However, the colonization of North America had serious negative impacts on Indigenous knowledge, culture, and practice. Settler policies and attitudes meant that Indigenous Peoples were cut off from their traditional cultures, languages, spiritualities, economies, systems of governance, and other important parts of their identity.

HOW WE CAN WORK TOGETHER

Several common themes emerge from the various perspectives on reconciliation presented in this chapter, including that it cannot occur without the meaningful engagement of Indigenous Elders and Knowledge Keepers. Furthermore, education around decolonization and the recognition that Indigenous Land Rights are a prerequisite for the process are essential. Comprehensive land claims negotiations are only a single step in the process. Reconciliation also cannot occur without justice, accountability, and substantive reparations for Indigenous Rights violations. It requires accepting individual and collective responsibility, and it will take time and require public awareness, engagement, and education. Reconciliation requires new forms of coexistence and trust-filled relationships between Indigenous and non-Indigenous Peoples.

Exploring the meaning of reconciliation from multiple perspectives benefits all of us. It helps us build a comprehensive understanding of various world-views, recognize multiple ways of knowing and doing, and develop bridging opportunities within and among cultures, knowledges, and practices. It also encourages us to protect the Earth and all lifeforms — humans, animals, the land, water, forest, and plants — and creates a sense of belonging with the land, the cultures, and the people who live on it. This exploration of multiple perspectives also increases our capacity by educating us about Indigenous knowledge, land, and culture.

Indigenous Peoples need capacity building at the community and individual levels as a key component of achieving long-term reconciliation. With regard to governance and leadership, all parties must be committed to ensuring capacity is developed to address the growing role of Indigenous leaders. As Indigenous scholars, Elders, and Knowledge Keepers note, Indigenous leaders, particularly in Canada, are taking on greater authority and responsibility as both federal and provincial governments recognize the jurisdiction of First Nation, Métis, and Inuit local governments (Assembly of First Nations 2018). Indigenous leaders frequently meet with senior government and private sector leaders and are often responsible for negotiating agreements on behalf of their communities (Wesley-Esquimaux and Calliou 2010), so we must ensure they have the capacity to negotiate agreements that benefit both sides and move reconciliation forward.

Appreciating Indigenous perspectives on reconciliation is essential for Canadians of all backgrounds and will assist us in understanding that we all have a collective responsibility for meaningful reconciliation. All of us, including new immigrants and refugees, share the responsibility to engage in genuine dialogue and action with Indigenous Peoples. We must all, Indigenous and non-Indigenous, listen to Indigenous Peoples and the TRC and actively follow their guidance to reach out to one another, crossing both the material and national boundaries that assign Indigenous Peoples to the margin.

TERMINOLOGY

The term *Aboriginal* is an umbrella term adopted by the Canadian federal government to include First Nations, Métis, and Inuit. It is recognized in section35 of the Canadian Constitution. Although Aboriginal is frequently used in government documents and is still an appropriate term, the term *Indigenous* has gained popularity in recent years. The use of Indigenous is often a choice made by Indigenous Peoples themselves. This term came into wide usage during the 1970s when Aboriginal groups organized transnationally and pushed for a greater presence in the United Nations (UN) (Anaya 2009). In the UN, Indigenous is used to refer broadly to peoples of long settlement and connection to specific lands who have been adversely affected by incursions by industrial economies, displacement, and settlement of their traditional territories by others. While many Canadian documents use Aboriginal and Indigenous interchangeably, the conscious decision has been made here to respect the choice that many Indigenous Peoples have made concerning terminology; therefore, wherever appropriate the term *Indigenous* will be used when referring to the Indigenous Peoples in Canada. When applicable, the terms *First Nations, Inuit,* and *Métis* are used when referring to those specific segments of the Indigenous Peoples in Canada.

We use the term *responsibility* throughout this book consciously because we want to suggest a consideration of accountability (what are we responsible for?) and obligation (to whom are we responsible?), as well as living (are we viewed as responsible by those we are obligated to?). The term *responsibility* used throughout this chapter is from Arendt's (2003) central notion of belonging. Arendt suggests that responsibility belongs to an individual who belongs to a community. Belonging is central to Arendt's concept of responsibility since she views all obligations as collective. Responsibility, therefore, includes both individual and collective acts (Morgan 2018), a process of unlearning and relearning on how to respect Indigenous knowledge.

In this book, the term *cross-cultural practice* emphasizes changing institutional structures, practices, and policies, as well as personal and professional ideologies to create environments that are committed to strengthening our relationships with Indigenous Peoples. In addition, this book suggests that we must support all learners as they develop their knowledge and understanding of Indigenous Peoples' worldviews and cultures as a basis for creating equitable and inclusive learning spaces.

A PREVIEW OF THE CHAPTERS IN THIS BOOK

The driving force behind this book is to respond to the TRC's calls to action, which recognize that meaningful engagement among Indigenous Peoples and non-Indigenous Canadians is necessary for advancing reconciliation. Through a presentation of various cross-cultural, community-oriented activities, the authors demonstrate how they have come to understand and take responsibility for reconciliation, as well as point to areas of opportunity and current obstacles to progress. The book is divided into two parts: Part One focuses on understanding reconciliation, while Part Two uses case studies to explore how the authors have begun taking responsibility for reconciliation.

Part One: Understanding Reconciliation

Part One focuses on understanding what reconciliation is and how it is defined. What are the challenges for achieving reconciliation? Why is it important? What role do immigrants and refugees have in reconciliation? The book opens with a discussion on the definition of reconciliation and invites a critical discussion on the challenges and possibilities in reconciliation. Through the words of Indigenous Elders and Knowledge Keepers, scholars, and youth, this chapter explores how Indigenous Peoples understand the challenges and their desire to redefine the concept of reconciliation. Following this discussion, Cree scholar Chris Scribe shares his poem, A Letter to John A. MacDonald (first prime minister of Canada), which speaks to the resiliency of Indigenous Peoples in the face of colonization.

Although this book focuses on the Canadian context, there are other struggles for reconciliation between Indigenous Peoples and settlers around the world, particularly in Australia, New Zealand, and Scandinavia, and we should understand those struggles in order to better understand our own. To this end, the third chapter looks at the experiences of the Sámi, the Indigenous People in Scandinavia, as they tried to build reconciliation with the Finnish state. The authors examine how assimilation and colonization processes affected the Sámi Indigenous People and how Sámi artists and the Sámi movement gave expression to such processes. They focus on the relationships between the state and the Sámi by examining the debates on how to define the Sámi and the Nordic Sámi Convention, including the lessons that can be learned from the Sámi and how their experience speaks to our own.

This section ends with another Cree scholar and activist, Colleen J. Charles, explaining the realities of colonialism with a discussion of the five stages of colonization and reflections from her own life. She explores the role of art in reconciliation, using her art workshop Colonialism on Canvas and other Indigenous art projects as inspiration.

Part Two: Taking Responsibility for Reconciliation

Part Two focuses on reconciliation in practice from various cross-cultural perspectives. Through a variety of case studies, these chapters speak to the intersections between critical anti-racist education and decolonization in different aspects of Indigenous, immigrant, and refugee lives with a focus on everyday practices, such as Indigenous education, environmental education, protecting Traditional Knowledge, and cultural and community resilience. Of special interest are discourses and practices around the issue of responsibilities for reconciliation, the local outcomes of cross-cultural bridges, culturally appropriate knowledge, social and environmental justice, and solidarity. These chapters are also an invitation for all of us to work together as Indigenists to build relational networks in the important work of intercultural bridging, move beyond cultural awareness and inclusion, and challenge racist ideology as we rethink and re-imagine ourselves in a relationship with one another in a sharing place.

In Chapters 5 and 6, Jebunnessa Chapola and I, both immigrants in Canada, share our experience of reconciliation as a lifelong ceremonial journey of unlearning and relearning on Treaty Six Territory. Through our ceremonial responsibility for reconciliation, we pay our respect, honour, and gratitude to the First Nations and Métis ancestors of this place and reaffirm our relationship and responsibility with them and with this land. We share our ceremonial stories regarding how we have learned the importance of reconciliation from our everyday actions and ask how those of us who invoke this term might most effectively address reconciliation and social challenges. Chapola explains how transnational perspectives offer us a significant step forward in exploring identity and justice in relation to immigrant responsibilities for reconciliation.

Many immigrant and refugee people in Canada are trying to take responsibility, as part of reconciliation, for building trustful relationships with Indigenous Peoples. For instance, in Chapter 7, Ali Abukar, a new Canadian and a former refugee, discusses his two years of community-based professional experience with reconciliation. Through these reconciliation activities, he claimed his identity as a global citizen and a promoter of diversity and multiculturalism. With the same focus on relationship building, Chapters 8 and 9 explore the role of reconciliation in the health care profession. Immigrant scholar Farzana Ali discusses why it is important for foreign health professionals to understand the Canadian context of colonialism and the residential school legacy, and how this awareness (or lack thereof) impacts the delivery of health care to Indigenous Peoples (TRC calls to action 22 and 24). Looking at community-based health research, immigrant health professional and scholar Valerie Onyinyechi Umaefulam explores reconciliation through the building of respectful relationships and community engagement when conducting research within Indigenous communities.

Offering the perspective of the white settler, Janet McVittie (Chapter 10) shares some of the lessons she has learned in establishing and cultivating a garden of plants native to Saskatchewan. Through this garden, she has worked to understand the concepts of decolonization, ally, and reconciliation, and to promote greater understanding among her (mostly) white settler teacher candidates. In Chapter 11, immigrant poet Khodi Dill offers two poems that reflect on reconciliation and argues that immigrants of colour are specially positioned to promote the work of reconciliation through new and/or revised settler perspectives regarding the land, as our connections to the land are more recently formed and contextualized differently than the historical white settler perspective.

Summarizing the contributions to this collection, the Conclusion reminds us that rebuilding and renewing a mutually respectful relationship between Indigenous and non-Indigenous Peoples is one of the most vital tools for transforming our relations. Reconciliation acknowledges the past but also attempts to offer us new ways forward. It reminds us that both parties are accountable to the process and that reciprocity is essential to strong, healthy relationships. Through their hard work and dedication to reconciliation, the contributors to this volume demonstrate the way forward, showing us that a different Canada is possible.

REFERENCES

Abu-Laban, Yasmeen. 2014. "Reform by Stealth: The Harper Conservatives and Canadian Multiculturalism." In J. Jedwab (ed.), *The Multiculturalism Question: Debating Identity in 21st Century Canada*. Montreal-Kingston: School of Policy Studies, Queen's University and McGill-Queen's University Press.

___. 2018. "Recognition, Re-distribution and Solidarity: The Case of Multicultural Canada." In J. Fossum, R. Kastoryano, and B. Siim (eds.), *Diversity and Contestations over Nationalism in Europe and Canada*. Palgrave Studies in European Political Sociology. London: Palgrave Macmillan.

Alfred, Taiaiake. 2018. "Don't Just Resist. Return to Who You Are: Let's Re-Experience Our Homelands the Way Our Ancestors Did and Regenerate That Culture." *Yes,* 14. <https://www.yesmagazine.org/issues/decolonize/peek-inside>.

Anaya, S. James. 2009. *International Human Rights and Indigenous Peoples*. Austin: Wolters Kluwer Law & Business.

Antaki Mark, and Kirkby Coel. 2009. "The Lethality of the Canadian State's (Re)cognition of Indigenous Peoples." In Austin Sarat, and Jennifer Culbert (eds.), *States of Violence: War, Capital Punishment, and Letting Die*. New York: Cambridge University Press.

Anuik, Jonathan, Marie Battiste, and Priscilla George. 2010. "Learning from Promising Programs and Applications in Nourishing the Learning Spirit." *Canadian Journal of Native Education*, 33, 1: 63–82.

Arendt, Hannah. 2003. "Collective Responsibility." In *Responsibility and Judgment*. New York: Schocken Books.

Assembly of First Nations. 2018. "Affirming First Nations Rights, Title and Jurisdiction." <https://www.afn.ca/wp-content/uploads/2018/09/Affirming-FN-Rights-Title-and-Jurisdiction_EN.pdf>.

Bang, Megan, Lawrence Curley, Adam Kessel, Ananda Marin, Eli S. Suzukovich III, and George Strack. 2014. "Muskrat Theories, Tobacco in the Streets, and Living Chicago as Indigenousland." *Environmental Education Research*, 20: 1, 37–55. DOI: 0.1080/13504622.2013.865113.

Barkaskas, Patricia, and Sarah Buhler. 2017. "Beyond Reconciliation: Decolonizing Clinical Legal Education." *Journal of Law and Social Policy,* 26, 20. <http://digitalcommons.osgoode.yorku.ca/jlsp/vol26/iss1/1>.

Barker, Adam, and Emma Battell Lowman. 2015. *Settler: Identity and Colonialism in 21st Century Canada*. Halifax: Fernwood Publishing.

Barker, Valerie. 2012. "A Generational Comparison of Social Networking Site Use: The Influence of Age and Social Identity." *International Journal of Aging and Human Development,* 74: 163–187.

Battiste, Marie. 2008. "The Decolonization of Aboriginal Education: Dialogue, Reflection, and Action in Canada." In P.R. Dasen and A. Akkari (eds.), *Educational Theories and Practices from the Majority World*. New Delhi: Sage.

___. 2017. "Decolonial Ways of Knowing and Doing at Banglar Gann O Katha at CFCR 90.5 Saskatoon Radio Program." <https://drive.google.com/file>.

___. 2013. *Decolonizing Education: Nourishing the Learning Spirit*. Saskatoon, SK: Purich.

Battiste, Marie, and James (Sa'ke'j) Youngblood Henderson. 2000. *Protecting Indigenous Knowledge and Heritage: A Global Challenge*. Saskatoon: Purich Publishing.

Cannon, Martain, and Lina Sunseri. 2011. "Not Disappearing: An Introduction to the Text." In Martain Cannon and Lina Sunseri (eds.), *Racism, Colonialism and Indigeneity in Canada: A Reader*. Don Mills: Oxford University Press.

CBC. 2016. "What Does Reconciliation Mean to You?" October 19. <http://www.cbc.ca/news/indigenous/what-does-reconciliation-mean-mb-1.3803617>.

___. 2017. "What Is the Significance of Acknowledging the Indigenous Land We Stand On?" July 17. <http://www.cbc.ca/news/canada/toronto/

territorial-acknowledgements-indigenous-1.4175136>.

____. 2018. "Educators Call on Universities to Help Fight Institutional Racism Following Stanley Verdict." February 13. <https://www.cbc.ca/news/indigenous/ antiracism-education-colten-boushie-gerald-stanley-verdict-1.4532233>.

Chandler, Michael, and Christopher Lalonde. 1998. "Cultural Continuity as a Hedge Against Suicide in Canada's First Nations." *Transcultural Psychiatry*, 35, 2: 191–219. DOI: 10.1177%2F136346159803500202.

Christian, Dorothy. 2011. "Reconciling with the People and the Land." In A. Mathur, J. Dewar, and M. Degagné (eds.), *Cultivating Canada: Reconciliation through the Lens of Cultural Diversity*. ON, Canada: Aboriginal Healing Foundation.

Clark, Tom, Ravi de Costa, and Sarah Maddison. 2017. "Non-Indigenous Australians and the 'Responsibility to Engage'?" *Journal of Intercultural Studies*, 38, 4. DOI 10.1080/07256868.2017.1341393.

Datta, Ranjan. 2016. "Community Garden: A Bridging Program Between Formal and Informal Learning." *Journal of Cogent Education*, 3, 1. DOI: doi.org/10.1080/2331 186X.2016.1177154.

____. 2017. "Decolonizing both Research and Researcher, and Its Effectiveness in Indigenous research." *Research Ethics*, 1–24. <http://journals.sagepub.com/doi/ pdf/10.1177/1747016117733296>.

____. 2018. "Traditional Story Sharing: An Effective Indigenous Research Methodology and Its Implications for Environmental Research." *Journal of AlterNative*, 14, 1. DOI: doi.org/10.1177/1177180117741351.

Donald, Dwayne. 2012. "Forts, Colonial Frontier Logics, and Aboriginal-Canadian Relations: Imagining Decolonizing Educational Philosophies in Canadian Contexts." In A.A. Abdi (ed.), *Decolonizing Philosophies of Education*. Rotterdam: Sense.

Dumont, Jim. 1997. "An Interview with Jim Dumont." In Dagmar Thorpe (ed.), *People of the Seventh Fire: Returning Lifeways of Native America*. Ithaca, NY: Akwe:kon.

Egan, B. 2011. "Resolving the 'Indian Land Question'? Racial Rule and Reconciliation in British Columbia." In A. Baldwin, L. Cameron, and A. Kobayashi (eds.), *Rethinking the Great White North*. Vancouver: UBC Press.

Ermine, W. 1995. "Aboriginal Epistemology." In M. Battiste and J. Barman (eds.), *First Nations Education in Canada: The Circle Unfolds*. Vancouver, BC: UBC Press.

Garcia, Jeremy, and Valerie Shirley. 2012. "Performing Decolonization: Lessons Learned from Indigenous Youth, Teachers and Leaders' Engagement with Critical Indigenous Pedagogy." *Journal of Curriculum Theorizing*, 28, 2.

Gebhard, Amanda. 2017. "Reconciliation or Reconciliation? Contemporary Discourses about Residential Schools in the Canadian Prairies." *Canadian Journal of Education*, 40, 1.

Gray, Bryn. 2016. *Building Relationships and Advancing Reconciliation through Meaningful Consultation*. <https://www.aadnc-aandc.gc.ca/eng/1498765671013/149876582 7601>.

Green, Joyce. 2011. "From Stonechild to Social Cohesion: Antiracist Challenges for Saskatchewan." In M.J. Cannon and L. Sunseri (eds.), *Racism, Colonialism, and Indigeneity in Canada*. Don Mills, ON: Oxford University Press.

Hansen, John George, and Rose Antsanen. 2017. "Elders Teachings: Wisdom We Need for

Addressing Social Exclusion and Building Better Relationships in Society." *Indigenous Policy Journal*, 28, 21: 1–18. <http://www.indigenouspolicy.org/index.php/ipj/article/view/410>.

Heleta, Savo. 2016. "Decolonisation of Higher Education: Dismantling Epistemic Violence and Eurocentrism in South Africa." *Transformation in Higher Education*, 1, 1. <https://thejournal.org.za/index.php/thejournal/article/%20view/9%20/31>.

James, Matt. 2012. "Carnival of Truth? Knowledge, Ignorance and the Canadian Truth and Reconciliation Commission." *The International Journal of Transitional Justice*, 6.

Knight, Keith. 2019. "Reconciliation." *Windspeaker Publication*, 26, 11. <https://ammsa.com/node/6874>.

Koebel, Joime. 2017. "Reconciliation with Canada's Indigenous People Has Been an Underlying Theme of Canada's Year-Long 150 Celebrations." <https://ottawacitizen.com/news/local-news/the-meaning-of-reconciliation>.

Kovach, Margaret. 2010. *Indigenous Methodologies*. Toronto, ON: University of Toronto Press.

Landry, Andrea. 2018. "This Reconciliation Is for the Colonizer." <https://indigenousmotherhood.wordpress.com/about/>.

McCrossan, Michael, and Kiera L. Ladner. 2016. "Eliminating Indigenous Jurisdictions: Federalism, the Supreme Court of Canada, and Territorial Rationalities of Power." *Canadian Journal of Political Science*, 49, 3: 411–431.

McGregor, E. Heather. 2018. "An Arctic Encounter with Indigenous and Non-Indigenous Youth as Pedagogy for Historical Consciousness and Decolonizing." *Historical Encounters: A Journal of Historical Consciousness, Historical Cultures, and History Education*, 5, 1.

McMahon, Ryan. 2016. "We Need Decolonization Before Reconciliation." CBC March 15. <http://www.cbc.ca/radio/the180/how-safe-cities-can-be-dangerous-the-problem-with-reconciliation-and-stop-saying-cuba-will-be-ruined-1.3507402/we-need-decolonization-before-reconciliation-argues-ryan-mcmahon-1.3507589>.

Moje, Elizabeth. 2000. "Changing Our Minds, Changing Our Bodies: Power as Embodied in Research Relations." *Qualitative Studies in Education*, 13, 1.

Morgan, Sloan. 2018. "Moving from Rights to Responsibilities: Extending Hannah Arendt's Critique of Collective Responsibility to the Settler Colonial Context of Canada." *Settler Colonial Studies*, 8, 3. DOI: 10.1080/2201473X.2017.1327011M.

Palmater, Pamela. 2014. "Genocide, Indian policy, and legislated elimination of Indians in Canada." *Aboriginal Policy Studies*, 3: 27–54.

Paperson, La. 2014. "A Ghetto Land Pedagogy: An Antidote for Settler Environmentalism." *Environmental Education Research*, 20, 1 (February). DOI: 10.1080/13504622.2013.865115.

Postmedia Network Inc. 2017. "The Meaning of Reconciliation: 'We're Not Anywhere Near That Word Called Forward. We're Not Even on the First Syllable.'" July 17. <https://ottawacitizen.com/news/local-news/the-meaning-of-reconciliation>.

Restoule, Jean-Paul. 2015. "On National Aboriginal Day, What Does Reconciliation Mean to You?" <https://www.ideas-idees.ca/blog/national-aboriginal-day-what-does-reconciliation-mean-you>.

Rice, Brian. 2005. *Seeing the World with Aboriginal Eyes*. University of Manitoba Press.

Ricochet. 2015. "10 Principles for Truth and Reconciliation." December. <https://ricochet. media/en/844/10-principles-for-truth-and-reconciliation>.

Sasakamoose, JoLee, and Pete Shauneen. 2015. "Towards Indigenizing University Policy kakwe-iyiniwasta kihci-kiskinwahamâtowikamikohk wiyasiwâcikanisa." *Education Matters*, 3, 1. <62922-Article%20Text-179779-1-10-20150706.pdf>.

Saskatoon Star Phoenix. 2018. "Decolonization through peaceful diplomacy needed after not guilty verdict, rally hears." February 12. https://thestarphoenix.com/ news/local-news/decolonization-through-peaceful-diplomacy-needed-after-not-guiltyverdict-rally-hears.

Shewaga, James. 2019. "People of the Plan: Uplifting Indigenization." <https://news. usask.ca/articles/people/2019/people-of-the-plan-uplifting-indigenization-.php>.

Simpson, Leanne. 2014. *Dancing on Our Turtle's Back: Stories of Nishnaabeg Re-creation, Resurgence and a New Emergence.* Winnipeg: ARP Books.

Sinclair, Murray. 2016. *What Is Reconciliation?* [video]. <http://www.trc.ca/websites/ reconciliation/index.php?p=312>.

Smith, Linda. 1999. *Decolonizing Methodologies: Research and Indigenous Peoples.* London: Zed Books.

___. 2008. "On Tricky Ground: Researching the Native in the Age of Uncertainty." In N.K. Denzin and Y.S. Lincoln (eds.), *The Sage Handbook of Qualitative Research.* Thousand Oaks, CA: Sage.

St. Denis, Verna. 2007. "Aboriginal Education and Anti-Racist Education: Building Alliance Across Cultural and Racial Identity." *Canadian Journal of Education*, 30, 4.

___. 2011a. "Foreword." In M. Cannon and L. Sunseri (eds.), *Racism, Colonialism and Indigeneity in Canada.* Don Mills, ON: Oxford University Press.

___. 2011b. "Rethinking Cultural Theory in Aboriginal Education." In M. Cannon and L. Sunseri (eds.), *Racism, Colonialism and Indigeneity in Canada.* Don Mills, ON: Oxford University Press.

St. Denis, Verna. 2012. "Silencing Aboriginal curricular content and perspectives through multiculturalism: 'There are other children here.'" *Review of Education, Pedagogy, and Cultural Studies*, 33, 4.

Steckley, John, and Bryan Cummins. 2008. *Full Circle: Canada's First Nations.* Toronto: Prentice Hall.

Tasker, John Paul. 2015. "Residential Schools Findings Point to 'Cultural Genocide.'" CBC News May 29. <https://www.cbc.ca/news/politics/residential-schools-findings-point-to-cultural-genocide-commission-chair-says-1.3093580>.

TD Economics. 2012. *Special Report: Debunking Myths Surrounding Canada's Aboriginal Population.* June 18. <www.td.com/document/PDF/economics/special/sg0612_aboriginal_myth.pdf>.

Teipar Rehena. 2018. "Turning Theory into Practice: What We Are Learning About the Work of Righting Relations." *Righting Relations.* <http://www.cawi-ivtf.org/sites/ default/files/key_learning_turning_theory_into_practice-_righting_relations.pdf>.

TRC (Truth and Reconciliation Commission of Canada). 2015. "Calls to Action." <http:// www.trc.ca/websites/trcinstitution/File/2015/Findings/Calls_to_Action_English2. pdf>.

Tuck, Eve, Marcia McKenzie, and Kate McCoy. 2014. "Land Education: Indigenous,

Post-Colonial, and Decolonizing Perspectives on Place and Environmental Education Research." *Environmental Education Research*, 20, 1: 1–23. DOI: 10.1080/13504622.2013.877708.

Tuck, Eve, and Wayne Yang. 2012. "Decolonization Is Not a Metaphor." *Decolonization: Indigeneity, Education & Society,* 1, 1.

Tully, James. 2000. "The Struggles of Indigenous Peoples for and of Freedom." In D. Ivison (ed.), *Political Theory and the Rights of Indigenous Peoples.* Cambridge, UK: Cambridge University Press.

Wesley-Esquimaux, Cynthia, and Brian Calliou. 2010. "Best Practices in Aboriginal Community Development: A Literature Review and Wise Practices Approach." The Banff Centre. <http://communities4families.ca/wp-content/uploads/2014/08/Aboriginal-Community-Development.pdf>.

Wildcat, Matthew, Mandee McDonald, Stephanie Irbacher-Fox, and Glen Coulthard. 2014. "Learning from the Land: Indigenous Land Based Pedagogy and Decolonization." *Decolonization: Indigeneity, Education & Society,* 3: I–XV.

Wilson, Shawn. 2008. *Research Is Ceremony: Indigenous Research Methods.* Winnipeg, MB: Fernwood Publishing.

___. 2011. "Indigenist Research." Community Presentation at Ryerson University, Toronto, ON, Canada.

___. 2013. "Using Indigenist Research to Shape Our Future.". In M. Grey, J. Coates, M. Yellow Bird, and T. Hetherington (eds.), *Decolonizing Social Work.* Burlington, VT: Ashgate Publishing.

___. 2017. "Writing up Indigenist Research." Presentation to the Indigenous Reading Group at Pacific Lutheran University, Tacoma, WA. October.

___. 2018. "Research as Reconciliation." Panel Discussion, University of Illinois. <https://icqi.org/pre-congress-days/a-day-in-indigenous-qualitative-inquiries/>.

Wolfe, Patrick. 1999. *Settler Colonialism and the Transformation of Anthropology: The Politics and Poetics of an Ethnographic Event.* London: Cassell.

Chapter Two

LETTER TO JOHN A. MACDONALD (FIRST PRIME MINISTER OF CANADA)

CHRIS SCRIBE

Dear John A Macdonald,
Today my children speak their language
Despite your approved assault on my family
Through an education system designed to kill us
Today my children still wear their regalia

Today my children sing our songs
Despite your railroad and the massacre of our buffalo
That brought us to the brink of starvation
Today my children feast on wild meat

Today my children go to ceremony
Despite your laws that fined us,
Jailed us and ripped our parents from our homes
Today my children give thanks for family

Today my children wear their hair in braids
Despite your policies to cut our
Children's hair and rip them from their mothers' arms
Today my children stand up with pride

Today my children would like to tell you
That you have failed in your attempts
to assimilate our people because
Today my children are still Indigenous

Chapter Three

SÁMI RECONCILIATION IN PRACTICE

A Long and Ongoing Process

IRJA SEURUJÄRVI-KARI AND PIRJO KRISTIINA VIRTANEN

In this chapter, we examine the Sámi reconciliation process in Finland by drawing on the effects of the colonization and assimilation processes. We focus especially on the relationship between the Sámi and the Finnish government and their socio-political changes; our case is contextualized transnationally, as the Sámi live in several different nation-states. The traditional living area of the Sámi people, Sápmi, covers the northern parts of Fennoscandia, totalling almost 400,000 kilometres: in Finland, it covers the municipalities of Utsjoki, Inari, Enontekiö, and the northern part of the municipality of Sodankylä; in Norway, the counties of North Trøndelag, Nordland, Tromsø, and Finnmark; and in Sweden, the provinces of Jämtland, Västerbotten, and Norrbotten. Today, the total number of Sámi is between 75,000 and 100,000 in four countries — Norway, Sweden, Finland, and the Kola Peninsula of Russia.

The Sámi have inhabited the northern and eastern parts of the Fennoscandian Peninsula since the first centuries CE (Aikio 2012: 102–106; Aikio 2006; Hansen and Olsen 2004). The Sámi did not arrive in their current territory, northern Fennoscandia and the Kola Peninsula of Russia, as a united people; rather, Sámi ethnicity has formed in the territory due to the processes of interaction, separation, and assimilation. Their cultures have continuously changed in relation to one another during the processes of migration — moving from east to west and from south to north. The Sámi migrated as far north as the North Cape, but proto-Sámi language studies show that the Sámi had inhabited areas much further to the south than they do today (Aikio 2006: 39-47). Evidence of Sámi settlement in the south of Finland can be found in historical documents, at archaeological sites, in local stories, in place names with the prefix *Lappi* (Lapland), as well as in loan words and substrate place names with a Sámi origin. Sámi presence in the southern part of Finland continued until the seventeenth century (Hansen 2011; Hansen and Olsen 2013; Saarikivi 2006).

Experts estimate that the Sámi language is spoken by over 30,000 people. In several contexts, the term *Sámi language* refers to the largest and most widely spoken Sámi language, North Sámi. However, there are currently nine Sámi languages, six of which have a writing system of their own and are used publicly to some extent. Table 3-1 demonstrates the languages and number of speakers in different areas.

Table 3-1: Sámi languages, areas where they are spoken, and estimated numbers of speakers (see, e.g., Seurujärvi-Kari 2013: 61).

Language	Area	Number of Speakers
Western Languages		
South Sámi	Norway, Sweden	300-500
Ume Sámi	Sweden	a few persons
Pite Sámi	Sweden	a few persons
Lule Sámi	Norway, Sweden	1,000-2,000
North Sámi	Norway, Sweden, Finland	30,000 (Norway: 23,000; Sweden: 5,000; Finland: 2,000)
Eastern Languages		
Inari Sámi	Finland	400
Skolt Sámi	Finland, Russia	300
Kildin Sámi	Russia	600
Ter Sámi	Russia	a few persons
Akkala Sámi	Russia	0

The linguistic landscape of the Sámi is highly diverse. Some Sámi people use their language both orally and in writing, while other Sámi speak their own language but cannot read or write it. There are also Sámi people with no knowledge of the Sámi language. Many have reactivated their passive mother tongue in adulthood through studying or by other means, such as by participating in the activities of Sámi associations or other common activities.

Motivation has increased along with the fact that the status of the Sámi has improved, and the Sámi language was recognized as an official language by law in the Sámi homeland at the beginning of the 1990s.

Today, the Sámi people are recognized as an Indigenous People by law, which guarantees them cultural autonomy, as implemented by the Sámi Parliament in Finland, Norway, and Sweden. They have more extensive rights than minorities. Currently, the concept of Indigenous Peoples is defined internationally in the International Labour Organization (ILO) Convention on Indigenous and Tribal Peoples (No. 169) of 1989. The essential elements of the definition are as follows:

- the person regards herself or himself as Indigenous;
- the peoples who have a historical continuity in a certain geographical region;
- the peoples who have a specific culture and way of life different from others of the national population;
- the peoples who do not have a dominant position.

Norway was among the first countries to ratify the Convention in 1990 and recognize the status of the Sámi as an Indigenous People. Finland and Sweden have not ratified the Convention because of unresolved land rights issues with the Sámi, but they have recognized the Sámi as an Indigenous People in their national legal frameworks. According to section 121(4) of the Constitution of Finland (1999), "Provisions on self-government in administrative areas larger than a municipality are laid down by an Act. In their native region, the Sámi have linguistic and cultural self-government, as provided by an Act."

The cultural autonomy of the Sámi is stipulated in more detail in the Act on the Sámi Parliament, which entered into force at the beginning of 1996 (No. 974/95). Section 1 of the Act on the Sámi Parliament stipulates the following: "The Sámi, as an Indigenous people, have linguistic and cultural autonomy in the Sámi homeland as provided in this Act. For the tasks relating to cultural autonomy the Sámi shall elect from among themselves a Sámi Parliament. The Sámi Parliament belongs to the purview of the Ministry of Justice" (Act on the Sámi Parliament [974/1995]).

COLONIZATION AND ASSIMILATION OF THE SÁMI

Indigenous Peoples have traditionally lived and moved around in their own territories, created their own livelihoods and ways of living, and spoken their own languages. The history of colonization and diverse assimilation processes have resulted in the change or disappearance of many of their traditional ways of life, communal values, and languages. We understand colonialism as more than the removal of people from their land; it is a process of hegemony, knowledge, and power with the aim of dominating different cultures in the global world (see, for example, Quijano 2007). These objectives have been assisted by policies of assimilation, a process by which various persons and cultures conform to mainstream national and/or global society.

Sámi assimilation processes have continued for hundreds of years (Hansen and Olsen 2004: 150–233; Minde 2005). For example, during the time of the Swedish Empire, the first two colonization proclamations of 1673 and 1695 given by the rulers for the combined area of Sweden-Finland provided the impetus for colonization and assimilation processes. Sápmi (the area inhabited by the Sámi) has been divided between four countries: Finland, Norway, Sweden, and Russia. As a result of this disintegration of the territorial integrity of Sápmi, the traditional social, economic, and legal systems of the Sámi, such as the traditional *siida* social system, were destroyed. *Siida*, a Sámi (earlier called Lapp) village, consisted of interrelated families with common livelihoods and territories and was guided by commonly held values of shared responsibility, equality, and support for disadvantaged members (Sara 2009: 153-154).

The Christianization efforts and missionary actions directed against the Sámi from the twelfth century until the eighteenth century were also important for spreading the ideas of colonization (Pulkkinen 2005: 218–221). Through the practices of the church, nations could maintain their paternalistic attitudes toward Indigenous Peoples living in small settlements throughout the northern Arctic region. The church introduced the Sámi to literacy and Christian texts. The missionary work and organizational activities of the church were initially ineffective in terms of Christianization, but the situation changed at the end of the sixteenth century and the beginning of the seventeenth century when a race for control of the northern territories and the Arctic Ocean began between the great powers of Sweden-Finland and Russia. Missionary work was one of the strategies employed by the crowns of the different northern kingdoms, in addition to taxation, to take over the northern areas where the

Sámi lived for the purposes of state-building and ideological reasons. By the end of the eighteenth century, the last undivided areas in Europe had been divided between the states (see e.g., Lähteenmäki 2004). Lappologist tradition often categorized the Sámi as people without history and drew from Eurocentric science, stereotypes and myths that placed the Sámi in the lower levels of development and evolution (Hansen-Olsen 2004: 11; Lehtola 2017).

The hundred years of assimilation policies practised by the nation-states between 1850 and 1950 resulted in a dramatic shift in identity and language. During this time, the Sámi minority had to capitulate to the decisions and authority of the majority populations in the Nordic countries. Their rights as individuals and as group members were not officially taken into consideration. This gave rise to an asymmetry between the dominated minorities and the dominant majority of the states. Assimilation measures targeted Sámi languages, which led to them being excluded from public use as well as from the school system. During the rise of nationalism, the Sámi were not the special target of assimilation, but as a result of the ideology of nationalism (*one nation, one language*), the languages of minority peoples were not used in schools and all the students were taught in the majority language (see e.g., Aikio 1987; Stordahl 2008: 253). Residential schools in particular, where most of the Sámi studied, but also Finnish students, became a symbol of state control of the Sámi and of other minorities (NOU 1980: 20; Seurujärvi-Kari 2008: 52). The Sámi pupils who attended residential schools lost close contact with their families because they could visit home only a couple of times a year. They learned to be ashamed of their background and often exchanged their Sámi identity for that of the majority population. This affected the development of parenthood and relationality. Assimilation efforts suppressed the will of the Sámi people for decades (Minde 2005). Recently, several Sámi people have started to openly to tell about their destructive experiences in residential schools.

The relationship between the majority people of the states of Finland, Norway, Sweden, and Russia and the minority Sámi meant that the majority population was not only in a governing position, but also owned the economic, social, and culture capital, which the minority could not possess or access. The majority population in such situations could also take over and control the resources of the minority population, as occurred in 1968 when the Norwegian state-owned energy company (NVE) put forward its first proposal for harnessing the water resources of Finnmark County, in the traditional Sámi homeland (see e.g., Paine 1982: 1–8). The proposal, however, never made it to the Norwegian Parliament because of strong resistance by the Sámi and many others.

In 1978, when the parliament voted in favour of regulating the waters of the Alta-Kautokeino River in Finnmark, a large civil rights movement emerged and several demonstrations were organized both in Oslo, the capital of Norway, and in the north against the construction of a hydroelectric power plant. This movement culminated in a hunger strike by five Sámi youths outside the Norwegian Parliament house in Oslo. In the end, the dam was built (1982–86), though it is smaller than originally planned. There are a few reasons that might account for the success that the Sámi had with the Alta-Kautokeino dispute. First, the movement was led by a group of Sámi who were trained professionals and who knew how to work with the media; and second, the movement worked side-by-side with international environmental activists. These two factors meant that the Sámi were able to garner national and international attention for their plight.

CREATING A SPACE FOR TELLING COLONIAL EXPERIENCES THROUGH ART AND THE ALTA CASE

Both the Sámi movement and Sámi artists have called attention to several forms of injustice in Sámi relations with the nation-states. In addition to the Sámi's own juridical practices and common law, such traditional practices as yoik singing (*juoigat*) and retelling oral stories have been ways of dealing with conflicts (Hämäläinen et al. 2017). By retelling stories or yoiking, the Sámi have had the chance to share, construct, and re-evaluate their colonial experiences with each other. Therefore, singing, yoiking, theatre, and visual arts have been used as a means to speak about individual and collective memories and experiences endured during the assimilation period. In producing such art, the Sámi raise important questions about who gets to write history and who decides what is remembered, what is forgotten, and what counts as truth.

Several Sámi artists, such as Nils-Aslak Valkeapää, Kirsti Paltto, and Ellen Maria Vars, began their careers and the process of emancipation by writing about their residential school memories in the 1970s and 1980s. Their childhood memories included being afraid of school, losing their relationships with their families, and becoming a lost generation — all common themes in their writings. They are personal in nature, but they also reflect collective experiences and feelings. Sámi political and artistic activism was a turning point in Sámi history and ushered in a period of ethnic revival and revitalization.

One such turning point was the Alta-Kautokeino conflict over the construction of a hydroelectric power plant in Sápmi, which ultimately influenced Sámi politics and the Sámi movement in Norway. The case was also addressed and discussed actively by Sámi artists, helping to bolster Sámi values and reinforce a sense of collective identity and community. Reunited, the Sámi leaders began to demand that the state recognize the Sámi people's special rights, such as the rights to their way of life, language, and culture as an Indigenous People (Magga 2000: 250; Paine 1982; Seurujärvi-Kari 2008: 63–64).

In Norway, the Alta case resulted in the establishment of Sámi committees on Sámi rights, culture, and language, the reform of legislation concerning the Sámi language and culture, and the ratification of international conventions concerning minority or Indigenous Peoples. Due to Norway's new Sámi politics, at the opening of the Norwegian Sámi Parliament in 1989, King Olav V apologized to the Sámi for their suffering at the hands of the state during the strongest period of assimilation and Norwegianization, 1850–1950. Furthermore, Norway ratified various international conventions and treaties that demanded stronger protection for Indigenous Peoples, being one of the first countries in the world to ratify ILO Convention No. 169 on June 20, 1990 (Seurujärvi-Kari 2011: 63–64; 2012: 44–46.) Overall, the Alta case and Sámi movement had significant consequences for Sámi politics in neighbouring countries as well.

One important factor for the rise of Sámi knowledge and telling the history from a Sámi perspective has been education and the development of higher education, including the establishment of the Sámi University of Applied Sciences in 1989 (Porsanger 2018). Since the 1990s, the Finnish state has given significant funding and support for teaching the Sámi language from kindergarten to senior high school in the Sápmi area. In recent years, Sámi language teaching has even been supported in the Helsinki Metropolitan Area as a result of requests by the Sámi community. At the opening ceremonies of the Finnish Sámi Parliament in 2004, then Finnish president Tarja Halonen and Samuel Salmi, the bishop of the Oulu diocese of the Lutheran Church in Finland, offered apologies to the Sámi people for the years of discrimination and the injustices committed against them, including wrongdoing during the time of assimilation. Yet, President Halonen stated that it was not an official apology.

The Sámi people's individual memories were rekindled by the rise of the

Sámi movement and the collective sharing of this knowledge through common events. In recent decades, Sámi artists and activists have turned their gazes inward, which has led to the use of Sámi images expressed not only in art but also in media and print. They realized that it was possible to recreate and bring back some Sámi traditions and also use new forms. Traditional rules and rituals, as well as other traditional repetitive practices, such as those related to reindeer herding, were used to strengthen values and norms to form a stronger Sámi community. Stories were retold, and the shared memories reconnected many people's presents with their pasts. The Sámi language played a fundamental role in this process. The Sámi people's narrative gradually created a strong Sámi identity and sense of togetherness. "Sáminess" is still changing, and Sámi media and art today are creating new stories about being Sámi. The interrelated processes of remembering and forgetting are in a constant state of flux and, despite the advances that have been made, the act of collective remembering still reveals many memories of exclusion and refusal. Several Sámi Elders say that these traditions and practices contain wisdom and practical guidance for moving toward reconciliation across the modern landscape.

THE SÁMI COUNCIL AND PARLIAMENT ESTABLISHED

In 2017, the Sámi celebrated the one-hundred-year anniversary of the first political gathering and the beginning of transnational cooperation among Sámi in Norway, Sweden, Finland, and Russia (Larsen 2017). The first Nordic Sámi assembly was arranged in 1917 in Trondheim, Norway. Since the beginning, one of the objectives of the Sámi movement and associations has been to reunite the dispersed Sámi people by means of transnational cooperation to create a common Sámi political agenda. The establishment of the Nordic Sámi Council (renamed the Sámi Council in 1992) in 1953 made the continuation of such gatherings possible on a formal level and encouraged conferences and seminars beyond national borders as a means of Sámi empowerment (Seurujärvi-Kari 2008). From the outset, the strategy of the Sámi Council was to influence national governments through the Nordic Council in order to reach a mutual understanding between the states and the Sámi people and promote Sámi affairs in countries with a Sámi population. The ideological and cultural-political objectives and strategies of the Sámi were included in several joint political and cultural declarations and programs approved at the general Sámi conferences in the 1970s and 1980s.

The Sámi movement grew in strength in the 1970s when it reacted to the prevailing intensive assimilationist policies. At that time, it was also linked to global political changes as well as to the growth of the civil society sector. As discussed in the previous section, Sámi agents gradually succeeded in creating a collective narrative, which led to a strong Sámi identity and feelings of togetherness. The struggle for change has led to many improvements for the Sámi and many political changes have occurred since the time of assimilation.

Finally, as a result of the long, hard work of the Sámi Council, Norway (1989), Sweden (1993), and Finland (1996) recognized the Sámi as an Indigenous People in their constitutions and established the Sámi Parliament (Sámediggi) to promote Sámi self-government. These hard-won gains include, for example, the right to cultural autonomy with respect to their language and culture as an Indigenous People (Finnish Constitution 1995: 121.4; 731/1999). Overall, the Sámi have become a legally recognized Indigenous People in the Nordic countries as a result of the resistance and struggles of the Sámi revitalization movement. Yet, there are still many political issues on the Sámi and Finnish governments' agendas that need to be resolved in order to make a more transformative leap. These issues include the ratification of the ILO Convention No. 169 and the Nordic Sámi Convention, as well as determining how to best define the Sámi and reform the Sámi law.

THE DEBATE ON DEFINING THE SÁMI

The laws concerning Sámi rights, the Act on the Sámi Parliament (974/1995; amendments up to 1026/2003 included) and Sámi Language Act (1086/2003) in Finland have protected and supported the Sámi language. However, in Finland, as in other countries, there is still a need to put the policies into practice in a more effective way. For example, in matters of major importance to the Sámi, negotiations should be held with the various Sámi parliaments before decisions are made by a public authority (Act on the Sámi Parliament 1995, Chapter 2, section 9). These negotiations between the state and Sámi should take place early enough to enable the Sámi parliaments to have a real influence over the proceedings and the result. The states should not adopt or permit measures that may significantly alter the basic conditions for Sámi culture, Sámi livelihoods, or Sámi society unless agreed upon by the appropriate Sámi parliament.

In Finland, the Sámi Parliament has not come up with a meaningful definition of what it means to be Sámi; therefore, renewing the Act on the Sámi Parliament has been suggested. The Act on the Sámi Parliament contains an expanded definition (section3:2) of who is entitled to participate in the elections of the Sámi Parliament (Act on the Sámi Parliament 974/1995). In Norway and Sweden, Sámi ethnicity is not based on ancestry, but primarily on self-identification; that is to say, on whether the person concerned first regards themselves as Sámi, and secondarily, on language (Lov om Sametinget og andre samiske rettsforhold (sameloven) 1989 [section 2-6], Sametingslag 1992: 1433 [1:section2]). However, language skills are not required from the person concerned; so-called retroactive language skills are sufficient. In Finland, the Act on the Sámi Parliament 1995, section3 (Act on the Sámi Parliament 974/1995) defines as Sámi any person who regards himself or herself as Sámi based upon the following conditions:

1. that he or she or at least one of his or her parents or grandparents has/had learned Sámi as his or her first language; or
2. that he or she is the descendant of a person recorded as a Fell, Forest, or Fisher Lapp in cadasters, tax records, or census registers; or
3. that at least one of his or her parents is listed or could have been listed as eligible to vote in the elections of the Sámi Delegation or the Sámi Parliament.

The Act on the Sámi Parliament (974/1995; amendments up to 1026/2003 included) evoked opposition even in its draft stages in the northern parts of Finland and led to years of debate in Finnish Lapland between local people, mainly those belonging to the Lapp Heritage Association, and the various Sámi organizations. The first point of contention was whether there was any actual need for the Act, and after it was passed, the debate turned to whether the descendants of the "Taxed Lapps of the old Lapp villages" should be included in the Sámi electoral roll. Taxed Lapps refer to people living in villages in the "Lapp Tax Lands," who were taxed since the Middle Ages by the Crowns of Sweden (including Finland), Russia, and Norway. This taxation system was abolished in the twentieth century, as was referring to the Sámi people as Lapps (Joona 2005: 186–189). Hence, the Taxed Lapps have provided evidence of Sámi descent dating back several centuries. However, the language criterion in the Sámi definition of Sámi origin can only go back two generations.

The debate on this Act led to numerous investigations by jurists and others concerning the proper definition of who is Sámi. In the autumn of 1999, the

Supreme Administrative Court of Finland issued rulings on the first appeals concerning the registering of persons in the electoral rolls, as stipulated in the Act. The main issue of the appeal was the fact that the appellants regarded themselves as Sámi based on the "Lapp" grounds of the Sámi definition of subsection 2 of the Act on the Sámi Parliament, maintaining that they were, therefore, entitled to vote in the Sámi Parliament elections in the autumn. Almost all the appellants based their claim on their ancestors being recorded as Lapps in the last tax records from the years 1739–1857. In the autumn of 1999, the Supreme Administrative Court granted the status of Sámi based on a Lapp ancestor to less than 1 percent of all 656 appellants. There had originally been over a thousand appeals, but the Court justified its rulings by noting that in defining a person as Sámi, retroactive language skills constitute the criterion for voting rights and Sámi roots cannot be searched further back in history than the language skills of immediate ancestors (Heinämäki et al. 2017: 94). Nowadays, the Sámi language is regarded as the most important indicator of Sámi culture, which differentiates the Sámi from other peoples in such Nordic documents as the Nordic Sámi Convention.

In 2011, the Supreme Administrative Court of Finland (decision KHO: 2011: 81) granted voting rights to ninety-nine appellants and the right to be registered in the electoral rolls of the Sámi Parliament on the basis of self-identification and an overall judgment of the Sáminess of an appellant. Thus, the criterion of self-identification provided important grounds for Sáminess but lessened the self-determination of the Sámi Parliament (Heinämäki et al. 2017: 121–122). The Sámi Parliament had been worried that some people would declare themselves Sámi even if they did not have a close connection with Sámi culture, and when granted the right to vote in Sámi elections, could potentially support decisions that weaken Sámi people's rights in Sápmi. Therefore, the Sámi Parliament demanded a renewal of the Act on the Sámi Parliament in order to remove the part (section3.2.) of the Sámi definition concerning the Taxed Lapps in the 1995 Act on the Sámi Parliament (Act on the Sámi Parliament 974/1995).

At the end of 2017, the Ministry of Justice set up a committee to prepare for the renewal process. The Sámi-State Renewal Committee formulated amendments of the definition and the state's duty to negotiate with the Sámi Parliament. In the Act proposal, being registered as a Sámi allows the right to register a person in the electoral roll of the Sámi Parliament of Finland or to vote in the Sámi Parliament election. The proposed Sámi definition follows the

Norwegian model as well as the rules of the Nordic Sámi Convention based on self-identification and retroactive home language. The committee sent a proposal to the Parliament on June 17, 2018, regarding the development of Sámi autonomy. However, ultimately the Sámi Parliament rejected the agreement on the grounds that the proposal should have included the prerequisites of land use or business. The international conventions concerning the rights of Indigenous Peoples deal with collective rights in particular. Similarly, the present Act on the Sámi Parliament (No. 974/1995:1) states that "the Sámi, as an Indigenous people, have linguistic and cultural autonomy in the Sámi homeland as provided in this Act," but the aim of re-examining the Sámi Parliament Act is to improve the operating conditions of the Sámi Parliament and Sámi cultural autonomy.

The Sámi Parliament also opposed the decisions of the Finnish Supreme Administrative Court to add a greater number of people to the electoral list of the Sámi Parliament and that the Sámi Parliament could not ultimately define who is a Sámi. It appealed officially to the UN Human Rights Committee, which reported the Sámi Parliament's communication in 2019 (Human Rights Committee 2019). However, the statement of the UN Human Rights Committee was criticized by some Sámi for being one-sided. Consequently, the discussions were lively in the media, communities, and academia, including the opinion that the rejected applicants by the Sámi Parliament had aimed at benefiting wrongly from being officially recognized as Sámi. In fact, some of the rejected applicants were individuals whose relatives were already registered as Sámi and who identified as Sámi, including participating in Sámi lifestyle and practices.

THE NORDIC SÁMI CONVENTION AS A PART OF SÁMI RECONCILIATION

The Sámi reconciliation process, which started with the rise of the Sámi movement, also includes the drafting, signing, and ratification process of the Nordic Sámi Convention between three Sámi parliaments and three states — Finland, Norway, and Sweden. This process has continued for over a decade. The draft for the Nordic Sámi Convention was submitted to the Nordic governments and the Sámi parliaments by an expert committee in October 2005. However, the Sámi were the first to take up the idea of drafting the Nordic Sámi Convention in the 1980s (Koivurova 2008). The draft for the Convention emphasizes the fact that the Sámi people are not the Indigenous People of one state, but of four nation-states. The central aim of the draft was to introduce issues that have resulted from the dispersion of the Sámi and decrease the significance of borders with respect to Sámi issues, making it possible for them to live in areas across national borders and to protect and strengthen the Sámi culture and Sámi knowhow without being restricted by nationality or place of residence. The draft for the Nordic Sámi Convention also includes a comprehensive survey of how the international human rights conventions, particularly the Convention No. 169 of the ILO on Indigenous and Tribal Peoples (1989) and the UN Declaration on the Rights of Indigenous Peoples (UNDRIP) (2007), are applicable to the Sámi as an Indigenous People.

At the end of 2016, the states reached a mutual agreement on the legal rules of the Convention and put them into effect in 2017 (Heinämäki and Cambou 2018). Now it is up to the Sámi Parliament to accept or abandon the rules before the signing and ratifying process can take place. If ratification occurs, this work would result in new legislation concerning all Sámi living in three countries, forming a basis for self-determination. According to Koivurova (2008), the Sámi Convention can be regarded more as a social contract than a normal international convention between three nation-states and the people who share a common region. Johanna Suurpää (2017), who has been the main representative of the Finnish national state in this long process, emphasizes that the draft Convention includes the obligation for the state to negotiate with the Sámi Parliament, with the aim of reaching a mutual understanding concerning Sámi affairs between the state and Sámi people. The Sámi definition of the rules of the Convention follows the Norwegian model, which is based on self-identification and retroactive home language (Nordic Sámi Convention 2005: Article 13, *The electoral list of the Saami Parliament)*. This joint Sámi definition could also serve as a good solution for the long-lasting conflict of defining who is Sámi and of registering a person in the electoral rolls of the Sámi Parliament of Finland (Koivurova 2008; Suurpää 2017).

The Nordic Sámi Convention between the Sámi and the three states of Norway, Sweden, and Finland (drafted in 2005, agreement reached in 2017), still awaits ratification. Ratifying the Convention would ensure the position of the Sámi as equals in the Nordic states, especially concerning Sámi identification issues, the criteria for defining membership, and the right to vote in Sámi elections. It could also help reconcile historical wrongs toward the Sámi by the states. Thus, among many, the pain of colonization, assimilation, and complex mistrustful relations continue to exist.

CURRENT RECONCILIATION PROCESSES AND PLANS

The generations of discrimination and trauma have taken a toll on the Sámi that cannot easily be overcome, and much more work needs to be done to help the Sámi deal with this transgenerational trauma. The Sámi parliaments in Finland, Norway, and Sweden filed motions for a Sámi Truth and Reconciliation Commission with the governments of their respective states in 2016 and 2017. For the Sámi Parliament, it was necessary to examine the wrongdoings and injustices against the Sámi during assimilation and let the people themselves tell their stories. There is a need to re-interpret history through texts written by the Sámi themselves since most of their history, similar to the history of other Indigenous Peoples, has not been written from their own perspective despite the fact that the Sámi people are one of the most researched Indigenous groups in the world. The Sámi and other Indigenous Peoples have a right to their own history and its interpretation on their own terms and from their own perspectives.

The model for this commission comes from the Final Report of the Truth and Reconciliation Commission of Canada (2015: 16), according to which "reconciliation is an ongoing process of establishing and maintaining respectful relationships." The Commission deals with, among other things, the wrongs done to Indigenous children as a result of residential schooling. It is notable that millions of Canadian dollars were spent on this process to work on reconciliation, and these millions could equally be applied to Indigenous populations' culture, language, and education. Unlike the Canadian Commission, the report from Greenland's reconciliation commission, *Vi forstås fortiden. Vi tager ansvar för nutiden. Vi arbejder for en bedre fremtid* (Grönlands Forsoningskommissionen 2017), emphasizes work that should be done in the future and does not focus as much on the past or on victimization. Truth and reconciliation work in South Africa (National Centre for Truth and Reconciliation: Internet Archives) and certain South American countries, where the human rights situation is much worse than in the countries mentioned above, also looks different. However, those last-mentioned truth and reconciliation commissions failed in achieving reconciliation between the states and the people.

Ethnological research on memory suggests that commonly shared and recognized cultural meanings are passed on to others and through generations via remembering and forgetting (see for example Assmann and Conrad 2010).

According to Pirjo Korkiakangas (2001), historically significant events can be perceived either through individuals' memories and oral histories or at a collective level. We have seen how youth struggle with their own experiences of colonization and assimilation, but they are also affected by transgenerational memories (see also Guttorm 2018). Despite the successes of the Sámi and the work that has been done to expose and reconcile the trauma experienced by the Sámi, young people are still haunted by transgenerational trauma. Additionally, many youth continue to experience trauma as the Sámi continue to fight for recognition and reconciliation. As a consequence, in Finland, the discussion regarding the Sámi and among the Sámi themselves has become quite aggressive, much more so than among the Sámi youth in Norway. We argue that this is because the Finnish government has agreed to support economic development from one perspective only, on its own terms, rather than with consultation and respectful negotiation with the Sámi. For example, a law was passed concerning the Deatnu River (in Finnish Teno) along the Finnish-Norwegian border that limits local people's rights to fishing but allows for more recreational or sport fishing (Finnish Parliament 2018). The law evoked opposition among some Sámi and gave rise to protests against the state, with the protestors stating that agreements with the Sámi were not being honoured and that the international conventions are that such rights should be better implemented.

Information and communication technologies play a significant role in political activism, and especially young people use the media to present their own ideas about the current Sámi situation and how the Sámi are represented and defined. This has been crucial for a public discussion on Sámi issues. However, even if social media raises awareness and mobilizes people among all age groups, some manifestations concerning Sámi politics, culture, and definitions have also become more restrictive and divisive for the Sámi themselves, as well as between non-Indigenous and Indigenous populations. Then representations of and debates on Sámi identity can be based on essentializing opinions, for example, highlighting cultural distinctiveness, and firmly protecting Sámi culture and language against acts of colonization can turn into forms of discrimination, even among the Sámi themselves. Those who express different opinions can be excluded from the notion of so-called "authentic" Sáminess, although they are recognized as Sámi within the community and have officially been recognized as being of Sámi descent.

It seems that the gaps between different factions, on the one hand between the Sámi and the Finnish state, and on the other hand between the local people in Sápmi, non-Sámi and Sámi, are growing. Furthermore, the relations and debates among the Sámi themselves are not unproblematic when Indigeneity and Sáminess are (re)conceptualized. The views on Sáminess and the Sámi definition are not shared by all, and that does not make reconciliation an easy path to walk. In Finland, Sáminess has recently become a contested concept and the definition of who is Sámi is dependent upon who is defining it.

The reconciliation process in Finland still has many unresolved questions, such as which issues should be reconciled and which leaders and members will be included in the process. Diverse voices are claiming to be Sámi, while others are denying or ignoring it. For these problematic reasons, several public hearings by the Prime Minister's office have been held in 2018 in various parts of the country to hear the opinions of the Sámi on the Truth and Reconciliation Commission's mandate, role, mission, and possible commissioners. We also would like to draw attention to reconciliation in the long run: What will happen after and alongside the truth discussions? The reconciliation process should not be used as a political tool to draw attention from other issues or treated as a parallel action that will diminish Indigenous Rights on other issues. Besides reconciliation discussions, an increasing number of economic projects are being conducted on Sámi lands without the mandatory negotiations established in Finnish law.

Sámi people have also commented in different media that reconciliation can also be crucial as a form of therapy to understand what has happened in a history that cannot always be easily understood and conceptualized. Others, however, are worried that the process can also create new traumas when people start (re-)remembering things from the past and things may look worse than they actually were, causing harm to some, or they might not have happened at all or have been the same experiences for everyone.

OUR RESPONSIBILITIES: RECONCILIATION THROUGH ACADEMIA

Scholars can also promote reconciliation work and influence the results so that reconciliation will not become just talk, but instead lead to proper changes at both the political and educational levels (Lightfoot 2017). Our academic institution, the University of Helsinki, and its Indigenous Studies program, which started in 2015, is aiming to take Indigenous histories and knowledge seriously, in ways that rarely have been regarded as academically valid (see Battiste 2013). Listening to Indigenous communities and voices can reveal the injustices in political processes. This includes reflections on whether real reconciliation is happening (Lightfoot 2017).

Our Indigenous Studies program at the University of Helsinki draws simultaneously from micro and macro levels, as well as insider points of view, through a focus on Indigenous concepts, values, and ideas. It welcomes indigeneity into academia, showing that Indigenous Peoples have too rarely been examined with their own view of history and social philosophies as a starting point. The starting point for teaching and conducting research through the Indigenous Studies program is Indigenous knowledge and knowledge-making processes. Therefore, the core focus of the program is informed by Indigenous epistemologies and ontologies as valid and legitimate forms of knowledge for critical discussion in relation to other forms. It encourages the creative use of Indigenous research methodologies in order to achieve more valid and sustainable research. The program also teaches about Indigenous Rights, including the international frameworks — such as UNDRIP, ILO, and the International Human Rights Covenants — and national laws and constitutions.

Another significant step and change that has been adopted as part of our teaching program emphasizes research ethics as a core aspect of the program and raises awareness about research protocols (Battiste 2008: 513). Taking responsive and reflective acts as the basis for teaching and research makes this discipline different from other study programs. Creating safe spaces for new dialogues and encounters is crucial, as well as promoting collaboration and respectful relationships with Indigenous Peoples, as Indigenous Peoples themselves have felt that there are several issues that must be addressed and heard outside of their communities (Wilson 2013). We invite students to look critically at the needs of Indigenous communities. This is implemented not only by teaching and conducting research but also by organizing seminars, conferences, and public debates, as well as by raising general awareness about these issues. At least these are the objectives, even if their realistic implementation is another issue due to financial and large geographical distances.

Consequently, during the first years, according to feedback, the program has greatly influenced many students' viewpoints. The courses have changed their ways of thinking about the world, making invisible power relations and structural discrimination visible, as well as contextualizing the histories of different actors. In fact, a study done by our program revealed that in the Finnish school system, very little information is offered about the Sámi people as an Indigenous People. Rather, they are represented as one of the minorities of

Finland, and the images of them often include stereotypes such reindeers, Sámi shaman drums, or traditional costumes, or a Sámi flag, but what the images symbolize is not described.

Sámi and Indigenous Studies have for a long time organized a Sámi National Day celebration: the Sámi flag is raised in front of the main buildings of the university, followed by the singing of the Sámi national song in the three different Sámi languages spoken in Finland (North Sámi, Skolt Sámi, and Inari Sámi). The event gathers together the Sámi community, civil servants, and researchers from different fields. In 2018, in the speeches, it was acknowledged and celebrated that the Sámi Parliament had produced teaching materials on the Sámi for use at different school levels and that the city of Helsinki had started a Sámi-speaking kindergarten group. From the perspective of our program, these changes were very good news, as increasing awareness and information about the Sámi and Indigenous Peoples is one of the most important results of the Indigenous Studies program at our university.

DIFFERENT STORIES OF RECONCILIATION AT THE PERSONAL LEVEL

Reconciliation means different things at the individual level. For the first author, teaching, researching, and participating in Sámi politics and the Sámi movement have been an important way to participate in the reconciliation process. Acting in the Sámi organizations opened her eyes to how strong the power of community can be when people focus their collective strength behind a common issue. They can change the world: from Sámi stigmatization toward restoration and revitalization. This process has also been captured in a poem by the first Finnish Sámi writer, Pedar Jalvi:

> *Muohtačalmmit* (Snowflakes): *Giddabeaivváš muoduid ovddas suddet smávva muohtačalmmit* šelges čáhcegoaikkanassan. *Goaikkanasas* čoggojit *dat* ájan, *deatnun, jávrin, mearran — stuoris lea dalle daid fápmu* (In front of the spring sun's face, the small snowflakes melt into clear water drops. From the water drop, they accumulate into small and big rivers, lakes, seas — enormous will their power then be). (1981 [1915]: 3)

Even if many of the first author's generation were forced to leave their home and family to study, for work or for some other reason, they could find another kind of home. In her journey, the circle and sense of family have grown larger and larger, so that it now encompasses the entire Indigenous world. However, Sámi identity is continuously reflected in my close relationship with my first home through the kin still living there and the Sámi language. This childhood landscape has been transferred as a topical lived experience throughout my whole life.

The most important teachers of the second author have been Amazonian Indigenous Peoples, especially the Apurinã and Manchineri, from different age groups and backgrounds. Co-living with these people has taught her the tragic experiences of colonialism — stories about invasions, even massacres, and the injustice still existing in various forms, especially unequal education and health services. This has provided the basis for understanding the similar experiences shared by Indigenous Peoples in various geographical locations and to teach about them. On the other hand, the Amazonian Indigenous teachers have taught the second author to experience relational ontologies and epistemologies at a very practical level. The Amazonian socio-philosophies underline relationality between humans and nonhumans and that existence is related to different life forms. They are crucial actors in order to understand Indigenous struggles and their relations to the land. The general ignorance of Indigenous histories is not only typical of Latin America but around the world (Mignolo 2011). The current academic work done in the name of decolonization and indigenization (Nakata 2006) through Indigenous Studies programs is a small personal step in achieving reconciliation between those who have dominated and those who have been oppressed.

CONCLUSION

In this chapter, we have depicted a long and continuous process of reconciliation in relations between the state and the Sámi, and also between several other actors. The vagueness of the reconciliation process is the result of two main issues: the longstanding and growing economic interests of the state, such as those of mining and logging companies, in the Sámi area; and the still unresolved question of who is Sámi.

In addition, the Finnish Sámi Parliament has continuously complained about a lack of resources to fulfill the aims of the Sámi Parliament Act to promote Sámi linguistic, cultural, and economic rights. At the same time, large economic projects are being planned for the Arctic region, often without a proper consultation process with the Sámi and other local actors. As a result, the Sámi are becoming less hopeful about the success of the reconciliation process. In fact, some of the former Sámi political leaders would rather use their limited resources to benefit Sámi communities through educational training and support for local livelihoods and economics than for a formal reconciliation process. However, those who would like to continue the reconciliation process have suggested that Finland might follow the example of Norway. In June 2018, a truth and reconciliation commission consisting of twelve experts from relevant fields was established with the aim of examining Norwegian politics and historical and contemporary wrongdoing not only toward the Sámi but also toward the Norwegian Finns, the Kvens. The Commission will submit its report by autumn of 2022.

Overall, through our research, we have learned that reconciliation must be actualized at various levels — personal, communal, regional, state — and in education institutions. Education and dialogue are the best methods for building trust and relationships between different persons and groups, and for transforming the world into a more humane and tolerant place. Merely including reindeer, Sámi drums, or the aurora borealis as depictions of the Sámi is not enough; a genuine dialogue between Finnish and Sámi politicians, Sámi communities, students, teachers, and researchers, as well as diverse local actors, is needed.

REFERENCES

Act on the Sámi Parliament (974/1995); amendments up to (1026/2003). <https://www.finlex.fi/fi/laki/kaannokset/1995/en19950974.pdf>.

Aikio, Ante. 2006. "On Germanic-Saami Contacts and Saami Prehistory." *Suomalais-Ugrilaisen Seuran Aikakauskirja*, 91. <https://www.academia.edu/1959273/On_Germanic-Saami_contacts_and_Saami_prehistory>. DOI: 10.33340/susa.81944.

___. 2012. "An Essay on Saami Ethnolinguistic Prehistory." In Riho Grünthal and Petri Kallio (eds.), *A Linguistic Map of Prehistoric Northern Europe*. Helsinki: Finno-Ugrian Society.

Assmann, Aleida, and Sebastian Conrad. 2010. *Memory in a Global Age: Discourses, Practices and Trajectories*. New York: Palgrave Macmillan.

Battiste, Marie. 2008. "Research Ethics for Protecting Indigenous Knowledge and Heritage: Institutional and Researcher Responsibilities." In N.K. Denzin, Y.S. Lincoln, and L. Tuhiwai Smith (eds.), *Handbook of Critical and Indigenous Methodologies*. Los Angeles: Sage.

Constitution of Finland. 1999. <http://www.finlex.fi/fi/laki/kaannokset/1999/en19990731.pdf>.

Finnish Parliament. 2018. HE 10/2018 vp. <https://www.eduskunta.fi/FI/vaski/KasittelytiedotValtiopaivaasia/Sivut/HE_10+2018.aspx>.

Grönlands Forsoningskommissionen. 2017. "Betenkningudgivet af Grönlands Forsoningskommission." *Vi forstås fortiden. Vi tager ansvar för nutide. Vi arbejder for en bedre fremtid.* Nuuk.

Guttorm, Hanna-Ellen. 2018. "Flying Beyond: Diverse Sáminesses and Be(com)ing Sámi." *Reconceptualizing Educational Research Methodology*, 9, 1: 43–54.

Hämäläinen, Soile, Frauke Musial, Ola Graff, Torjer A. Olsen, and Anita Salamonsen. 2017. "Yoik Experiences and Possible Positive Health Outcomes: An Explorative Pilot Study." *International Journal of Circumpolar Health*, 76, 1. <https://www.ncbi.nlm. nih.gov/pmc/articles/PMC5328371/>.

Hansen, Lars Ivar. 2011. "Näkökulmia saamelaisten historiaan." In Irja Seurujärvi-Kari, Petri Halinen and Risto Pulkkinen (eds.), *Saamentutkimus tänään*. Helsinki: Finnish Literature Society.

Hansen, Lars Ivar, and Björnar Olsen. 2004. *Samenes historie fram til 1750*. Oslo: J.W. Cappelens Forlag as.

___. 2013. *Hunters in Transition: An Outline of Early Sámi History*. Brill.

Heinämäki, Leena, and Dorothee Cambou. 2018. "New Proposal for the Nordic Sámi Convention: An Appraisal of the Sámi People's Right to Self-Determination." *Retfærd: nordisk juridisk tidsskrift*, 41, 2: 3–18.

Heinämäki, Leena, et al. 2017. *Saamelaisten oikeuksien toteutuminen: kansainvälinen oikeusvertaileva tutkimus*. Helsinki: Valtioneuvoston kanslia.

Human Rights Committee. 2019. "Views adopted by the Committee under article 5 (4) of the Optional Protocol, concerning communication No. 2668/2015." International Covenant on Civil and Political Rights CCPR/C/124/D/2668/2015 (1 February). <https://tbinternet.ohchr.org/Treaties/CCPR/Shared%20Documents/FIN/ CCPR_C_124_D_2668_2015_28169_E.pdf>.

ILO–Indigenous and Tribal Peoples Convention (No. 169). 1989. <https:// www.ilo.org/dyn/normlex/en/f?p=NORMLEXPUB:12100:0::NO::P121 00_ILO_CODE:C169>.

Jalvi, Pedar. 1981 [1915]. *Muohtačalmmit*. Sámiráddi. Ohcejohka.

Joona, Juha. 2005. "Lapp Villages and Lapp Tax Lands." In Ulla-Maija Kulonen, Irja Seurujärvi-Kari, and Risto Pulkkinen (eds.), *The Saami. A Cultural Encyclopaedia*. Helsinki: Finnish Literature Society.

Koivurova, Timo. 2008. "The Draft Nordic Saami Convention: Nations Working Together." *International Community Law Review*, 10: 279–293.

Korkiakangas, Pirjo. 2001. "Historia muistina ja muisti historiana." *Historiallinen aikakauskirja*, 99: 2–18.

Larsen, Vibeke. 2017. "Lea sápmelaččaid jahki." <https://avvir.no/se/ oddasat/2017/01/2017-lea-sapmelaccaid-jahki>.

Lehtola, Veli-Pekka. 2017. "Vanishing Lapps, Progress in Action: Finnish Lappology and Representations of the Sámi in Publicity on the Early 20th Century." *Arktika I Sever*, 27: 83–102.

Lightfood, Sheryl R. 2017. "Revealing, Reporting, and Reflecting. Indigenous Studies Research as Praxis in Reconciliation Process." In Chris Andersen and Jean M. O'Brien (eds.), *Sources and Methods in Indigenous Studies*. London: Routledge.

Lov om Sametinget og andre samiske rettsforhold (sameloven). 1989. <https://lovdata.

no/dokument/NL/lov/1987-06-12-56>.

Magga, Ole Henrik. 2000. "The Alta Conflict and Its Significance for Sámi Culture." In Jukka Pennanen and Klementti Näkkäläjärvi (eds.), *Siiddastallan: siidoista kyliin. Luontosidonnainen saamelaiskulttuuri ja sen muuttuminen.* Oulu: Pohjoinen.

Mignolo, Walter D. 2011. *The Darker Side of Western Modernity: Global Futures, Decolonial Options.* Durham & London: Duke University Press.

Minde, Henry. 2005. "Assimilation of the Sámi — Implementation and Consequences." *Journal of Indigenous Peoples Rights,* 3.

Nakata, Martin. 2006. "Australian Indigenous Studies: A Question of Discipline." *The Australian Journal of Anthropology,* 17, 3: 265–275.

National Center for Truth and Reconciliation: Internet Archives. <http://nctr.ca/map.php/>.

Nordic Sámi Convention. 2005. "Luonnos pohjoismaiseksi saamelaissopimukseksi" [draft for the Nordic Sámi Convention]. <https://www.regjeringen.no/globalassets/upload/aid/temadokumenter/sami/sami_samskonvensjonen_finsk_h-2183-f.pdf>.

___. 2017. "Saamelaissopimus parafioitu 2017." <https://samiidguovddassearvi.files.wordpress.com/2018/10/saamelaissopimusparafoitu_2017suomi.pdf>.

NOU. 1980: 59. *Sámegiella vuoddoskuvllas.* Oslo–Bergen–Tromsø: Universitetsforlaget.

Paine, Robert. 1982. *Dam a River, Damn a People? Saami (Lapp) Livelihood and the Alta/ Kautokeino Hydro-Electric Project and the Norwegian Parliament.* Copenhagen: IWGIA Document 45: 1–24.

Porsanger, Jelena. 2018. "Building Sámi Language Higher Education: The Case of Sámi University of Applied Sciences." In Elizabeth McKinley and Linda Smith (eds.), *Handbook of Indigenous Education.* Singapore: Springer.

Pulkkinen, Risto. 2005. "Missionary Work: History." In Ulla-Maija Kulonen, Irja Seurujärvi-Kari, and Risto Pulkkinen (eds.), *The Saami: A Cultural Encyclopaedia.* Helsinki: Finnish Literature Society.

Quijano, Anibal. 2007. "Coloniality and Modernity/Rationality." *Cultural Studies,* 21, 2: 168–178.

Saarikivi, Janne. 2006. "Substrata Uralica: Studies on Finno-Ugrian Substrate in Northern Russian Dialects." Doctoral dissertation. Helsinki: University of Helsinki.

Sametingslag. 1992. 1433. SFS nr: 1992:1433. <http://www.riksdagen.se/sv/dokument-lagar/dokument/svensk-forfattningssamling/sametingslag-19921433_sfs-1992-1433>.

Sámi Language Act. 1086/2003. <https://www.finlex.fi/en/laki/kaannokset/2003/en20031086.pdf>.

Sara, Mikkel Nils. 2009. "Siida and Traditional Sámi Reindeer Herding Knowledge." *Northern Review,* 30: 153–178.

Seurujärvi-Kari, Irja. 2008. "'We Took Our Language Back' — The Formation of a Sámi Identity within the Sámi Movement and the Role of the Sámi Language from the 1960s until 2008." In Riho Grünthal and Magdolna Kovács (eds.), *Ethnic and Linguistic Context of Identity: Finno-Ugric Minorities.* Helsinki: University of Helsinki.

___. 2012. *Ale jaskkot eatnigiella. Alkuperäiskansaliikkeen ja saamen kielen merkitys saamelaisten identiteetille.* Doctoral dissertation. University of Helsinki.

___. 2013. "Saamelaisdiskurssi, kieli ja valta. Alkuperäiskansaidentiteetin rakentaminen."

In Pirjo K. Virtanen, Lea Kantonen, and Irja Seurujärvi-Kari (eds.), *Alkuperäiskansat tämän päivän maailmassa*. Helsinki: Suomalaisen Kirjallisuuden Seura. Tietolipas 244.

Stordahl, Vigdis. 2008. "Nation Building: Through Knowledge Building. The Discourse of Sámi Higher Education and Research in Norway." In Harald Gaski, S. Jentoft and G. Midré (eds.), *Indigenous Peoples: Self-Determination Knowledge Indigeneity*. Delft: Eburon.

Suurpää, Johanna. 2017. Interview by Irja Seurujärvi-Kari. January 17 in Helsinki.

TRC final report. 2015. *Honouring the Truth, Reconciling for the Future. Summary of the Final Report of the Truth and Reconciliation Commission of Canada*. <http://www.trc.ca/websites/trcinstitution/index.php?p=890>.

UNDRIP (United Nations Declaration on the Rights of. Indigenous Peoples). 2007. <https://www.un.org/esa/socdev/unpfii/documents/DRIPS_en.pdf>.

Wilson, Shawn. 2013. "Using Indigenist Research to Shape Our Future." In Mel Grey, John Coates, Michael Yellowbird, and Tiani Heatherington (eds.), *Decolonizing Social Work*. Burlington: Ashgate.

Chapter Four

RECONCILIATION THROUGH DECOLONIZATION

*Returning to a First Nations Way of Life
Through Art and Recognition of Land*

COLLEEN J. CHARLES

My identity as Cree is an important part of my reconciliation. I am from the Lac La Ronge Indian Band, Treaty Six Territory of the Woodland Cree, with the "TH" dialect in the north-central area. There are five Cree dialects, with three in Saskatchewan alone. The Swampy Cree reside in the northeast and the Plains Cree reside south of Prince Albert, Saskatchewan. The Dene resides in the North-West and far-North regions as well. My grandparents on my mother's side, Betsy Ratt (nee Ross), Cree from Montreal Lake, and Denver Joseph Ratt (often called D-Joe Ratt), Dene from the Black Bear Island Lake area, north-west of Missinipi (Otter Lake) had eighteen children in total. His mother, my great-grandmother Annie, was married three times with surnames Ratt, Halkett, and Hamilton. She was Dene from Wollaston Lake, in the far north of Saskatchewan. My mother, Hannah, was born in 1951 at McTavish Lake, on my grandparents' trapline, as they called it. A place where they hunted, fished, trapped, and gathered berries. It was their home. There was no highway at that time so they travelled their trapline by canoe, paddling up the Montreal River from Montreal Lake to Lac La Ronge. Today, one would have to travel one hour by car north of La Ronge, then hop on a small plane for twenty minutes to reach McTavish Lake in northern Saskatchewan. My biological father is Gregg Charles; his parents are Lizzie "Betsy" Charles (nee Eninew), Cree from Nemeiben (Sucker) River, twenty minutes north of La Ronge, and Adam Charles, Cree from Potato River/Bow River area, south of La Ronge. My biological father is the youngest of twelve children. He married my mother in 1968 when she was eighteen and he was nineteen. I was born a year later, followed by two younger brothers. My parents separated when I was five years old so I did not grow up with my biological father's side of the family. I have a stepfather, Brian Bathgate, and a stepbrother, whom I refer to as my brother. My grandmother from my stepfather's side, Gwen (Daintree) Bathgate, English, was born in Kettleston, Saskatchewan. According to my stepfather, this town does not exist anymore. She lived to be ninety-eight years old. My grandfather, William Claire Bathgate, a Scottish man, was born in Sarles, North Dakota and only became a Canadian citizen in the 1970s. They had four children; my stepfather has three sisters. He finally married my mother in 2015, and they had been together for forty years.

Residential school experiences have negatively impacted my family and my identity. My mother and biological father both attended residential school, as did I for a short time. The experience still haunts me to this day. If you have the chance to see the movie *Indian Horse,* then you will have an idea of what I went through. I remember having to wear a dress for Sunday church services and sit on one side of the benches while the boys were dressed in suits and sat on the other side. We had to clean the bathrooms with a toothbrush and when you are only seven years old, it takes a long time. They made me wear clothes that were tight and if they ripped, it was deemed my fault and I was beaten. I tried to tell them but they would not listen. My mom came to visit me after one month at the school, and when I told her I wanted to go home with her, she took me out of that place. Her little brother, who was only two years older than me, asked her if he could come home with her as well, but she could not take him because she was not his mother. He had to stay there — I still remember the look on his face when we left.

Recognizing the importance of land is another significant part of my identity. I remember picking berries with my grandmother, mother, and aunties south of La Ronge. The stories they told and the laughter — those were the best days to be out on the land among the trees, small rivers, and the smell of campfire. Margaret Kovach (2009: 94) suggested that "stories remind us of who we are and of our belonging.... They tie us with our past and provide a basis for continuity with future generations." Stories, passed down through oral traditions, tell the children about the wihtikow (a monster in the woods) in order to teach us to respect the land, animals, plants, and medicines. As children, the story of the wihtikow keeps us close so we do not wander off in the woods. This was my experience, but my children know very little about the ancient stories. There are certain stories that are told at different times of each season. The Woodland Cree have six seasons: summer, fall, freeze-up, winter, break-up, and spring. Colonialism, residential schools, and the Sixties Scoop have greatly impacted the way of life for Indigenous Peoples in Canada. Land, language, culture, and children were taken away — and those children were adopted into white families — resulting in the loss of many of these stories and the tradition of sharing them. In the following, I explain how my art has been an important part of my process of reconciliation. I believe that my art is a means of returning to this way of life — art and recognition of land are part of my decolonization and reconciliation.

ART AS DECOLONIZATION

To me, the terms *decolonization* and *reconciliation* are about healing, moving forward, recreating oneself, and understanding the *other*. But before someone can understand decolonization, they must first understand what colonialism is and how it struck its mighty whip to try and "break the Indian" inside the child. I have found Winona Stevenson (now Wheeler) and Rodolfo Pino's (1997) *The Five Stages of Colonialism* helpful for understanding the brief history and contemporary aspects of colonialism. I have used their ideas to create an art workshop called Colonialism on Canvas, which utilizes art to teach people about colonialism and decolonization.

The Five Stages of Colonialism

Before colonization, the land was pristine, with clear rivers flowing, trees thriving, and wild animals in abundance; more than enough for the Indigenous Peoples across Canada. (Saysewahum) Sylvia McAdams (2015: 22) notes that prior to the arrival of the Europeans, a child would have been taken into a ceremony, a form of welcoming him/her into the Nation, but "since European contact, the Indigenous birth has been disrupted, and much of the teachings that are involved were illegalized through the *Indian Act,* along with the ceremonies." This criminalization of ceremonies is just one example of colonialism. In *The Five Stages of Colonialism,* Stevenson and Pino (1997) describe the process of colonialism as having the following stages: steady state, first encounter, colonial relations, internalized colonialism, and decolonization. In what follows, I will define each stage and then use my family's experience and perspective to examine how First Nations have experienced the movement through these stages.

Steady State

Indigenous scholars Winona Stevenson and Rudolfo Pino (1997) explained steady state with the following stages: i) traditional worldviews, philosophies, and spirituality intact; ii) Aboriginal laws and customs function to maintain social cohesion in families and communities; iii) Aboriginal family structures are healthy and balanced; and iv) Aboriginal communities are autonomous and self-sufficient. At night, my father told me, they used to walk in the forest by moonlight so they could see where they were going. His trapline is fifteen minutes south of La Ronge by car and five minutes east of the Creighton Junction by Bow River. As a young girl, I went to visit him on his trapline. I remember he caught a rabbit and gave it to me as a pet. But two days later, he killed it and showed me how to skin it. Supper was rabbit stew. That is how it was and, for him, how it continues to be. He still hunts and traps animals.

In northern Woodland Cree area, they hunted moose and small animals, fished, and gathered berries and medicines. Further south, the Plains Cree, largely in central Saskatchewan, relied on the bison for their main source of food; bison were interpreted as buffalo by Europeans. Through non-disruptive bison hunting and the preservation of beaver meat to ensure a reliable supply of food and water, plains bison hunters not only averted the hardship endured by their neighbours in the eastern woodlands but also appear to have flourished in the centuries before contact (Daschuk 2013: 8).

First Nations people live in harmony with the land, animals, and water. Respect is shown through ceremonies to give thanks to the Creator. Everything has a place and a purpose. To be born Cree is to be born into the lands, cultures, and languages of the people as well as to the responsibilities and obligations (McAdam 2015: 27). Stories are often told to keep the traditions alive. Herman Michell from the Peter Ballantyne Cree Nation wrote that:

> The North is fully alive at this time of the year. Sacred and mysterious ancient voices from the land travel in whispers through air entering dreams and thoughts of storytellers where there is no beginning and no end. Winter is a time when certain stories are told in northern Bush Cree trapping families. (2015: 172)

First Encounter

First encounter was defined by Stevenson and Pino (1997) as the following: i) colonial agents (merchants) arrive seeking economic profits; ii) Aboriginal Peoples enter the global market system, created by the Europeans, as producers of resources; and iii) Aboriginal Peoples become increasingly dependent on foreign commodities which draw them further into the colonial economy. With the arrival of the Europeans came the destruction of the lands and demise of the First Nations way of life. The fur trade era took its place and "firewater" (alcohol) was introduced to the First Nations people. The Numbered Treaties were established with the colonizer starting from 1871 onwards. First Nations cultures, languages, and lands were disrupted. As we learned in our history books, Christopher Columbus arrived in the Americas in 1492 and for years to come, many explorers and missionaries decided to leave their mark as well. Early European maritime explorers found the Indigenous Peoples fascinating because they felt that they illustrated what people were like when stripped of Christian and civilized behaviour (Oswalt and Neely 1988: 35). With this pervasive mentality toward the original inhabitants came strategies for wiping them off the land. Descriptions of game scarcity and human losses from newly introduced diseases have been present since the earliest written accounts from western Canada (Daschuck 2013: 11). The colonizers were motivated first and foremost by economic profit. To achieve this, they befriended and persuaded First Nations people by any means possible, including using trinkets, alcohol, guns, etc., to join in the fur trade — a market that continues today. My father still hunts animals for food and sells their fur. I met him in Prince Albert a few months ago as he and other First Nations hunters brought in their furs in large canvas bags to sell. Not surprisingly, the buyers were of Caucasian descent.

Colonial Relations

Colonial relations can be defined by the following: i) colonial presence increases (settlement); ii) demand for Aboriginal land increases (displacement); and iii) Aboriginal labour and skills are not needed anymore and the colonial economy shifts from trade to agricultural; relationship shifts from interdependence to dominant/subordinate (Stevenson and Pino 1997). By the 1900s, treaties were signed between some First Nations tribes and the Canadian government under false pretences, which is another story. The purpose of treaty signing, according to Yale Belanger (2010: 79), was dispossession: "Colonial leaders were beginning to aggressively try to displace Indigenous Peoples from their lands, outright dispossess them, so that those lands could be open to settlement." The land was taken away from them and sold or given to newcomers to make way for a new life. The newcomers recorded and portrayed the land as they saw it: empty. The First Nations people were bound to small pieces of land called reserves. In relation to art and colonial relations, the artists known as the Group of Seven, based out of Toronto, Ontario, were landscape painters whose artwork consisted of beautiful sceneries from across Canada. Through their depictions of the land as "ideal," "empty," and "there for the taking," they painted the erasure of First Nations people.

Internalized Colonialism

The concept of internal colonialism is complex and varies according to the people, place, and situation. However, I use the term *internal colonialism* similar to the way it was described by Robert Blauner (1969). with four components that are common to both external and internal processes of colonization. First, how the racial group enters into the dominant society; colonization begins with a forced involuntary entry. Second, the impact on the culture and social organization of the colonized people, which is more than just a result of such "natural" processes as contact and acculturation. Rather, the colonizing power carries out a policy that constrains, transforms, or destroys Indigenous values, orientations, and ways of life. Third, colonization involves a relationship by which members of the colonized group tend to be administered by being managed and manipulated by outsiders in terms of ethnic status. Fourth, racism as a form of social domination by which a group seen as inferior or different in terms of alleged biological characteristics is exploited, controlled, and oppressed socially and physically by a superordinate group. Indigenous scholars Stevenson and Pino (1997) describe the following manifestations of internalized colonialism: i) economic marginalization (high unemployment); ii) environmental exploitation and destruction; and iii) violent crimes, high suicide rates, incarceration, social assistance, chemical dependency, low education levels. While in residential school, my mother was physically abused whenever she spoke her Cree language, as was my father. They did not talk about it much. As a mother, my mom tried to protect my brothers and me by not teaching us to speak our language. She did not want the same abuse to happen to us when we went to school. I went to residential school. It was deemed a good idea by my grandmother. The place where I stayed was in a big building in Timber Bay, Saskatchewan, a remote community farther east of Montreal Lake Cree Nation. I was cramped in a small bedroom with four bunk beds, punished by washing the bathroom floor with a toothbrush, and forced to walk two miles each way to attend school every day. In the end, the memories lingered.

Intergenerational trauma and its effects still echo strongly in people's' lives. The resulting mental and physical health problems can be hard to treat if the stories are not told in some form or another. The effects of physical and sexual abuse continue, resulting in intergenerational trauma. In a qualitative study among forty-three service providers who worked with individuals and communities affected by the Indian residential school (IRS) system, the widespread sexual abuse suffered by generations of children while attending these schools was implicated as a key factor contributing to high rates of sexual abuse in some communities (Bombay, Matheson, and Anisman 2014: 325).

Residential schools had lasting impacts that are still felt to this day: "Although numerous historically traumatic events occurred earlier, the 19th century in Canada was marked by government policies to assimilate Aboriginal peoples based on the assumption that Whites were inherently superior to the 'Indians' and they considered them to be savage and uncivilized" (Bombay, Matheson, and Anisman 2014: 322). This assumption still appears in newspapers, television, and on the radio. News reports often show us images of Indigenous men or women who have broken the law or have been involved in a domestic violence incident, often emphasizing the presence of alcohol. Similar incidents involving white individuals will often be framed quite differently in the media, with little to no discussion on their ethnicity or background.

In the past decade, there has been an increase in First Nations scholars, artists, and activists writing and talking about issues from the IRS system and other colonization-related traumas. Numerous movies, books, and documentaries have come out that offer personal stories of peoples' experiences. Some powerful examples include Richard Wagamese's book *Indian Horse*, which was turned into a movie of the same name, and the 2012 documentary film *We Were Children*. Tasha Hubbard's *Birth of a Family* depicts the journey of four siblings trying to build a life together as a family after they were taken from their family and placed with white families in what is known as the Sixties Scoop.

Decolonization

Decolonization was defined by Stevenson and Pino (1997) as the following: i) individual rejection of the colonizer and their victimization; ii) appropriate tools (such as schooling, life skills, etc.) of the oppressor to challenge oppression; iii) resist in direct and indirect ways; and iv) reclaim languages, culture, spirituality, ceremonies, and communities. Decolonization is an essential element of reconciliation (Battiste 2017). The individual needs to change their own perspective of the colonizer and no longer be a victim of oppression. One way of doing this is through education. For some First Nations people, this means getting a high school education. When I graduated with my Grade 12 diploma in 1987, at the age of eighteen, I was the first to graduate from both my mother's and father's sides of the family. My son is another example. He dropped out of school ten years ago when he was in Grade 11, but now, at the age of twenty-seven, he is working to complete his high school diploma and plans to become an electrician. Other First Nations people are acquiring higher education and becoming lawyers and professors so they can utilize the colonial system to fight back.

Changing the system of education is important for decolonization. Marie Battiste, a Mi'kmaw professor at the University of Saskatchewan, has been critiquing and arguing against Eurocentric education for more than twenty-five years. In her book, *Decolonizing Education: Nourishing the Learning Spirit*, she wrote, "I have aimed my research and discursive arrow not at teachers or their methods, but largely at the federal and provincial systems and the policies and inequities coming from them" (2017: 2). In other words, decolonization needs to start not only with the people at the grassroots level but also with the individuals who are in power and are able to create new policies and strategies for reconciliation.

Decolonization can also emerge from political activism. The Idle No More movement, for example, sparked Indigenous Peoples to come together as one against colonialism. Missing and Murdered Indigenous Women and Girls (MMIWG) activists demanded that the Canadian government establish an inquiry on this issue and hear women's stories. First Nations people are rallying against the pipelines along with taking a stark look at the oil sands in Alberta. These activities raise public awareness about the trauma experienced by First Nations people, and they also help to bring First Nations people together to struggle toward a common goal.

Reclaiming one's language and practising ceremonies are ways of decolonization as well. In 1973, the Indian Group of Seven was created on the heels of the famous Anishinaabe artist Norval Morrisseau, who painted works of art displaying First Nations spirituality as, for some, healing in nature (Adese 2012). The Indian Group of Seven — Norval Morrisseau, Jackson Beardy, Alex Janvier, Carl Ray, Eddy Cobiness, Daphne Odjig, and Joe Sanchez — created the Professional National Indian Artists Inc. The group started with a small circle of artists who were dissatisfied and frustrated at the lack of exhibition opportunities for Indigenous art within the contemporary gallery system, but their interests quickly matured into a critique of the assumptions, then common in Canada, about Indigenous Peoples and their art (Devine 2015).

There are many different paths to healing and therapies that help people get there. One such approach is art therapy. Though people often associate art therapy with children, healing through art is a good choice for people of different ages and cultural backgrounds. The interpretation of art can be a form of healing from the intergenerational impacts of residential schools and the Sixties Scoop. John Dewey, a philosopher and author of *Art as Experience*, suggested that "a primary task is thus imposed upon one who undertakes to write upon the philosophy of the fine arts" (1958: 3). Dewey also says that "this task is to restore continuity between the refined and intensified forms of experience that are works of art and the everyday events, doings, and sufferings that are universally recognized to constitute experience."

As in art, one needs to hear the stories behind the creation in order to fully understand the artworks. Whether it be children, youth, or adults, their drawings or paintings give insights into their souls. Dewey further stated that:

> It is quite possible to enjoy flowers in their coloured form and delicate fragrance without knowing anything about the plants theoretically. But if one sets out to *understand* the flowering of plants, he is committed to finding out something about the interaction of soil, air, water and sunlight that condition the growth of plants. (1958 [1934]: 4)

My youngest daughter, Jewel Charles, who is sixteen, has been painting since she was three years old. She paints abstracts and landscapes, and encourages the viewer to consider their own interpretations of her art. She relays how she feels about them but respects the feelings of the other person. Jewel received a SaskTel Indigenous Youth Award of Excellence in 2018 for fine and performing arts and has started teaching children between the ages of 4 and 12 years old the basics of painting. She was asked to teach the immigrant and refugee children of University of Saskatchewan students. She agreed, but she wanted to teach First Nations children as well. So, we invited First Nations children to participate in her sessions. The idea of bringing international and First Nations children together is a way to help foster positive friendships and build capacity. This could constitute the beginnings of art therapy. Dan Hocoy wrote,

> The history of Western therapeutic traditions is replete with instances in which legitimate cultural expressions are pathologicalized, marginalized or misinterpreted ... Art therapy in its conscious consideration of these issues has a unique opportunity to depart from this heritage and to serve as a tool of cultural enrichment rather than oppression. (2002: 141)

Children and people in general will paint what they feel to express their creativity. Getting to know one another and where a person comes from is a form of decolonization.

Colonialism on Canvas

As a visual learner myself, I know the importance of offering learning opportunities in a variety of forms. To this end, I have created an interactive art workshop called Colonialism on Canvas, which incorporates the themes of healing, learning, and understanding to teach audiences about First Nations history and colonialism. Colonialism on Canvas walks participants through Stevenson and Pino's (1997) *Five Stages of Colonialism* while doing a painting exercise. The exercise asks them to create freely, then paint as told, then blend the colours, then destroy, before being invited to a new creation of their own. To further understand this path, I will explain the process of the interactive workshop. The participants will sit at a table with a small canvas, a plate with five colours of paint (blue, yellow, red, white, and black), a paintbrush, and a cup of water. Each paint colour represents one of the stages of colonialism. The first three stages (steady state, first encounter, and colonial relations) are painted with blue, red, and yellow as circles, triangles, and squares respectively on the canvas. While the participants are painting each shape, I am describing the stages as they go along. The fourth stage, internalized colonialism, uses the white paint to draw squiggly lines horizontally to blend the colours. At this point, participants have created a nice picture. The fifth stage, decolonization, uses the black paint to cover the entire canvas. The participants are shocked and dismayed to have to cover up their picture. So, I tell them to paint their picture half black or put some black in it. The significance of black is change. Once the paint has dried, by painting over the black, the participant can create a whole new picture. That is, they can reinvent or recreate themselves and move forward in life — such as reclaiming their language or getting a higher education. My art workshop is mainly for educators, staff, managers, faculty, and business owners. It is geared toward adults. However, I asked Jewel to create a youth version and it is called Colonialism on Canvas: A Youth Perspective.

A study by Barbara Davies (2010) similarly showed how art as a communicative resource moved participants beyond dialogical differences into a richer understanding of respective worldviews. An intervention for community leaders and artists to engage in interracial dialogue. Davies developed the Talking, Race, Engagement, Creatively (TREC) program, where she introduced metaphors and symbols to penetrate deeply held beliefs and attitudes. These served to transcend language and cultural barriers in attempting to grasp their commonalities and differences. Importantly, the study showed how art facilitated thought organization in a second language system beyond relying on words (2010: 180). As a former Building Bridges Coordinator for the Aboriginal Student Centre at the University of Saskatchewan, I found, after facilitating a Colonialism on Canvas workshop, that international and Aboriginal peoples have commonalities when it comes to the term *colonization*.

Another example of decolonization through art can be found in the work of Kent Monkman, an artist of Swampy Cree, English, and Irish descent from the Fisher River Cree Nation in northern Manitoba. In 2015, Kent Monkman began working on *Shame and Prejudice: A Story of Resilience,* which first showed at the Art Museum at the University of Toronto and is now booked through 2020 across Canada. Monkman's art is a clear critique of Canadian history. "It was a pretty deliberate effort to have people reflect on the last 150 years in terms of the Indigenous experience," said Monkman of the show (Morgan-Feir 2017: 1). He continued:

> Canada's 150 years old — what does that mean for First People? When I thought about it, I thought it includes the worst period, because it goes all the way back to the signing of the treaties, the beginning of the reserve system, the legacy of incarceration, residential schools, sickness, the removal of children in the 60s, missing and murdered women. (Morgan-Feir 2017: 10)

Monkman went on to say, "I can't think about the Indigenous experience without being critical of the colonial policies that were genocidal." Once people learn about First Nations history, they will understand the stereotypes and labels given to them. Monkman's art reworks colonial-era paintings to represent the land as no longer empty and shows First Nations peoples in new ways. In my workshop, people see their own work; in Jewel's paintings, she invites them to see their own meaning, a new meaning in her work. Jason Chalmers (2017: 108–109), from the University of Alberta, argued that "for the decolonizing researcher, this means addressing how knowledge is used to reproduce colonial order and the way we can use knowledge to challenge the order." This can be done through art and is much needed in the elementary, middle, and high schools, too. In the future, I would like Jewel to present her workshop, Colonialism on Canvas: A Youth Perspective, to youth and students. This interactive session on the historical and contemporary aspects of First Nations people through art will benefit them. Jewel facilitated this particular art workshop at the Canadian Roots Exchange Youth Conference in Saskatoon, Saskatchewan, in November 2018. She had twenty-seven participants and was very well received. I believe we need to tap into youth's passions, whether it be sport, culture, or recreation. Some work has started in the postsecondary system and some organizations, too. But there is much more work to be done.

CONCLUSION

Decolonization in its literal sense is to give back the land to First Nations people. However, it is not feasible due to urbanization intertwined with colonial policies. The next best thing is to reclaim one's language and cultural ceremonies that were banned by the colonizer. Tipi teachings is one tool that helps First Nations people to get back to their roots. Tipi teachings reflect the values that First Nations people taught their children in the steady state in Stevenson and Pino's (1997) *Five Stages of Colonialism*. Some of these teachings include respect and care for the land, plants, animals, and people — especially, the Elders. Making time to stretch out onto the land (my father's trapline) for short or long periods of time will help you in this process. He will show you the First Nations ways of life and tell you stories. He will have you laughing most of the time, as humour was a coping mechanism for the intergenerational trauma experienced by residential school Survivors. There are many terms to describe First Nations people, such as Indian, Aboriginal (refers to First Nation, Métis and Inuit), and Native; the more internationally phrased Indigenous is widely utilized today. If one is not sure about what term to use, please ask the person what they prefer, and they will tell you. Lastly, when researchers stride into First Nations communities, they need to research Indigenous methodologies because it is crucial to maintain relationships and build capacity. In doing so, the researcher engages in the First Nations Protocol of Reciprocity. It is hard for urban people to understand land-based practices if they cannot go on the land. But if you can make your way to Wanuskewin Heritage Park, a little north of Saskatoon, this will give you a glimpse of how First Nations people lived off the land. Wanuskewin hosts interactive sessions all year round. Learning bits and pieces every now and then helps build an understanding of the history and contemporary contexts of First Nations people. In relation to art, think of landscapes — the beauty of the trees, rivers, plants, and animals. First Nations language and cultures are important for understanding the historical traumas: decolonization must occur before reconciliation.

REFERENCES

Adese, Jennifer. 2012. "Aboriginal™: Constructing the Aboriginal and Imagineering the Canadian National Brand." Unpublished doctoral dissertation, McMaster University. <https://macsphere.mcmaster.ca/bitstream/11375/15246/1/fulltext.pdf>.
Battiste, Marie. 2017. *Decolonizing Education: Nourishing the Learning Spirit*. Vancouver: UBC Press.
Belanger, Yale D. 2010. *Ways of Knowing: An Introduction to Native Studies in Canada*. Toronto: Nelson Education Ltd.
Blauner, Robert. 1969. "Internal Colonialism and Ghetto Revolt." *Social Problems*, 16, 4: 393–408.
Bombay, Amy, Kimberley Matheson, and Hymie Anisman. 2014. "The Intergenerational Effects of Indian Residential Schools: Implications for the Concept of Historical Trauma." *Transcultural Psychiatry*, 31, 3: 320–338
Chalmers, Jason. 2017. "The Transformation of Academic Knowledges." *Socialist Studies*, 12, 1: 97–116.
Daschuck, James. 2013. *Clearing the Plains: Disease, Politics of Starvation, and the Loss of Aboriginal Life*. Regina: University of Regina Press.
Davies, Barbara. 2010. "Hermeneutic Methods in Art Therapy Research with International Students." *The Art of Psychotherapy*, 37: 179–189.
Devine, Bonnie. 2015. "Professional Native Artists Inc., or the 'Indian Group of Seven.'" Edited November 16. <www.canadianencyclopedia.ca>.
Dewey, John. 1958 [1934]. *Art as Experience*. New York: Capricorn Books, G.P. Putnam's.
Hocoy, Dan. 2002. "Cross-Cultural Issues in Art Therapy." *Art Therapy*, 19, 4: 141–145. <https://doi.org/10.1080/07421656.2002.10129683>.
Kovach, Margaret. 2009. *Indigenous Methodologies: Characteristics, Conversations, and*

Contexts. Toronto: University of Toronto Press.

McAdam, (Saysewahum) Sylvia. 2015. *Nationhood Interrupted: Revitalizing Nehiyaw Legal Systems*. Saskatoon: Purich Publishing Ltd.

Michell, Herman. 2015. "Bush Cree Storytelling Methodology: Northern Stories that Teach, Heal, and Transform." *In Education*, 21, 2: 171–178.

Morgan-Feir, Caoimhe. 2017. "Kent Monkman: History Painting for a Colonized Canada." Edited January 26. <www.canadianart.ca>.

Morley, Sam. 2015. "What Works in Effective Indigenous Community-Managed Programs and Organisations." Australian Institute of Family Studies, CFCA paper No 32. <https://aifs.gov.au/cfca/publications/what-works-effective-indigenous-community-managed-program/background>.

Oswalt, Wendell, and Sharlotte Neely. 1988. *This Land Was Theirs: A Study of North American Indians*, Fifth edition. Mountain View, CA: Mayfield Publishing Co.

Stevenson, Winona, and Rudolfo Pino. 1997. "The 5 Stages of Colonialism." Saskatoon: University of Saskatchewan. <https://piazza.com/class_profile/get_resource/hka84p6teuz6k6/ho7h0mkh9cjqo>.

Truth and Reconciliation Commission of Canada. 2015. *Truth and Reconciliation Commission of Canada: Calls to Action*. 1–11.

PART TWO

TAKING RESPONSIBILITY FOR RECONCILIATION

Chapter Five

RECONCILIATION AS CEREMONIAL RESPONSIBILITY

An Immigrant's Story

RANJAN DATTA

In this chapter, I share my experience of reconciliation as a lifelong ceremonial journey of unlearning and relearning on Treaty Six Territory and the Homeland of the Métis in Saskatchewan, Canada. Through my ceremonial responsibility for reconciliation, I pay my respect, honour, and gratitude to the First Nations and Métis peoples of this place, past and present, and reaffirm my relationship and responsibility with them and with this land. In this chapter, I share my ceremonial stories of how I have learned the importance of reconciliation from my everyday actions and ask how those of us who invoke this term might most effectively address reconciliation and social challenges. This chapter takes a significant step forward in exploring identity and justice in relation to immigrant responsibilities for reconciliation. It is also an invitation for all of us to work together as Indigenists to build relational networks in the important work of intercultural bridging, moving beyond cultural awareness and inclusion and challenging racist ideology as we rethink and re-imagine ourselves in relation with one another in a sharing place — a sacred land.

INTRODUCTION

Although the national discussion on reconciliation started more than fifteen years ago, many immigrants do not know the meaning of it in our everyday lives as discussion on how to practise reconciliation has been absent from our everyday activities (Abu-Laban 2018, 2014). While the Canadian government has undertaken various initiatives on reconciliation, many Indigenous and non-Indigenous scholars argue that these initiatives have been limited to discussion, research, and reports (Abu-Laban 2018; Marom 2016; Yu 2011). While the government's initiatives have received extensive critique by reconciliation scholars, initiatives for new immigrant involvement in reconciliation have been even more neglected than initiatives involving other groups (i.e., settlers and Indigenous Peoples) (Abu-Laban 2018). As Yu's (2011: 301) work on new immigrants explains:

> Many new arrivals in Canada received very little information about the history of Aboriginal people and, in particular, of the devastating effects of governmental policies such as residential schooling; therefore, through no intention of their own, they [new immigrants] were often left only with stereotypes and the negative images of popular culture as the basis for their knowledge about Aboriginal people.

New immigrant communities often do not get adequate opportunities to learn about Indigenous Peoples, their history, and their perspectives on reconciliation (Abu-Laban 2018, 2014; Datta 2017; Marom 2016). These gaps lead to many misconceptions about Indigenous communities and Canadian history (Yu 2011).

This chapter discusses my ceremonial journey by sharing how I have come to understand the importance of reconciliation and how I started my reconciliation learning journey on Treaty Six Territory. Through this journey, I learned that reconciliation for me is a process of empowering, belonging, and becoming. A ceremonial journey to me is the ceremony of maintaining accountability to my all relationships, including relationships with the land, people, culture, plants, animals, and so on (Wilson 2008). This process can also be explained as lifelong unlearning and relearning ceremonies.

WHY IS RECONCILIATION SIGNIFICANT FOR ME?

Situating yourself and taking a position is an important starting point for understanding reconciliation. I was born in a minority and Indigenous family in Bangladesh, which resulted in my family having been displaced several times from their land. Like my family, many minority and Indigenous communities face discrimination in their everyday lives, such as being displaced from their ancestral lands, seizure of traditional cultivation rights, and racial attitudes in education and employment, among others (Human Right Report 2017). Many minority Indigenous Peoples in Bangladesh have been displaced from their land but very few have the opportunity or the financial means to migrate to another country. In addition, many Indigenous Peoples in Bangladesh do not want to migrate as we (Indigenous Peoples) think of our ancestral land as our parents and our God, and we do not want to leave our motherland. However, in most cases we (i.e., minority and Indigenous Peoples) do not have any choice as mainstream people displace us, killing our relatives to confiscate our land (Adnan 2004).

Living far from the motherland is one of the hardest, most painful, and unwanted tasks for many Bangladeshi minority and Indigenous Peoples. I did not want to leave my motherland either. For our community, leaving our land is like separating our identity from our body (the land). Like many minority and Indigenous Peoples, my father was one of the land and water protectors. Around the time I was born, my father and some of my close family members were killed and our land was stolen, displacing us from our ancestral land. Since my family had been displaced several times, we did not have a place to stay. My mother was forced to move to the city and became a very low-paid worker. Many of my relatives have become refugees in neighbouring countries such as India.

Although education is very expensive and hard, it is the only social capital available to Bangladeshi minority and Indigenous Peoples. My community Elders and Knowledge Keepers always inspired me to obtain both traditional and Western educations. The Elders and Knowledge Keepers in our Indigenous and minority communities have been educated by our land and traditional culture. They have lived sustainably on our land for centuries. However, the majority population (i.e., Muslims) in Bangladesh and the Bangladeshi government do not want to recognize our traditional education or our land-water rights. Therefore, our community wanted me to get an education so that we could fight for our rights. Like other minority and Indigenous Peoples, I faced discrimination at each step of my education. However, I was successful in creating a number of opportunities for university scholarships in Norway, the United States, and Canada for my master's and PhD studies. As I was the youngest in my family, my sisters and brothers worked hard to send me to school.

There are few countries in the world that welcome immigrants to their land. Finding a home away from home is one of the hardest and most expensive journeys for many immigrants. For my postgraduate studies (MA, MPhil, and PhD), I had the opportunity to live in various cities, including Bergen, Norway; New Jersey and New York City in the United States; and Toronto and Saskatoon in Canada. It was only at the University of Saskatchewan that I had an opportunity to learn about Indigenous colonial history and Indigenous contributions to environmental and social justice.

Why have I decided to be an immigrant in a foreign land? This was an important question for me and for our minority community in Bangladesh. The first reason is that, although I have a national and international education, I do not have fair job opportunities in my homeland. The second reason is that I could be killed if I work (conduct research) with our Indigenous and minority communities in Bangladesh as the majority population would prefer to keep these truths hidden from the international community (Datta 2019). Therefore, our community and my family suggested I find a new home from which to do this important work for my community. My mom used to tell me that "sun and moon are our land and mother. Wherever you go, they will be with you to guide and protect you." Based on my community and family's suggestion, I was desperately looking for a second home where I could work for our community and at the same time create a sense of belonging with my new land.

I have learned from my fifteen years abroad in various large and small immigrant-based cities that there are not enough opportunities for us (particularly new immigrants and refugees) to learn about Indigenous colonial history and Indigenous worldviews on environment and social justice. Local residents have many misconceptions about Indigenous Peoples, their history, and their ongoing oppression. They unconsciously and consciously participate in many racist activities.

I have seen many new immigrants and refugees become involved in racist activities toward Indigenous Peoples without being aware they are racist. Many Indigenous and immigrant scholars warn that immigrants' false consciousness on Indigenous history and lives in Canada may not only create misconceptions about their own identity as new immigrants but can also lead to racist attitudes toward immigrant and Indigenous communities (Abu-Laban 2018, 2014). As a result, immigrants participate in the maintenance of systemic colonial processes (St. Denis 2007). There is also a tendency in many new immigrant and refugee communities to become neo-white — to believe themselves superior to other immigrant or minority populations, including Indigenous communities. This leads to negative assumptions that the other groups are less important (Said 1993; St. Denis 2007). Not only does this create misunderstandings about Indigenous Peoples and their lives, but it also leads to misrepresentations about who we are and what we should do in our new land (Yu 2011). As new immigrants, we need to decolonize neo-white racialized concepts through cross-cultural learning, participation, and action. Once we recognize neo-white tendencies, we will understand the importance of reconciliation.

CHALLENGES IN MULTICULTURAL COUNTRIES

New immigrants' conscious and unconscious racist attitudes and activities toward Indigenous Peoples and other immigrants in multicultural countries (particularly in Canada and the United States) may create a false belief that we will gain power and status in our new country (Abu-Laban 2018). The term *multiculturalism* is problematic for many immigrant and Indigenous communities in Canada as historically the term has been used to hide racism, inequality, and discrimination (Burman 2016; MacDonald 2014). For instance, MacDonald (2014; 67) argues that "multiculturalism and its promise of 'tolerance' (within Western institutions) and formal equality insufficiently recognize the *sui generis* or inherent rights of Aboriginal peoples which existed before colonization and continue still." Multiculturalism is then a tool to legitimate and strengthen state power while seeming on the surface to be relatively benign, even positive. In my nine years as an immigrant in Canada and fifteen years abroad, I have seen that new Canadians, particularly new immigrant and refugee communities, have limited knowledge of Indigenous Peoples, colonial history, treaties, the impact of residential schools, missing and murdered Indigenous women, and the colonial impact on Indigenous sustainable livelihoods. This lack of knowledge creates many misconceptions and can lead to racist attitudes toward Indigenous Peoples. In the following section, I discuss six short personal stories to explain why I feel it is urgent to learn about reconciliation, to obtain a deeper understanding, and to take responsibility for this concept. My stories are not, of course, reflective of every new immigrant's life, attitude, or culture, and it is not my intention to create any generalizations about them. Rather, I want to share my personal stories as they relate to the importance of reconciliation for immigrants. Stories are important and I believe that through our stories we can learn from each other and appreciate each other's needs and responsibilities.

MISCONCEPTIONS AND NEW IMMIGRANTS

New immigrants may have many misconceptions about another new immigrant's community and people. For instance, when I first came to the United States for higher education, my family and I were invited to visit a university professor's new house with other newcomer guests. This professor was known to me from back home and currently a university professor in the United States. He has become a religious leader for a South Asian Islamic organization and leads thousands of youth. After lunch, the professor was showing us his new house and neighbourhood. The neighbourhood housed a number of Black Americans and many of the guests began making extremely negative comments, such as "Your area is full of *Koula* [a negative expression in Bangla]. There are not enough whites [not merely white but also educated, wealthy, etc.] yet." The professor replied, "Yes, *Koula* is everywhere nowadays. They have occupied all the places; it's difficult to get rid of them." I was surprised by these comments, which I understood to be affirming of their own superior race/nationality through the expression of racist attitudes toward other minorities. As a newcomer in the United States at that time, I was not educated and strong enough to protest their comments and attitude. This event was not unique, in my fifteen years abroad, I have experienced many similar racist attitudes.

My minority Indigenous identity and anti-racist and social justice education helped me to understand that we hold many misconceptions in our day-to-day lives. Since most new immigrants need to fight for their survival and have few opportunities to obtain an anti-racist education in their new land, they want to think that they are in a better position in regards to their race/nationality/gender/culture than their fellow immigrants. In my fifteen years as an immigrant, I learned that this misconception comes mostly from a lack of anti-racist education, a lack of appropriate knowledge about Indigenous and immigrant communities in Canada. For instance, although the host was a professor of sociology, his perspectives on non-white and other new immigrants were different as he did not get an anti-racist education. Although most South Asian immigrants in North America are themselves non-white, many new immigrants use the term *white* to mean educated, rich, and cultured, while *non-white* refers to the stereotyped assumptions that the majority population makes about people of colour — that they are uneducated, poor, and uncultured. I learned from my ten years of anti-racist education that all these misconceptions come from a lack of systematic anti-racist education in our institutions. I learned that anti-racist education not only creates many learning opportunities for minimizing misconceptions but is also able to make us responsible to each other.

INDIGENOUS ISSUES AND NEW IMMIGRANTS

As mentioned previously, immigrant and refugee communities tend to lack knowledge of Indigenous issues. When I arrived in Canada from the United States in the skilled immigrant category, I needed to find a place to live in Saskatoon, Saskatchewan. When I asked for help from another immigrant who had been living in Saskatoon for more than ten years, he asked us why we wanted to come to Saskatoon instead of going to a big city, such as Toronto or Vancouver. I told him we were currently living in Toronto, but I needed to move to Saskatoon to pursue postgraduate studies at the University of Saskatchewan. He warned me that Saskatoon has several "unexpected" communities that are actively involved in various criminal activities. I asked him to explain what he meant by this. In reply, he mentioned the names of some of the Indigenous communities. Looking for further clarification, I asked him how he came to know this, where he had learned it. I asked him if he had personally experienced any of these incidents. Did he talk to any Indigenous community members about this? Did he have any contacts, relationships, or friends from any Indigenous communities in Saskatoon? He replied that he had learned about all the negative issues around Indigenous Peoples in Saskatoon from his non-Indigenous fellow immigrants and refugees. He had not faced any issues personally with any Indigenous person here and he did not know anything about them. Since he had heard many negative stories from his fellow immigrants, he did not want to become friends with them. I asked him to explain why he believed these stories if he did not have any personal experience and did not receive any information from authentic sources. His response was that he needed to trust his fellow immigrant and refugee workers, and that he had also seen a lot of stories in the local newspapers and on television. Moreover, one of his supervisors, who is of European descent (i.e., white), had told him similar stories. I remember strongly challenging his perspective at that time by providing my country's misconceptions about our Indigenous Peoples. I have now lived in Saskatoon for almost seven years and I have developed strong relationships with Indigenous communities here. Now that my friend has seen that most of my best friends and mentors are from Indigenous communities, he understands. He has apologized several times for his mistaken views of Indigenous

Peoples. He and his family now live in an Indigenous area, and he has several Indigenous friends. We both agree that there are not enough opportunities for immigrant and refugee communities to learn about Indigenous Peoples and their history. This lack of opportunity can lead to many misunderstandings and stereotyped attitudes toward Indigenous Peoples.

SOCIAL JUSTICE MOVEMENTS AND NEW IMMIGRANTS

While I was doing my PhD at the University of Saskatchewan, my family and I were actively involved with various Indigenous and minority movements in Canada, including Idle No More, Black rights, Two-Spirit rights, and Indigenous Land Rights movements. Although there are many immigrants and refugees in Saskatoon, very few people from minority communities have been involved in Indigenous movements. However, I have seen that many Indigenous, settler, immigrant, and refugee communities were actively involved with other rights-based movements. I asked several immigrants and refugees who have been very active in the Muslim rights movement but not Indigenous movements for an explanation. They provided several reasons why they do not participate in Indigenous movements and are not concerned with Indigenous issues in Canada. Many immigrants and refugees said that they did not understand why land and water rights are an important issue for Indigenous Peoples in Canada, which is one of the richest countries in the world. Immigrants and refugees in Canada are concerned about their own country and their religious issues, which they learn about from their communities and the international media, but they are not aware of Indigenous issues. This lack of information can lead to this kind of disconnect between Indigenous and immigrant communities.

The lack of knowledge on Indigenous issues can lead to prejudiced activities toward Indigenous Peoples (Burman 2016). For instance, one of my fellow immigrants who recently became a Canadian citizen and is a PhD student at a university in Canada gently asked me one day in 2016 why I get involved with so many negative movements, meaning Indigenous Rights movements. Before I answered her question, I wanted to know more, and so I asked her why she was asking this question, what did she want to know, specifically. Responding from a neo-white perspective, she replied that she wanted to see me as "white." I asked her to clarify. She boldly replied that by white, she meant Euro-Canadian. She suggested that I should forget about Indigenous

Peoples if I wanted to get a job in Canada, that being white is the easy way. She explained that she had learned many positive things about whiteness from a number of sources, including her Canadian citizenship book during her citizenship exam, from her Caucasian friends, and from her professors at the university. She further told me that if I wanted to have a good job and a good life in Canada, I should have good knowledge and relationships with white people. She also said I needed to "respect what they [white] have done and are doing for Canada, including for Indigenous Peoples." When I strongly disagreed with some of her arguments on Indigenous issues, she was not happy with me. I realized that she was not alone in being misinformed and not having an opportunity to learn about Indigenous Peoples in Canada. Many people, such as my fellow immigrants, pick up a great deal of incorrect information about Indigenous Peoples, both formally and informally.

SETTLEMENT ORGANIZATIONS AND NEW IMMIGRANTS

Settlement organizations in Canada have major impacts on new immigrants' settlement. When I first arrived in Canada in 2009–10, I went to a new-comer centre in Toronto, a city with a large immigrant population, to build a network and learn about the Canadian job market. One of my mentors at the newcomer centre (who was of European descent) told us (twenty-five to thirty skilled new immigrant students) that we need to be civilized to get a job in Canada. As a newcomer to Canada, I respectfully asked her, "What do you mean by civilized?" In response, she showed us a large photo on the classroom wall. In this photo there were two white men in formal dress in a formal setting, greeting each other by exchanging a handshake. She suggested that we should be like them and learn from them. I asked her again, "Is this the meaning of civilization in Canada?" I could see that she was not happy with my question. She explained that this photo is symbolic. If we can speak like them, communicate like them, and know their success stories, we will be more likely to get a good job in Canada. I replied, "Okay, I get your point from a skill development perspective, but not from a civilization perspective. Would you please explain this a little bit more? What about other communities, such as Indigenous Peoples, and their success stories?" I saw that she did not like my curiosity about this and suddenly changed our discussion to another topic. Since I was a new immigrant at the time, I could not challenge her on this anymore. However, I saw that none of the other immigrants in my class (who had immigrated to Canada in the highly educated/skilled immigrant category) asked any questions. Some of my classmates explained after class that, as new immigrants, they were afraid. For instance, they were afraid that if the instructor got angry with them, they might not get a good reference letter for their first job in Canada (the reference letter plays a significant role in obtaining a job in Canada).

INDIGENOUS WAYS OF LIFE IN CANADA AND NEW IMMIGRANTS

Many settled immigrants have misunderstandings about Indigenous Peoples and Indigenous ways of life in Canada (Abu-Laban 2018). For instance, I went to a children's birthday party in 2014 at the home of an immigrant from my homeland. The host is a faculty member at one of the universities in Canada and completed his MA and PhD at two different Canadian universities. The host family had invited almost fifty immigrant families to the party, most of whom were his international MA and PhD students. Most of his international students were planning to apply for Canadian citizenship at that time, and I know that all of them are now Canadian citizens. My family and I were among the few guests who were not his students. During the birthday party, we discussed many issues. At one point, one of his students wanted to know why there was so much criminal activity in Saskatoon, particularly within the Indigenous communities. The guests were interested in learning the host's perspective on this issue and the discussion took on a classroom format. At one point, the host said that Indigenous Peoples in Canada get so many benefits; therefore, they do not work, and they have time to become involved in criminal activities. He went on to say that they do not work hard like white, immigrant, and refugee people. I was seriously shocked by his comments about Indigenous Peoples and with the way he was sharing this information with many new immigrant families. I challenged his perspective by referring to my four years of positive experiences with Indigenous communities. Most of his students did not want to hear what I had to say. The faculty member was trying to justify his perspective by saying that he had been living here for a long time and he knew more about Indigenous Peoples than I. I am from an Indigenous community back home in Bangladesh and I have been studying Indigenous issues for a long time, but my opinion was ignored. After the party, I could not sleep for several nights. I have learned from eight years in Saskatoon and one year in Toronto that there are many immigrant engineers, doctors, educators, and professionals who think and act like the host of that party. They are not new to Canada, but they either have no knowledge of Indigenous issues in Canada or they have incorrect information. I have observed that many of these individuals not only demonstrate a racist attitude but also share their racist attitude with other newcomers. Within my own immigrant community, I have realized that racist attitudes are not an individual problem. Racism is a part of our everyday lives; we learn it through our education institutions, our daily experiences, and knowledge sharing.

These stories demonstrate that there is a significant lack of opportunities to learn about Indigenous issues within many immigrant and refugee communities and this lack of knowledge leads to negative assumptions. While the stories happened at different times, they are interconnected and demonstrate how racism is embedded, both consciously and unconsciously, in new immigrants' day-to-day beliefs, thoughts, and activities. The result is the development of racist attitudes toward both Indigenous Peoples and immigrants. Although these stories are from my own personal experience, they demonstrate why we (immigrant and refugee communities) need more formal opportunities to learn about Indigenous issues.

RECONCILIATION AS A CEREMONY OF RESPONSIBILITY

My ceremonial learning journey has shown me that reconciliation is a lifelong process of unlearning and relearning. My perspective on reconciliation is that it is a responsibility to learn, act, and share. As a researcher, my journey of reconciliation started with anti-racist theory and practice, cross-cultural research methodology, critical investigations, and a land-based approach, particularly during my interdisciplinary PhD program at the University of Saskatchewan. I learned how to see and use the term *researcher* in a way that is very different from the Western research tradition. I learned that every act of reconciliation is a story, and each story has power and impacts who I am as a researcher (King 2003). My reconciliation stories are neither chronological nor history; rather they are lived, influential, and relational. My stories have a great deal of influence on my thinking and doing. Sharing reconciliation stories can benefit others who are not only conducting research with Indigenous, immigrant, refugee, and settler communities but also seeking social and environmental justice.

Critical anti-racist education furnished me with an analytical approach to reconciliation. For instance, although my home department was the School of

Environment and Sustainability at the University of Saskatchewan, my PhD research training courses, including cross-cultural and postcolonial research methods courses, were through the Department of Educational Foundations. Faculty in the Department of Educational Foundations had diverse interests, and I learned not only anti-racist, postcolonial, Indigenous methodologies and methods but also how and why to build relationships with participants. I had the opportunity to instruct and participate in a variety of courses and worked closely and collaborated with the nationally and internationally known Indigenous scholars Drs. Marie Battiste, Verna St. Denis, Alex Wilson, and Margaret Kovach. These faculty members relied on me for research and teaching assistance and I had opportunities to guest lecture. Working with these colleagues exposed me to their contributions in social phenomena, such as Indigeneity, Indigenous education, experiential learning, anti-racist theory and practice, cross-cultural learning and management, social and environmental justice, and Indigenous research methodology and methods. Knowing Indigenous faculty and their academic contribution to decolonization helped me to dream, think, act, and reclaim four dimensions of the research process — decolonization, healing, transformation, and relearning— as well as the four major stages of reconciliation — survival, recovery, development, and self-determination.

My involvement with various Indigenous communities' social and environmental justice activities and movements enriched my understanding of reconciliation. My concept of research began to shift from a scientific one to one of cross-cultural, anti-racist, and critical eco-justice environment commitments. Anti-racism, decolonization, and critical ethnography were crucial elements of my research mindset and helped me to understand the meaning of *otherness* in research (Foucault 1978; Said 1993; Spivak 1988), as well as the colonization of the mind, which normalizes the whole project (Fanon 1961). I began to question the very existence of research and academia.

Identifying the processes of decolonization has also been a significant part of my reconciliation. I learned that calling for the decolonization of research and the strategic use of research as a tool of decolonization continue to resonate for me as I attempt to answer the question, "What might a decolonization of research entail?" In my PhD and research work, I had opportunities to instruct and participate in a variety of courses in Indigenous education, anti-racist theory and practice, social inequality, and the like. These decolonizing courses inspired me to become involved in community justice activities beyond the university. I have actively participated in social well-being and justice movements, including the Idle No More movement, Indigenous Land Rights movements, the Climate Justice movement, Standing Rock, and anti-racist movements. I expect to continue with community service for the rest of my life because I am, by necessity, a vehement critic of injustice.

My Indigenous identity, cross-cultural socialization, unique interdisciplinary education, interdisciplinary research skills, and passion for understanding reconciliation have served me well in my life as an immigrant living on Indigenous Land. For example, my PhD and postdoctoral research became part of a reconciliation learning journey. I learned from my participant communities that we need to deconstruct the concepts of research and researcher from the research participants' perspectives before we can move toward reconciliation (Datta 2017). The meanings of both these terms have changed

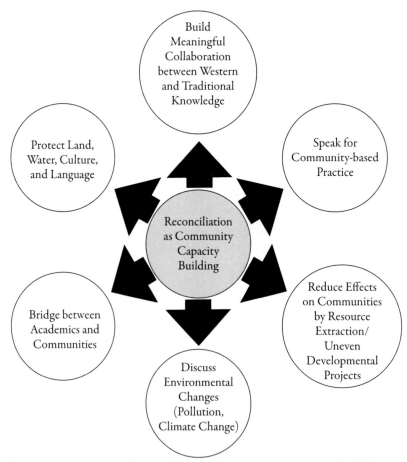

Figure 5-1. Meanings of reconciliation as community capacity building.

from their traditional definitions to a Western, colonial one (Smith 2008) and have become exploitative, separated, and other to many Indigenous communities (Datta 2019; Kovach 2010; Smith 2008). As an Indigenous person from Bangladesh, my fifteen years of professional research and teaching activities in various Indigenous communities in Canada, Norway, New Zealand, the United States, Japan, and Bangladesh have provided me with the background and experience to understand the concept of reconciliation from the perspective of community capacity building (Figure 5-1).

I also learned that there are multiple challenges to reconciliation, such as the politics of recognition of Indigenous scholarship; the dominance of the Western worldview over an Indigenous worldview; historical and ongoing racism; the separation of knowledge and practice; and the unclear delineation of researcher responsibilities.

As a researcher, I have learned that reconciliation is not a checklist because knowledge is relational; it must be constantly communicated, negotiated, and agreed upon with honest and sincere hearts. As an Indigenous scholar from Bangladesh, I see my responsibilities for reconciliation as decolonizing both research and researcher; adopting critical anti-racist theory and practice; bridging Indigenous and non-Indigenous worldviews; recognizing multiple ways of knowing; providing culturally appropriate education; adopting land-based education and practice; honouring and respecting Indigenous knowledge; and rethinking research as action.

As I reflect on my ceremonial journey as an immigrant on Treaty Six Territory and the Homeland of the Métis and on my transformation as a researcher, I am reminded that being a minority Indigenous researcher working with Indigenous Peoples and communities involves a journey of learning that is both empowering and rewarding. Along this journey, it is vitally important that I form authentic relationships with the people I work with. I am not worried about challenges to my research training and ways of being. I know that as an immigrant I am responsible for a meaningful application of reconciliation, including learning Indigenous perspectives on Canadian history, understanding the history and legacy of residential schools, exploring the connection between Treaty and constitutional Rights, and recognizing the rich contributions Indigenous Peoples have made to Canada. I am also responsible for taking action to address historical injustice and present-day wrongs and teaching and sharing my acquired knowledge with future generations of Indigenous Peoples, immigrants, refugees, and settlers.

My cross-cultural involvement has inspired me to learn about and take responsibility for reconciliation. Reconciliation, even in a new land, is not just for other people. It is our responsibility to incorporate it in our everyday thoughts and actions. For example, in the last seven years, I have created a cross-cultural community garden with individuals, particularly immigrants and refugees, from twenty-eight different countries. During my seven-year learning journey, I have had several opportunities to learn about reconciliation from Indigenous Elders and Knowledge Keepers. Their stories help to decolonize — unlearn and relearn — by providing us with true stories about Indigenous Land, language, and history that can create a sense of belonging for newcomers like myself. They help us build relationships between Indigenous and non-Indigenous (settler, immigrant, and refugee) Peoples; take responsibility for protecting the land, water, and environment; learn how to build solidarity among ourselves and understand each other's rights; and speak up for social and ecological justice.

In our cross-cultural community garden, besides harvesting food, we have tried to develop a cross-cultural bridge for reconciliation. To do this, we have developed relationships among ourselves (immigrant, refugee, and Indigenous communities) using three different Indigenous research methods: blanket exercise, relational storytelling, and deep listening. We had many learning opportunities with Indigenous Knowledge Keepers, and this proved to be an effective process for learning and acting on reconciliation.

Learning About Decolonization

What does decolonization mean to me? Why does it matter for me? How should I teach our children about decolonization? We have seen that the concept of decolonization can create opportunities to learn Canadian colonial stories directly from Indigenous Elders and Knowledge Keepers, helping us to unlearn negative assumptions about Indigenous Peoples and relearn Indigenous success stories.

Knowing

What does bridge building mean to us as immigrants and refugees in a foreign land? Why is it important? By appreciating multiple ways of being and doing, Indigenous and non-Indigenous communities can learn about each other's cultures, challenges, and successes. Communities can share their land-based stories on ways of growing food, networking, and caring. Gardeners also had several opportunities for building bridges: critical discussion of the ongoing racism toward Indigenous Peoples and visible minorities; speaking up against all forms of injustice; learning about land-based food security; and developing land-based social networks.

Thinking and Acting Responsibly

Through thinking and acting responsibly, we develop diverse understandings of the concept of reconciliation. We learn how to grow food, how to respect each other's culture, and how to support each other's education. Through deep listening to the stories of Indigenous Elders and Knowledge Keepers, we build trustful relationships and learn about protecting and caring for the land, water, and environment, and taking responsible action.

As an immigrant in the Indigenous Land known as Canada, the concept of reconciliation is important for me personally. I have seen from my ten years in Canada that multiculturalism did not inspire me to learn Canadian colonial histories. I was not inspired to learn the meanings of reconciliation from Indigenous Peoples, to learn in-depth meanings of Indigenous culture and language, or to learn how I can take responsibility to decolonize my conception. I was not inspired to practise decolonization in my everyday life in an immigrant country like Canada. For instance, immigrant and refugee communities are expected to integrate into and participate in mainstream society without questioning the rules that guide that society, and by so doing, we become complicit in the colonial project. By integrating into such a societal culture with the eventual attainment of citizenship status, we participate in and "further the cultural and political elimination of Aboriginality" (Thobani 2000: 98).

CONCLUSION

Through my ceremonial journey, I have learned that it is high time for all of us to be responsible for the land on which we live. It is time to change our ways and understand our roles and responsibilities to ourselves, to our land, to our relationships, and to creation. Everyone benefits if we do this work together.

For me, as a new immigrant in Canada, reconciliation has meant taking the time to build respectful relationships and learn alongside the Indigenous Peoples of this land. It has created opportunities to develop a new model of interrelating, a model that takes us beyond the usual multicultural sharing and food and dance, in order to walk toward a responsible reconciliation. I know this process requires a complex, continuous, multi-faceted approach; however, I believe that if we (immigrants and refugees) can accept responsibility for this issue, Indigenous Peoples will be with us and we can collectively create the political will to make this Indigenous Land and its people part of who we are and where we belong.

My ceremonial journey in reconciliation, then, is a process and an ongoing journey of learning, building relationships, and accepting responsibility. Within this process, I am responsible for my actions and my relationships with Indigenous and non-Indigenous Peoples in Canada. A love of learning will give us the courage to relearn the diverse meanings of reconciliation from an Indigenous perspective, to rethink our actions, re-imagine our dreams and hopes, and teach these to future generations. This will involve challenging colonial attitudes inside our own hearts and minds and using our political voice to advocate and bear witness, following the lead of Indigenous Peoples. It requires learning when our actions are helpful and when they interfere. Reconciliation, as a ceremonial journey, is an act of love that generates responsibilities, activism, passion, and empathy. Reconciliation is, then, a call to action for all of us, both Indigenous and non-Indigenous, to take responsibility for meaningful actions in our everyday lives.

REFERENCES

Abu-Laban, Yasmeen. 2014. "Reform by Stealth: The Harper Conservatives and Canadian Multiculturalism." In J. Jedwab (ed.), *The Multiculturalism Question: Debating Identity in 21st Century Canada*. Montreal-Kingston: School of Policy Studies, Queen's University and McGill-Queen's University Press.

___. 2018. "Recognition, Re-Distribution and Solidarity: The Case of Multicultural Canada." In J. Fossum, R. Kastoryano, and B. Siim (eds.), *Diversity and Contestations over Nationalism in Europe and Canada*. London: Palgrave Studies in European Political Sociology. Palgrave Macmillan.

Adnan, Shapan. 2004. *Migration Land Alienation and Ethnic Conflict: Causes of Poverty in the Chittagong Hill Tracts of Bangladesh*. Dhaka, Bangladesh: Research & Advisory Services.

Battiste, Marie. 2008. "Research Ethics for Protecting Indigenous Knowledge and Heritage: Institutional and Researcher Responsibilities." In N.K. Denzin, Y.S. Lincoln, and L. Tuhiwai Smith (eds.), *Handbook of Critical and Indigenous Methodologies*. Berkeley, CA: Sage.

___. 2013. *Decolonizing Education: Nourishing the Learning Spirit*. Saskatoon, SK: Purich.

___. 2017. "Decolonial Ways of Knowing and doing." Banglar Gann O Katha at CFCR 90.5 Saskatoon Radio Program. <https://youtu.be/wFw5gqdKCAs>.

Burman, Jenny. 2016. "Multicultural Feeling, Feminist Rage, Indigenous Refusal." *Cultural Studies Critical Methodologies*, 16, 4: 361–372.

Datta, Ranjan. 2017. "Decolonizing Both Research and Researcher, and Its Effectiveness in Indigenous Research." *Research Ethics,* 14, 2: 1–24. <http://journals.sagepub.com/doi/pdf/10.1177/1747016117733296>.

___. 2018. "Traditional Story Sharing: An Effective Indigenous Research Methodology and Its Implications for Environmental Research." *Journal of AlterNative,* 14, 1: 35–44. DOI: doi.org/10.1177/1177180117741351.

___. 2019. *Land-Water Management and Sustainability: Indigenous Practices.* London: Routledge.

Fanon, Frantz. 1961. *The Wretched of the Earth.* New York, NY: Grove Press.

Foucault, Michel. 1978. "The History of Sexuality, Vol. 1: The Will to Knowledge." New York: Pantheon Books.

Human Rights Report. 2017. <https://www.state.gov/reports/2016-country-reports-on-human-rights-practices/bangladesh/>.

King, Thomas. 2003. *The Truth about Stories.* Minneapolis, MN: University of Minnesota Press.

MacDonald, David Bruce. 2014. "Reforming Multiculturalism in a Bi-National Society: Aboriginal Peoples and the Search for Truth and Reconciliation in Canada." *Canadian Journal of Sociology*, 39: 65–86.

Marom, Lilach. 2016. "A New Immigrant Experience of Navigating Multiculturalism and Indigenous Content in Teacher Education." *Canadian Journal of Higher Education*, 46, 4: 23–40.

Said, Edward. 1993. *Culture and Imperialism.* London: Chatto & Windus.

St. Denis, Verna. 2007. "Aboriginal Education and Anti-Racist Education: Building Alliance Across Cultural and Racial Identity." *Canadian Journal of Education*, 30, 4: 1068–1092.

Smith, Linda. 2008. "On Tricky Ground: Researching the Native in the Age of Uncertainty." In N.K. Denzin and Y.S. Lincoln (eds.), *The Sage Handbook of Qualitative Research.* Thousand Oaks, CA: SAGE.

Spivak, Gayatri Chakravorty. 1988. "Can the Subaltern Speak?" In C. Nelson and L. Grossberg (eds.), *Marxism and the Interpretation of Culture.* University of Illinois Press.

Thobani, Sunera. 2000. "Nationalizing Canadians: Bordering Immigrant Women in the Late Twentieth Century." *Canadian Journal of Women*, 12.

Wilson, Shawn. 2008. *Research Is Ceremony: Indigenous Research Methods.* Halifax, NS: Fernwood Publishing.

Yu, Henry. 2011. "Nurturing Dialogues Between First Nations, Urban Aboriginal, and Cultivating Canada: Reconciliation Through the Lens of Cultural Diversity." In Ashok Mathur Jonathan Dewar Mike DeGagné (eds.), *Immigrant Communities in Vancouver.* Ottawa, ON: Aboriginal Healing Foundation.

Chapter Six

RECONCILIATION THROUGH TRANSNATIONAL LITERACIES

An Immigrant Woman's Transformative Learning Journey

JEBUNNESSA CHAPOLA

In this chapter, I share my reconciliation learning experiences through transnational literacy based on my eight-year journey of unlearning and relearning as a newcomer immigrant woman in Treaty Six Territory, Saskatchewan, Canada. Throughout her academic texts, Gayatri Spivak (2003) uses the term *transnational literacy,* though she never clearly defines the term and instead leaves it to her readers to find the meaning. Other scholars, such as Diane Brydon (2010: 21), have provided a working definition, "This is a form of literacy that dominant cultures need to learn. It is a revised form of literacy that recognizes the power relations built into knowledge production in cross-cultural contexts. It requires in learners an ability for self-critique, vigilance, and openness to challenge." Transnational literacy as a concept, however, needs deeper cross-cultural understanding as it carries significant potential beyond the contexts used by Spivak. Brydon goes on to explain how colonial powers suppressed all other forms of knowledge and literacy and enforced the dominance of their own. This then created the myth that there is only one way to practise literacy, when in fact there are many ways of practising and knowing that are being unearthed by decolonization.

In this chapter, I use a framework of transnational literacies based on Spivak's ideas of "learning to unlearn, learning to learn, learning to listen and learning to reach out" (Andreotti 2014: 40). Informed by the scholarship of transnational feminist scholars Brydon (2014), Mohanty (2003), and Spivak (1992), I understand that the learning processes of reconciliation through transnational literacy are varied, complex, and partial. They arise out of intercultural experiences and require a dialogic exchange between theory and practice achieved through repositioning and co-positioning projects. I learned from my eight years of cross-cultural activities that providing education on transnational literacy requires a deep understanding of who I am, where I am, and my responsibility in this Indigenous Land. In this chapter, I share my learning and implications processes of reconciliation through transnational literacies, including decolonization, subalternity, hybridity, otherness, and intersectionality. These concepts are helpful for developing a critical inter-sectional approach to transnational literacy because they foreground issues of colonization, nationalism, global capitalism, and empire in an analysis of gender and sexual oppression, resistance, and other socially constructed biases.

Constructing the meanings of reconciliation through transnational literacy challenges the idea that reconciliation can be understood as a static and uni-form entity (Spivak 1992). However, my intention is not simply to outline the diverse meanings of reconciliation using these concepts (i.e., decolonization, subalternity, hybridity, otherness, and intersectionality). Rather, I want to uncover and learn how the complex and variable meanings of reconciliation can be applicable in diverse contexts, grounding intersectional thinking in meaningful and community-engaged actions. To do this, I use my eight-year cross-cultural learning journey, particularly my experience in a cross-cultural community garden, as a case study. Here I share my autoethnography of lived experiences of learning about reconciliation.

RECONCILIATION THROUGH THE LENS OF DECOLONIZATION

Understanding decolonization is essential for understanding reconciliation in our everyday practices (Battiste 2013). Indigenous scholars Marie Battiste (2017, 2013) and Eve Tuck and Wayne Yang (2012) suggest that reconciliation requires a continuous, lifelong process of decolonizing that is grounded in the unlearning of dominating processes and the relearning of reciprocal processes. Tuck and Yang (2012: 2) explain that decolonization means "the repatriation of Indigenous land and life," and they are clear that this "is not a metaphor." Decolonizing means moving away from the institutions of colonialism, white supremacy, racism, and capitalism, but specifically through a feminist lens, in order to govern today's nation-states through the reclamation and recognition of Indigenous identities. As Tuck and Yang (2012: 35) suggest, "Decolonization is not accountable to settlers, or settler futurity. Decolonization is accountable to Indigenous sovereignty and futurity." Therefore, in the Canadian context and beyond, transnational literacies require the decentralizing of dominant perspectives and the questioning of normative discourses. Decentring settler colonialism within academia and formal-informal social institutions could have powerful effects, making visible what decolonization might look like for all peoples. Decentring dominating practices will help to develop new forms of feminist activism and critically articulated alliances.

Many Indigenous scholars emphasize decolonization first because it involves dismantling structures, institutional policy, and everyday practices (Battiste 2017; Simpson 2014; Tuck and Yang 2012). Marie Battiste (2017: n.p.) suggests that decolonization has two pillars that are important for reconciliation; we need to understand that "our system of education is deeply colonial" in order to "help people to understand where colonialism came from and ... colonial histories and unpack these histories from our own [Indigenous] perspectives." It is important to understand and take responsibility for the process of learning decolonization and reconciliation for everyone (i.e., Indigenous, settlers, "new" Canadians, immigrants, and refugees) and part of that is understanding everyone's roots or migration history as well. Battiste added that "decolonization education needs to not just be a colonial experience ... but it has to be a way to help people to understand their situation where they are and how they are in an inequitable situation." Through this quotation and the concept of decolonization, Battiste challenged the dominance of Western thought and created a space to bring the Indigenous worldview to the forefront. Battiste (Datta 2018: 12) suggested that we all need to learn the second pillar of decolonization as it is the process of "recovery from colonial impact, restoration of Indigenous people's identities, Indigenous people's languages, Indigenous people's experiences, and all things that we [Indigenous people] need for restoring us in this country [Canada] which builds in treaties that have been signed, ignored, marginalized for many, many years in Canada." Decolonization is a process of empowerment for all of us. For instance, Battiste (2017: n.p.) suggests that decolonization can inspire us to ask questions like: "How are we related to the colonial oppressions? Who are the people who belong to colonial cultures? Who are the people benefiting from the oppressive systems? Who is gaining privilege by oppressing others?" As Datta (2017) notes, by decolonizing research, which is to say by understanding colonial legacies of oppression and their impacts, researchers will be able to reaffirm their relationship to the discipline of academic research.

Decolonization needs to take place in all our relationships, not just in research and education. For example, both Battiste (2013, 2000) and Datta (2017) invite scholars to decolonize their research — to look at their own cultural histories, contexts, positionalities, and complicities, to unlearn our privileges, to relearn transnational identity construction processes, to establish ethical relationships in the context of so many socially constructed differences, and to learn more about where we came from. Their work points toward the relevance of critical reconciliation in education, especially that which is concerned with issues of global and social justice. The concept of decolonization helps illuminate how Indigenous knowledges have been suppressed, oppressed, and dismissed by white, European, and other non-Indigenous settlers. Decolonization helps to reclaim and re-establish Indigenous and non-Indigenous voices, particularly those of women (Battiste 2000, 2017; Tuck and Yang 2012), whose subordination undergirds the formation of all modern nation-states. Thus, feminist researchers, educators, and activists need to develop transnational literacies, drawing not only from our own thoughts, experiences, work, localities, and positioning, but also by respecting Indigenous ways of knowing and being, and understanding how the processes of subordination work in the lives of the most disadvantaged, who often live on the verge of danger and death.

Decolonization Lens in Practice

Eight years with the cross-cultural community garden have helped me to understand the process of decolonization. As a newcomer racialized immigrant woman, I got involved with the McKeown Park community garden at the University of Saskatchewan campus in the city of Saskatoon, for reasons of survival and poverty. Using participatory action research (PAR) as a research methodology, I have been involved with cross-cultural community garden activities for the last eight years. This project started in 2012 with twenty garden plots, worked by people from three different countries. In 2018, this program space had extended to 120 garden plots with over twenty-five countries and cultures represented among community gardeners. Another six sharing plots were created, two for the local food bank, two for students and neighbours without access to garden space, and two for children. In 2012, we started our garden with ten families, including eighteen adults and five children. In 2018, approximately 120 families, including 400 adults and 60 children, were involved in this diverse, cross-cultural garden program. Many of the children were there daily, particularly during weekends and the two months of summer when schools close. The garden had operated for six months of each of the last seven years. Engagement with this land helped me to start thinking about who I am and about my history. I questioned whose land this is and what my relationship with this land is as a newcomer. Why am I here and who are these people here in Canada? I began this learning process based on understanding theories of decolonization; then I realized decolonization is an Indigenous way of thinking, questioning, and knowing.

In our community garden, I have observed that many newcomer immigrants and international students do not know that Indigenous Peoples in Canada have undergone hundreds of years of colonization. They do not know the history and consequences of colonization, such as the realities of residential schools. Newcomers are full of misconceptions about Indigenous Peoples and their history. I have also observed that newcomers do not have the opportunity to access information about decolonization and reconciliation (Abu-Laban 2014). Many of us are not aware of the Truth and Reconciliation Commission of Canada (TRC). Therefore, as the cultural coordinator of the community garden, I volunteered to take responsibility for organizing many informal workshops around the community garden under the open sky. I invited many Indigenous Elders, Knowledge Keepers, and Indigenous scholars and educators to share their knowledge about decolonization and reconciliation with newcomer immigrants. I invited Indigenous speakers because I wanted to learn the meaning of reconciliation from Indigenous Peoples. Indigenous educators taught newcomer gardeners why it is necessary to learn about reconciliation and how non-Indigenous people should be responsible for it.

I also took the opportunity to organize many trips for gardeners to Wanuskewin Heritage Park and the Gordon Oakes Red Bear Student Centre. Wanuskewin Heritage Park in Saskatoon is a non-profit cultural and historical centre of the Indigenous Peoples in Saskatchewan. The Gordon Oakes Red Bear Student Centre is an intercultural gathering place at the University of Saskatchewan situated on Treaty Six Territory and the Homeland of the Métis. This centre brings together the teachings, traditions, and cultures of the peoples of Saskatchewan. The centre's purpose is to facilitate the coordination of effective student services for Métis, First Nations, and Inuit students and build relationships within and outside the university with Indigenous Peoples. The centre also functions as the university's hub for on-campus Indigenous engagement and initiatives. Both community resources provide opportunities for non-Indigenous learners to engage in and learn about the history, culture, and worldview of Indigenous Peoples.

Learning about decolonization has helped me to understand the meaning of reconciliation. Reconciliation is not about hiding my own history and life story. If I do, others will continue to reproduce the similar religious racism and colonial approaches that I have experienced and witnessed in my life. For example, when I first arrived in Canada around 2010, I perceived the term reconciliation to mean the coexistence of multiple religions, races, castes, creeds, and all sexual orientations, gender identities, gender expressions, abilities, bodies, cultures, languages, and backgrounds. Through the TRC, Indigenous literature, and my eight years of cross-cultural activities, I am constantly working to learn reconciliation as a process of personal decolonization. Through the process of decolonization, I have taken the responsibility to share my own story because I need to know why, whether in Bangladesh or Canada, we always learn colonial histories instead of Indigenous ones. I need to know why and how the religions, institutions, and education in the Indian sub-continent and in Bangladesh became colonized. I am also curious to know how our thoughts are being colonized generation after generation without questioning. Is there any similarity or connection between the colonized history of India, Bangladesh, and Canada? I have learned that we need to make a connection with the land before we can work together as a community. This process helps align my own resilience with these life-sustaining forces, reinforcing my responsibility to serve the land and take up my treaty role as an ally with Indigenous Peoples, who are its most informed protectors. I have learned to decolonize my thoughts and self through this community garden and its intercultural activities, cross-cultural mingling, and connection with nature and the land. I also learned that decolonization is a lifelong process through which we can unlearn and relearn. Through land-based education, we can start to learn about decolonization and reconciliation, and it is empowering for us all.

RECONCILIATION THROUGH THE LENS OF SUBALTERNITY

When learning about the meaning and value of reconciliation, the concept of subalternity has significant relevance. Spivak (1988: 78) proposes subalternity in her essay "Can the Subaltern Speak?" By subaltern, Spivak (1988: 283) means the oppressed subjects, or more generally, those "of inferior rank." She provides an example from the Indian context where subaltern groups do not have the privilege of representing themselves. As Spivak explains, the subaltern groups in India are socially subordinate. They do not have any decision-making power and do not participate in social and state decision-making processes.

Spivak (1988) illustrates her point through a discussion of the traditional *sati* practice, which was outlawed by the British. *Sati,* which translates to "true" or "honest" refers to a funeral ritual common in some Asian communities where a recently widowed woman commits suicide by fire, typically on the husband's funeral pyre. Outlawing this fading practice served as a means of securing British power in India. The British formed an anti-*sati* law to stop the traditional practice by consulting with Indian men, arguing that more "modern" and "civilized" ways of engaging women would be learned from their own culture. Women's voices were not heard, and they were effectively excluded from the decision-making process, even though it was about them. Spivak (1998: 93) argues that the abolition of the Hindu rite of *sati* in India by the British can be described as "white men saving brown women from brown men," which also explains how it serves to justify colonial interventions. The process was never about brown women, or white ones for that matter. It was about asserting the superiority of white men, as was the case in the context of Canadian colonization. Therefore, the concept of subalternity is helpful for reconciliation; it helps to explain the relationships of colonial powers with any person or groups of people who hold inferior rank or positions in their society due to race, class, gender, sexual orientation, ethnicity, or religion. Understanding the subalternity position is important because it helps us to learn the process of raising our voices for our rights and the rights of other marginalized groups. It might also help us to explore our own social and political agency, which then helps us in taking responsibility to learn the meaning of reconciliation.

Subalternity Lens in Reconciliation Practice

Using the subalternity lens was one of the most effective ways of learning my responsibility for furthering the process of reconciliation. In this garden, subaltern groups included international students and their spouses, immigrant families, the queer community, and Indigenous Peoples. These groups of gardeners cannot afford or do not have access to organic foods and fresh vegetables in the market. They also do not have adequate opportunities to learn about Canadian history and culture, and do not have sufficient access to university and community resources. I have seen that, through the development and fostering of a cross-cultural garden, subaltern groups of people can find their voices and contribute to decision-making processes.

The cross-cultural community garden activities helped subaltern groups to speak up for their rights and to learn about social justice issues. For example, in 2013, the university administration decided to suspend the community garden because of a lack of resources. As a coordinator, I worked to mobilize most of the gardeners to protest this administrative decision. Many gardeners came forward and raised their voices against the administration's decision, even though they were scared to do so. Because of the strength of our voices, we were able to garner considerable media attention and force the university to give back the land and resources for the community garden. From this activity, we, as community gardeners, have learned how to fight against injustice and to raise our voices to achieve our rights. As a member of a subaltern group of people in my community, I personally learned to speak up for my own rights and how to deal with the complex administrative structures of an institution. For example, when the garden was re-opened, as a community organizer I was identified as a front-line protestor and leader and was not re-hired for the garden coordinator position, even though I had the experience for this casual student summer job position. As a result, I had to find other ways to maintain my work within and my passion for the garden. I took the initiative and wrote the garden support proposal and searched for other community resources to continue my work as a cultural coordinator. As a cultural coordinator, educator, and activist for our garden community, I have learned how a community garden can empower women like me and can help give a voice to the subaltern.

RECONCILIATION THROUGH THE LENS OF HYBRIDITY

Hybridity is an important concept for understanding the complex, socially constructed identities of women, which in turn helps to foster an understanding of the everyday practice of reconciliation (Anand 2009; Bhatia and Ram 2004; Bhatia 2002; Davies 2007; Ghosh 2013; Kibria 2012; Mirza 2013; Samuel 2010; Sundar 2008). Postcolonial scholar Homi Bhabha (2004) is responsible for conceiving of one of the major contributions to the concept of hybrid identities: having access to two or more ethnic identities. He examines the social context and historical effect of various intersections and avoids simply listing them or elevating one aspect of his analysis over others. He goes on to explain how the concept of hybridity challenges colonial fixity and rigidity since the very definition of hybridity involves blending compounds, and the whole of European colonialization was founded upon the belief in the superiority and purity of European culture. For Bhabha, hybridity takes meaning as a continuous process, which disobeys any colonial fixed authenticity by mixing partial (limited) and subjective viewpoints. Therefore, the concept of hybridity has many implications in understanding the meanings of reconciliation from multiple perspectives.

Hybridity Lens in Practice

Through eight years of community garden activities, I have come to understand this cross-cultural garden as a hybrid space. A community garden can encourage food sovereignty, feminist consciousness raising, social justice activities, and leadership skills. It can also provide some psychological benefit and create a sense of belonging with the new host society. A community garden provides science and environmental education and helps us engage in research, which ultimately leads to community action. It is a sharing space for women's daily struggle of coping with this new host society, and it is a land-based relational learning space. Immigrant women can share their ethnic history, heritage, and their socially constructed hybridized story with other immigrant women.

A community garden is not just a piece of land that produces organic vegetables. It is a space that helps to deconstruct the capitalistic ways of seeing the world, particularly the idea of individual property ownership. It can serve many purposes and has diverse meanings for different age groups. For example, it can be a recreational and relaxing space for elderly people. Many cross-cultural elderly people bring their grandchildren to the garden. These children work as translators for their non-English-speaking grandparents and help them enjoy the garden to the fullest. The children themselves can spend time in the kids' section, where they work independently at their own assigned plots rather sharing their parents' plot. Children may also engage in garden arts activities and educational workshops. This shared hybrid community garden space offers a unique opportunity for cross-cultural sharing and educational social activities, which cultivate the hope of learning the meaning of reconciliation together.

RECONCILIATION THROUGH THE LENS OF OTHERNESS

According to Edward Said (1993), *otherness* is a colonial idea, which positions one group of people as inferior to another group of people, making them the *other*. Examples of this are plentiful: developed vs. developing countries, East vs. West, women vs. men, Indigenous vs. non-Indigenous, and so on. This attribution of *otherness* is the representation of Western hegemonic knowledge politics, which privileges the Westernized self. The term, Andreotti (2014) explained, justifies superiority and supports domination. Said's *Culture and Imperialism* (1993) demonstrates how Western scholars purposely stereotype and dehumanize the East to construct an imaginary *other*. Said's *otherness* concept has created a framework and opportunity to produce new scholarship using non-dominant lenses or methods to examine the power held by scholars of the West and its capacity to reproduce colonial misrepresentations of the East. Said explains that Western scholars and media portray the so-called Orient as inferior, regressive, primitive, and irrational, whereas the West is represented within its own framework as superior, progressive, and rational. According to Said, *other* translates as inferior, less significant, less important.

In feminist literature, we need to move away from categories of others to a more inclusive *we*. Within *we* there shouldn't be *other*. Said (1993) argues that we can move away from the objectification of the *other* and the conception of *them* by instead using the terms *we* and *us*. He emphasizes the culturally authoritative process through which constructs of the Orient and Oriental people are made by Western scholars and imperialists and notes that *otherness* undermines local people's experiences and their everyday cultural practices. According to Said, the concept of *otherness* is not a fact of nature but is rather a hegemonic cultural production of the dominant institutions, which is constructed through language and the systematic production of experts. In the Canadian context, where Indigenous Peoples are perceived of as the other, otherness is an important concept for understanding reconciliation.

Otherness Lens in Reconciliation Practice

Through my experiences in the cross-cultural community garden, I was able to understand my identity through the otherness lens. For example, as a newly arrived visible minority, I felt socially isolated from the majority population, who do not acknowledge my voice and experiences. This small shared land helped me to challenge the concept of *otherness*. Our community of gardeners was very supportive in creating a shared community space — a shared piece of land with community-shared funding, shared garden equipment, and shared seeds, plants, and harvests. The gardeners come from many countries but together have built a new community. Sharing harvests, particularly the year-end harvest potluck party, with the wider community is the best part of our community gardening. The sense of belonging that has emerged from this shared space and shared equipment has been empowering. The belief we hold that sharing can bring caring has made this a space where we are no longer othered. This *we* feeling will help the gardeners to learn the meaning of reconciliation together.

RECONCILIATION THROUGH THE LENS OF INTERSECTIONALITY

Intersectionality as a concept focuses on recognizing the many connected facets of social identities that impact experiences of discrimination, including racism, ableism, ageism, sexism, xenophobia, and religious or other belief-based bigotries (Crenshaw 1989; Maillé 2010; Mirza 2013; Zaman 2012, 2006), all of which operate to compound one another. Intersectionality is the recognition that people have multiple identities — and that these identities intersect to create a particular experience of the world. I am an educator, brown-skinned feminist, mother of three non-religious daughters, Muslim woman, having an inter-religious married life, unpaid community activist, and volunteer. These identities intersect with each other to create a particular experience of the world.

Heidi Mirza's (2013) study examines the narratives of three transnational Muslim women of Turkish, Pakistani, and Indian heritage who have multiple place attachments (The Netherlands, Bombay, Pakistan, Britain, Canada, and

Bangladesh) and have identities shaped by living and working in Britain. Her study shows how these transnational groups of women are using embodied practices such as choosing to wear the *hijab* or *burqa*, which one woman describes as her "second skin." According to Mirza, transnational groups of women are being gendered, othered, and racialized owing to biases projected onto their use of the *hijab*, even though they have been raised in the Western world since their childhood. Transnational groups of women in this study were conscious of the disjunction between how they see themselves as Muslim women and how they are racially constructed as Asian because of their appearance, food, culture, and accents. Mirza shows how Muslim women's agency challenges and transforms hegemonic discourses of race, class, gender, and religion in some transnational diasporic spaces. Drawing from Crenshaw (1989) and Mirza (2013), the concept of intersectionality shows how white women and privileged women of colour can also play a role as an oppressor at different complex experiential intersections or crossroads. Intersectionality is a form of literacy and proposes the use of methodologies that identify multiple threats of discrimination when an individual's identities overlap with many minority structures such as class, race, gender, age, and other components of social bias.

Intersectionality Lens in Reconciliation Practice

Through the cross-cultural community garden activities, I also came to understand reconciliation through the lens of intersectionality. For instance, I was born into a Muslim faith-based family. Growing up, I was not exposed much to other religious faiths because, in Bangladesh, Muslims are a majority. I have observed that there is more religious racism in Bangladesh than Canada because of socially constructed systemic and institutional racism and unequal social practices. The partition of India in 1942 and a long history of colonization are the root causes of the ongoing religious discrimination and prohibitions against inter-religious mingling (Pandey 2001). As a result, I did not have the opportunity to mingle with groups of people of other faiths due to my social class and the limitations of diverse socialization. However, my partner and his family are Hindu, which is considered a minority and oppressed religious community in Bangladesh. It was through our inter-religious marriage that I started to learn about other religious traditions.

Bangladeshi diasporic and newcomer community members, leaders, and our own family members ostracized me, our children, and my partner due to our inter-religious marriage. We dared to mix faiths and family, which is extremely unacceptable in Islam and is not appreciable even in Hinduism, though there are some exceptions. I was never congratulated when I became a new mother. Bangladeshi Muslim community members still consider our children "*haram*" (illegitimate) and do not socialize with my family because they consider our union, life practices, and advanced degrees, or scholarships, to be *haram,* as well. I have a new hyphenated identity (Bangladeshi–Canadian), I am a mother of three daughters, a wife, a sister, and a feminist activist. Through all of these intersectional identities and lenses, I have learned that, because of my brown skin colour, my diasporic identity, and my ex-Muslim identity (Islam is not a part of my everyday practice anymore, and I am not attached to any religious identity), I have been labelled as a visible minority immigrant woman both within the diasporic, newcomer Bangladeshi community and the community at large. I have been gendered, othered, and racialized even though I have been living in the Western world since 2003.

Through the cross-cultural community garden, I have learned that I do not need to be ashamed of my inter-religious relationship and brown skin colour. I now know that I should be proud of my relationships and inform others about the benefits of inter-religious and intercultural relationships. I also learned that I am a newcomer guest on Treaty Six Territory and the Homeland of the Métis. I came to appreciate that the original (i.e., Indigenous) Peoples of this land have never asked me about my faith or my religious identity to undermine me. By using these intersectional lenses in our community garden activities, I feel I have empowered myself, increased my self-esteem, and acquired the strength to break any kind of socially constructed barriers. My community work and contributions have been recognized and honoured by several provincial and community organizations, and our gardeners' community also took the time to appreciate my effort. Through community garden activities and intersectional lenses, I understood the term reconciliation in my own way. To me, reconciliation means the peaceful coexistence of multiple faiths and races (in my case, Hindu vs. Muslim and my brown skin) and coming together to find common ground to move forward from any difficulties, such as the indoctrinated dogmas that keep us separate.

DISCUSSION AND CONCLUSION

I have seen from my eight-year learning journey with the community garden that understanding reconciliation through transnational literacies can have various meanings and implications for our everyday practices. These meanings and implications vary according to place, land, situation, relation, perspectives, culture, and one's own knowledge and positionality. In this chapter, I have discussed transnational literacies by mobilizing some of the concepts and implications informing decolonizing feminist theories.

In the community garden activities, I have learned how reconciliation can be understood through transnational literacies (such as decolonization, subalternity, hybridity, otherness, and intersectionality), which is helpful in transforming my everyday practice of solidarity and advocacy for myself and others. I understand that there are many ways we can discuss the concept of transnational literacies and that it is not fixed. Rather, as Bhabha (2004) has said, it is achieved through a hybrid process of becoming. It changes according to people's needs, practices, and cultures. I would say that the baseline of transnational literacy requires engagement with more than one culture and an understanding of the role of nation-states in shaping identities.

Many newcomer immigrants are not aware of the 2008 UN Declaration on the Rights of Indigenous Peoples and know little about the Truth and Reconciliation Commission's calls to action in 2015 or about the colonial history of Canada with First Nations, Inuit, and Métis people. As a newcomer, I did not know these either. This lack of knowledge can lead to the perpetuation of negative and damaging stereotypes about Indigenous Peoples and their cultures. Non-Indigenous Canadians and newcomers need to appreciate that reconciliation represents only the minimum standard for the survival, dignity, and well-being of Indigenous Peoples in Canada. Working with community garden members over many years, I became hopeful and came to understand how to work with settlers, international students, newcomer immigrants, and refugees to enhance their knowledge and to lay the groundwork for reconciliation. Through eight years of cross-cultural community garden activities, I have learned that all of us (Indigenous and non-Indigenous) should be responsible for honouring and acknowledging Indigenous treaties and putting this into our everyday practice. And as non-Indigenous people, we must recognize our positionality and privileges in order to begin to reconcile.

Although our community garden is community driven, it clearly has political implications for reconciliation. I learned that meaningful engagements with the land can help gardeners to understand Canada's colonial history. It helps to inspire gardeners to transform Canadian society into a collaborative and harmonious place so that our children and grandchildren can live together in dignity, peace, and prosperity on the land we are now only beginning to learn how to share through our community garden activities. For example, we have been learning Canadian history through many activities: the blanket exercise, storytelling/cultural teachings with the Indigenous Elders and Knowledge Keepers, workshops with children, music, artworks, and recycling.

When approaching reconciliation through transnational literacies, it is helpful to keep an open mind. It is important to ask about what challenges are shaping capacities to learn about transnational feminist practices and knowledge. I would respond that feminist scholars are still in the process of learning, unlearning, and relearning through decolonization processes. Educators and scholars are developing new ways to learn how to decolonize our understandings, our knowledge, our research methods, and our actions toward social justice and reconciliation.

Reconciliation through transnational literacy helps to increase the ability to better read the world in all its complex differences. Chandra Talpade Mohanty (2003: 122) insists that feminist work must be "deeply collective" and this deep collectivity calls for a continuous process of feminist/ intellectual struggle and consciousness raising. She suggests that our thinking and doing should involve "knowing without borders" (123). I support Mohanty and her invitation to create collective empathy and solidarity for understanding and practising reconciliation from and within transnational lenses.

Reconciliation through transnational literacies crosses borders to study the intellectual, political, and institutional contexts that inform our own shifts and new commitments to creating transnational solidarity networks and activism. As a feminist, I am aware of the need to take responsibility to create awareness around achieving Indigenous sovereignty by connecting with Indigenous understandings of land. I am also aware that decolonization is not a metaphor (Tuck and Yang 2012). We need to take up our responsibility to decolonize the meanings of transnational literacies in practical terms by situating local knowledge, through historical materialisms, land use, marriage customs, repro-ductive labour, commodification and decommodification processes, various community engagements (for example, community gardening, community radio, cross-cultural activities, cross-cultural networking etc.), intercultural education, social work, academia, policy implications, and the transnational literacies that are already in a process of decolonization.

As an immigrant woman on Indigenous Land, I argue that there is an increasing need for meaningful dialogue across borders and boundaries. Building transnational solidarity for reconciliation requires transnational literacy for articulating and preserving differences without silencing anyone. But what constitutes meaningful, transformative, feminist, and decolonized dialogue and under what conditions can it be realized? Does it mean translating someone's words into my own language? Transnational scholars suggest being open to creating a new language that all can share easily. This can be achieved through more empathy for the other. We must revisit the arguments that support the need for transnational dialogue. There is a possibility of overcoming language and cultural differences by reaching a shared understanding.

Therefore, reconciliation through transnational literacy is complex. It includes learning one another's histories, genealogies, cultures, and languages, and understanding that this can play a vital role in building shared understanding and reconciliation. Transnational scholars have been arguing that no nation-state has been founded on gender justice or has managed to learn the real meaning of reconciliation or Indigenous sovereignty. Therefore, understanding reconciliation through transnational literacies is required. In the Canadian context, and beyond, reconciliation through transnational literacies requires decentralizing dominant perspectives and questioning normative discourses.

REFERENCES

Abu-Laban, Yasmeen. 2014. "Reform by Stealth: The Harper Conservatives and Canadian Multiculturalism." In J. Jedwab (ed.), *The Multiculturalism Question: Debating Identity in 21st Century Canada*. Montreal-Kingston: School of Policy Studies, Queen's University and McGill-Queen's University Press.

Ahmed, Sara. 2014. *Cultural Politics of Emotion*. UK: Edinburgh University Press.

Anand, Dibyesh. 2009. "Diasporic Subjectivity as an Ethical Position." *South Asian Diaspora*, 1, 2: 103–111.

Andreotti, Vanessa. 2014. "Critical and Transnational Literacies in International Development and Global Citizenship Education." *Sisyphus Journal of Education*, 2, 3: 32–50. DOI: <https://doi.org/10.25749/sis.6544>.

Barndt, Deborah (ed.). 2011. *Viva! Community Arts and Popular Education in the Americas*. Albany and Toronto: State University of New York Press and Between the Lines Press.

Battiste, Marie (ed.). 2000. *Reclaiming Indigenous Voice & Vision*. Vancouver: University of British Columbia Press.

___. 2013. "Decolonizing Education: Nourishing the Learning Spirit." Saskatoon, SK:

Purich Publishing.

___. 2017. "Decolonial Ways of Knowing and Doing at Banglar Gann O Katha at CFCR 90.5 Saskatoon Radio Program." https://www.youtube.com/watch?v=wFw5gqdKCAs

Berry, Jhon. 2005. "Acculturation: Living Successfully in Two Cultures." *International Journal of Intercultural Relations*, 29: 697–712.

Bhabha, Homi. 1985. "Signs Taken for Wonders: Questions of Ambivalence and Authority Under a Tree Outside of Delhi." *Critical Inquiry*, XII, 1: 89–106.

___. 1991. "The Third Space: Interview with Homi K Bhabha." In J. Rutherford (ed.), *Identity: Community, Culture, Difference*. London: Lawrence & Wishart.

___. 2004. *The Location of Culture*. London and New York: Routledge.

Bhatia, Sunil. 2002. "Acculturation, Dialogical Voices and the Construction of the Diasporic Self." *Theory and Psychology*, 12, 1: 55–77.

Bhatia, Sunil, and Anjali Ram. 2004. "Culture, Hybridity, and the Dialogical Self: Cases from the South Asian Diaspora." *Mind, Culture, and Activity*, 11, 3: 224–240.

Brydon, Diana. 2010. "Critical Literacies for Globalizing Times." *Critical Literacy: Theories and Practices,* 4, 2 (June): 16–28.

___. 2014. "Canada and Brazil: Shifting Contexts for Knowledge Production." ("Canadá e Brasil: Contextos de mudança para a produção de conhecimento.") *Interfaces Brasil/Canadá*, 13, 16: 201–221.

Carr, Summerson E. 2003. "Rethinking Empowerment Theory Using a Feminist Lens: The Importance of Process." *Women and Social Work*, 18, 1: 8–20.

Crenshaw, Kimberle. 1989. "Demarginalizing the Intersection of Race and Sex: A Black Feminist Critique of Antidiscrimination Doctrine, Feminist Theory and Antiracist Politics." *University of Chicago Legal Forum*, 8.

Datta, Ranjan. 2016. "Community Garden: A Bridging Program Between Formal and Informal Learning." *Cogent Education*, 3, 1. <https://doi.org/10.1080/2331186X.2016.1177154>.

___. 2017. "Decolonizing Both Research and Researcher, and Its Effectiveness in Indigenous Research." *Research Ethics*. Advance online publication. DOI: 10.1080/13549839.2013.818957.

___. 2018. "Decolonizing Methodologies: A Transformation from Science-Oriented Sociology Researcher to Relational/Participant-Oriented Researcher." *American Indian Culture and Research Journal,* 42, 1. <http://uclajournals.org/doi/pdf/10.17953/aicrj.42.1.datta>.

Davies, Rebecca. 2007. "Reconceptualising the Migration: Development Nexus: Diasporas, Globalisation and the Politics of Exclusion." *Third World Quarterly*, 28, 1: 59–76.

Foucault, Michel. 1978. *The History of Sexuality, Vol. 1: The Will to Knowledge*. New York: Pantheon Books.

Gardner, Katy. 1999. "Women and Islamic Revivalism in a Bangladeshi Community." In Patricia Jeffery and Amrita Basu, *Appropriating Gender: Women's Activism and Politicized Religion in South Asia*. UK: Routledge.

Ghosh, Sutama. 2013. "Am I a South Asian, Really? Constructing 'South Asians' in Canada and Being South Asian in Toronto." *South Asian Diaspora*, 5, 1: 35–55.

Gramsci, Antonio. 1971. *Selections from the Prison Notebooks of Antonio Gramsci*. New York: International Publishers.

Gutierrez, Lee. 1995. "Understanding the Empowerment Process: Does Consciousness Make a Difference?" *Social Work Research*, 19: 229–237.

Hobbs, Margaret, and Carla Rice (eds.). 2013. *Gender and Women's Studies in Canada: Critical Terrain.* Toronto: Women's Press.

Kabeer, Naila. 2012a. "Empowerment, Citizenship, and Gender Justice: A Contribution to Locally Grounded Theories of Change in Women's Lives." *Ethics and Social Welfare*, 6, 3: 216–232.

____. 2012b. "Women's Economic Empowerment and Inclusive Growth: Labour Markets and Enterprise Development." <http://www.idrc.ca/EN/Documents/NK-WEEConcept-Paper.pdf>.

Kaminski, Michelle, Jeffrey S. Kaufman, Robin Graubarth, and Thomas G. Robins. 2000. "How Do People Become Empowered? A Case Study of Union Activists." *Human Relations,* 53: 1357–1383.

Kearney, Shanon. 2009. "The Community Garden as a Tool for Community Empowerment: A Study of Community Gardens in Hampden County." Master's thesis. <http://scholarworks.umass.edu/theses/361>.

Kibria, Nazli. 2012. "Transnational Marriage and the Bangladeshi Muslim Diaspora in Britain and the United States." *Culture and Religion*, 13, 2: 227–240.

Kieffer, Charles. 1984. "Citizen Empowerment: A Developmental Perspective." In J. Rappaport, C. Swift, and R. Hess (eds.), *Studies in Empowerment: Steps Toward Understanding and Action.* New York: Hayworth Press.

Maile, Arvin, Eve Tuck, and Angie Morrill. 2013. "Decolonizing Feminism: Challenging Connections between Settler Colonialism and Heteropatriarchy." *Feminist Formations*, 25, 1, (Spring): 8–34. Johns Hopkins University Press. DOI: <http://doi.org/10.1353/ff.2013.0006>.

Maillé, C. 2010. "Critical Race Feminism for the 21st Century." In Sherene Razack, Malinda Smith, and Sunera Thobani (eds.), *States of Race: Critical Race Feminism for the 21st Century.* Toronto: Between the Lines.

Mirza, H. 2013. "'A Second Skin': Embodied Intersectionality, Transnationalism and Narratives of Identity and Belonging among Muslim Women in Britain." *Women's Studies International Forum*, 36: 5–15.

Mohanty, Chandra Talpade. 2003. "Feminism Without Borders: Decolonizing Theory, Practicing Solidarity." Durham and London: Duke University Press.

Nelson, G., J. Lord, and J. Ochocka. 2001. "Empowerment and Mental Health in Community: Narratives of Psychiatric Consumer/Survivors." *Journal of Community and Applied Social Psychology*, 11: 125–142.

Pandey, Gyanendra. 2001. *Remembering Partition: Violence, Nationalism, and History in India.* Cambridge: Cambridge University Press.

Ross, Luana. 2009. "From the 'F' Word to Indigenous/Feminisms." *Wicazo Sa Review*, 24, 2 (Fall): 39–52. University of Minnesota Press. DOI: 10.1353/wic.0.0041.

Rublee, C., and S.M. Shaw. 1991. "Constraints on the Leisure and Community Participation of Immigrant Women: Implications for Social Integration. *Loisir et société,* 14, 1.

Said, E. 1993. *Culture and Imperialism.* London: Chatto & Windus.

Samuel, Lina. 2010. "Mating, Dating and Marriage: Intergenerational Cultural Retention and the Construction of Diasporic Identities among South Asian Immigrants in

Canada." *Journal of Intercultural Studies,* 31, 1.

Simpson, L. 2014. *Dancing on Our Turtle's Back: Stories of Nishnaabeg Re-Creation, Resurgence, and a New Emergence.* Winnipeg: ARP Books.

Solomon, B. 1976. "Black Empowerment." New York: Columbia University Press.

Spivak, G.C. 1988. "Can the Subaltern Speak?" In C. Nelson and L. Grossberg (eds.), *Marxism and the Interpretation of Culture.* University of Illinois Press.

___. 1992. *An Aesthetic Education in the Era of Globalization.* Cambridge, MA: Harvard University Press.

___. 1999. "A Critique of Postcolonial Reason: Toward a History of the Vanishing Present." Cambridge, MA: Harvard University Press.

___. 2003. "Death of a Discipline." New York: Columbia University Press.

Subramaniam, M. 2012. "Grassroots Groups and Poor Women's Empowerment in Rural India." *International Sociology,* 27, 1: 72–95.

Sundar, Purnima. 2008. "To 'Brown It Up' or to 'Bring Down the Brown': Identity and Strategy in Second-Generation, South Asian-Canadian Youth." *Journal of Ethnic & Cultural Diversity in Social Work,* 17, 3.

Tuck, Eve, and Marcia McKenzie. 2015. "Decolonizing Perspectives on Place." In *Place in Research: Theory, Methodology, Methods.* New York: Routledge.

Tuck, Eve (Aleut), and K. Wayne Yang. 2012. "Decolonization Is Not a Metaphor." *Decolonization: Indigeneity, Education, Society,* 1, 1: 1–40.

Walia, Harsha, and Andrea Smith. 2013. *Undoing Border Imperialism.* Chico, CA: AK Press.

Zaman, Habiba. 2006. *Breaking the Iron Wall: Decommodification and Immigrant Women's Labor in Canada.* Lanham, MD: Lexington Books.

___. 2012. *Asian Immigrants in "Two Canadas": Racialization, Marginalization and Deregulated Work.* Halifax: Fernwood Publishing.

Zimmerman, M. 1995. "Psychological Empowerment: Issues and Illustrations." *American Journal of Community Psychology,* 23: 581–598.

Chapter Seven

RECONCILIATION AND NEW CANADIANS

ALI ABUKAR

In this chapter, I share stories explaining why, as a new Canadian and a former refugee, I feel so grateful to live and work on Treaty Six Territory and the Homeland of the Métis. I discuss my two years of community-based professional experience with reconciliation in Saskatoon, Saskatchewan. Through my reconciliation activities in Saskatoon, I claimed my identity as a global citizen and a promoter of diversity and multiculturalism. In this chapter, I argue that reconciliation means working together to meet shared needs and celebrate shared successes through dialogue and relationship building. I also believe that reconciliation means standing together against injustices, remembering and learning from the past, ensuring past injustices are not repeated, and moving toward healing as a community and as a country. Through my work with newcomers to Canada, I will continue the important process of truth and reconciliation, and community and nation building.

The welcoming atmosphere of this country, which I now call home, was established when its Indigenous Peoples greeted the initial newcomers to Canada centuries ago. The Indigenous Peoples of Canada showed the early settlers generosity and shared their land and resources with them. However, as a country, we have a history of colonialism, racism, and injustice in the way that our government systems have treated our Indigenous sisters and brothers and this land. After a long struggle, we finally have the Truth and Reconciliation Commission (TRC) report, which documents the cultural genocide that residential schools inflicted upon Indigenous Peoples. It also brings to light what can be done to bring about reconciliation between Indigenous and non-Indigenous Peoples, as immense suffering and damage were inflicted upon the Indigenous children who were sent to the residential schools and on their families. It also noted that these schools were funded and operated by the Canadian government and Canadian religious institutions (TRC 2015).

The impact of the residential schools left Indigenous Peoples, both Survivors and those indirectly affected, with intergenerational trauma. The experiences and the related trauma resulted in the loss of language, culture, Traditional Knowledge, and ways of doing things for many generations. As a new Canadian social activist and refugee advocate, I care about reconciliation and relationship building in Canada because it rights the wrongs done to our Indigenous sisters and brothers, and I believe it is an important way to promote diversity and inclusion in our community and our country.

This chapter will explore some of the commonalities in the cultural practices of newcomers to Canada and Indigenous Peoples, and their shared understanding of the importance of maintaining one's culture and identity. I discuss this commonality to establish a relatability between the two groups in the hopes of promoting relationship building and reconciliation. I also touch on the importance of cultural bridging and relationship building between newcomers to Canada and our Indigenous sisters and brothers, specifically regarding the role that settlement agencies and ethnocultural community organizations can play in reconciliation, community building, and nation building. In order to see these commonalities, I must first situate myself, acknowledge my privileges, and explore what reconciliation means to me. Through my own experiences, both my lived experience and the work I do with other new Canadians, I explore what reconciliation means to a new Canadian and how newcomers approach reconciliation by trying to establish relatability between Indigenous, newcomer, and new Canadian communities so as to create a potential for relationship building, alliances, and reconciliation.

SITUATING THE SELF

I am a young black man who was born and raised in Somalia. I have lived and worked in various countries and I consider myself a global citizen. Global citizenship is a way of living that recognizes our increasingly complex, connected, and interdependent world where our actions and choices may have an impact on people and communities locally, nationally, and globally (IDEAS for Global Citizenship n.d.). As political scientist Michael Byers said in a talk at the University of British Columbia in 2005:

It empowers individual human beings to participate in decisions concerning their lives, including the political, economic, social, cultural and environmental conditions in which they live. It includes the right to vote, to express opinions and associate with others, and to enjoy a decent and dignified quality of life. It is expressed through engagement in the various communities of which the individual is a part, at the local, national and global level. And it includes the right to challenge authority and existing power structures, to think, argue and act with the intent to change the world.

Having fled my home country as a teenager, I developed empathy for the concerns of my fellow humans. This empathy grew as I learned about my own privileges and the importance of equity and social justice for humanity in the course of my postsecondary education. I am university educated and earn a decent wage at my job. My family and I have a home in a safe neighbourhood, clean drinking water, and access to basic services. I acknowledge my privileges and I am grateful for the life I live as a Canadian citizen. However, being aware of my privileges makes me question the ongoing inequities and injustices perpetrated against our Indigenous sisters and brothers. What continues to happen in the Indigenous communities is unacceptable and goes against what Canada should stand for, to me as an immigrant and new Canadian.

It is unacceptable that historical injustices against the Indigenous Peoples of this great land should persist. Although former prime minister Stephen Harper issued an apology for the residential schools in June 2008 (Harper 2008), the legacy of the schools has contributed to social problems that continue to exist in many communities today. In addition, this 2008 apology was not extended to the Survivors of the residential schools in the province of Newfoundland and Labrador; however, these Survivors did receive an apology in 2017 when Prime Minister Justin Trudeau addressed hundreds of former students and their families in Goose Bay:

> Saying that we are sorry is not enough. It will not undo the harm that was done to you. It will not bring back the language and traditions you lost. It will not take away the isolation and vulnerability you felt when you separated from your families, communities and cultures. (McIntyre 2017)

Trudeau apologized on behalf of the Canadian government and all Canadians, including new Canadians like me. He also acknowledged that there is still a lot to be done to engage in reconciliation and fix the systems, such as the current foster system, which removes so many Indigenous children from their homes in a continuation of the country's colonial policies.

WHAT RECONCILIATION MEANS TO ME

As a new Canadian, I see reconciliation as acknowledging the past, respecting the land on which we live, and building relationships based on respect, equity, and inclusivity. I am grateful to live and work on Treaty Six Territory and the Homeland of the Métis and the Cree Nations. I stand with our Indigenous sisters and brothers against the injustices and inequities they continue to face. To me, reconciliation will only work if we acknowledge the truth of the past, build meaningful relationships, and stand with one another against injustices and inequities. The process of reconciliation involves both Canadian society as a whole and all levels of government. Furthermore, it must be nation-to-nation, as our current government promised, and action-based (Liberal Party of Canada 2015). I acknowledge that there is encouraging work being done toward reconciliation and bettering the conditions in Indigenous communities, yet not much has been achieved thus far. It remains to be seen whether these promises will come to fruition.

NEWCOMERS AND RECONCILIATION

Newcomers to Canada may relate to some of the experiences of Indigenous Peoples. Many new Canadians and newcomers to Canada come from countries that were colonized by European nations. Some countries are still fighting and sacrificing many lives to protect their land and people from ongoing colonization; for example, Palestine and Somalia. The land of origin of many of these newcomers to Canada was taken by force, its resources exploited, and its people deprived of their rights. Unlike Indigenous Peoples, however, the European colonizers to these countries of origin did not stay and continue to colonize the inhabitants. This is not to say that colonization did not leave many of those countries with lasting, devastating effects. For instance, European colonizers from Britain, France, and Italy, along with Ethiopia, divided Somalia, where I was born, among themselves (Sosinski 2014). Although Somalia gained independence in 1960, parts of it are still occupied by Ethiopia and Kenya. The people living on that occupied land are of Somali origin but llive under either Ethiopian or Kenyan rule. What countries like Somalia and Palestine underwent at the hands of colonizers and settlers may not be the same as the Indigenous experience, but it may facilitate a relatability between the struggles of Indigenous Peoples and those of newcomers to Canada/new Canadians, whether the struggles resulted from inequality, racism, and underemployment or from colonization and oppression prior to arriving in Canada.

Many newcomers to Canada, mainly refugees and other forced migrants, witnessed forms of systemic oppression and violence that forced them to flee their home countries and seek safety and security elsewhere. For examples, we can look at what is happening in Syria, Myanmar, Somalia, and Afghanistan, among others. As a refugee, I can relate to some of the injustices that my Indigenous sisters and brothers continue to face. As shared earlier, I fled my home country of Somalia as a teenager due to civil war and violence following the fall of Somalia's central government in the early 1990s. I lived in Cairo, Egypt, as a refugee and experienced racism and discrimination firsthand. After moving to Canada as a permanent resident and completing my graduate degree, I faced barriers to entering the labour force. I can relate to some of the struggles that other immigrants and refugees face as newcomers to Canada. However, what I found missing in educating newcomers to Canada was the history of the Indigenous Peoples — the history of colonialism and residential schools in Canada. As a new Canadian, I have an obligation to engage in reconciliation and relationship building here because I am a treaty person.

Systemic oppression has been another effect of colonialism for both Indigenous Peoples and many newcomers to Canada (Circles for Reconciliation 2017). The residential schools run by the Canadian government and settler religious institutions, which were intended to break the Indigenous children's links to their culture and identity, are a particularly poignant example of this systemic oppression (TRC 2015). The use of colonial policies by Canada's colonial governments, including the Indian Act and residential schools, were intentional, systemic attempts to eliminate Indigenous governments, ignore Indigenous Rights, terminate treaties, and, through a process of assimilation and elimination, cause Indigenous Peoples to cease to exist as distinct legal, social, cultural, religious, and racial entities (TRC 2015). This is evident in the words of one senior government official in 1920: "Our object is to continue until there is not a single Indian in Canada that has not been absorbed into body politic" (TRC 2015: 6).

The Indian residential schools have all closed now, but their legacy and the devastating impacts of them on the Indigenous communities remain, including intergenerational trauma. As an example, I want to share what I learned from a session by an Indigenous educator. He said that, although he did not go to a residential school, he and his siblings were still affected, due to his parents, other relatives, and community members being Survivors. He said that growing up, he witnessed a lot of drinking in their house and his parents struggled to parent him and his siblings. There was a lot of hurt and suffering in the community where he grew up. He believes that things have now changed, and people use political correctness in general when engaging in discussions around Indigenous Peoples and reconciliation, despite the apparent racism faced by members of the Indigenous community. He was sharing his experience of residential schools and engagement with reconciliation through storytelling with some non-Indigenous community members, including newcomers to Canada and new Canadians. It was fascinating to see how engaged the immigrants were in this session, which was organized by our volunteer management program at the Saskatoon Open Door Society.

To engage in reconciliation, we need to confront the impact of ongoing racism and discrimination on marginalized communities (Circles of Reconciliation 2017). We must also recognize the stigma, myths and stereotypes that abound about these communities: "they do not pay taxes"; "bogus refugees/queue-jumpers"; or "they are here to abuse our welfare system and take our jobs" (Circles of Reconciliation 2017: n.p.). The colonialism and systemic oppression of these communities include forced and unforced assimilation, capitalism, exploitation, and the degradation of resources. As discussed above, Indigenous Peoples experience forced assimilation, whereas newcomers to Canada are expected to assimilate into Canadian society. Thanks to colonial multiculturalism (MacDonald 2014: 70) and Canada's use of the so-called integration policies to promote the full participation of immigrants in Canada's social, economic, and political life, integration policies are not applied as strictly as in other immigration-based societies. This was evident when, in 1969, the Royal Commission on Bilingualism and Biculturalism clarified the distinction between assimilation and integration, noting that "man is a thinking and sensitive being; severing him from his roots could destroy an aspect of his personality and deprive society of some of the values he can bring to it" (Griffith 2017: n.p.). This was not applied to the Indigenous Peoples. Instead, they were forced to assimilate through systemic oppression and colonialist policies. Current newcomers to Canada are favoured in this regard because this integration policy was put in place when immigration to Canada was not as diverse as it is currently. Most of the immigrants were European, white, and primarily Christian. In addition, it is argued that multiculturalism, albeit a good thing as a concept, is used by Canada as a tool to assimilate newcomers into the mainstream society. David MacDonald (2014: 69) argues that "a critical approach [to multiculturalism] seeks to uncover the unspoken assumptions about assimilation at the heart of some multicultural policies, while unpacking whiteness as an invisible norm by which other ethnicities are judged." This Canadian multiculturalism fails to recognize "the histories of oppression experienced by Indigenous Peoples and people of colour and there is a little talk of colonialism, racism, white privilege, sexism, patriarchy, heteronormativity and capitalism" (Dhamoon, as quoted in MacDonald 2014: 69).

CULTURAL COMMONALITY

On the cultural level, there are shared perspectives between the Indigenous Peoples in Canada and newcomers to Canada. I share this principle of cultural commonality because it helps to bring communities closer together when they have more commonalities than differences — it facilitates connections and relationship building. In the course of my professional career in the settlement sector, I have seen both newcomers to Canada and Indigenous members of our community connect through sharing their common experiences. For example, at one of the orientation sessions organized for a group of newcomer men with our local police services, a Sudanese refugee shared that in his culture they have a tribal lineage, and one of the police officers who identified as Indigenous shared that she too has a tribal lineage in her culture. The orientation session was intended to introduce newcomers to policing in Canada; at first, there was a tension and some mistrust, but after establishing the shared cultural experience between the Indigenous police officer and the newcomer, the two groups realized that they have a lot in common, more than they initially thought.

Other shared cultural practices include naming oneself in relation to family or ancestors, drumming and dancing, the use of traditional herbs as medicine for healing, storytelling, and placing emphasis on oral tradition. Knowledge and traditional ways of life are preserved and passed on through the generations by grandparents sharing their wisdom with their grandchildren. In many newcomer cultures, grandchildren spend time with their grandparents to learn these traditions. Celebrations of coming of age, fasting, piercing, and tattooing are also traditions common to Indigenous and newcomer communities (Circles of Reconciliation 2017). It is worthwhile to note similarities in important cultural practices, such as the celebration of the seasons, a relationship to the land (and the loss of that relationship through colonialization and/or forced migration/capitalism and land grabbing), tribal identity, and respecting Elders as Knowledge Keepers (Circles of Reconciliation 2017). I cite these examples of commonalities among our Indigenous Peoples and newcomers to further illustrate what the newcomers to Canada may have in common with their Indigenous counterparts. Newcomers cannot only relate to Indigenous experiences but may also contribute to building bridges and engaging in reconciliation.

Like Indigenous Peoples, many newcomers to Canada see the importance of keeping one's culture and identity (Circles for Reconciliation 2017). This is evident in how many newcomers to Canada stay within their own community for interaction and to preserve their cultural heritage. Culture and identity help both Indigenous Peoples and immigrants maintain their ways of life. This is what makes us human beings. We tend to seek familiarity, and this tendency is greater when we move to a new community or a new country. The importance of keeping your culture and identity has to do with maintaining your heritage so that your offspring do not lose it. This was made possible through multicultural policy and the recognition of cultural and ethnic identities of immigrants as a key feature of Canadian immigration policy (Griffith 2017); however, as discussed above, this opportunity was not afforded to Indigenous Peoples in the early settler-Indigenous relationships. There seems to be a sense of familiarity between the Indigenous and newcomer communities whenever there are opportunities for storytelling and sharing through cultural activities and celebrations. There is a strong sense of relatability between the two, and I believe the reason is that they share an understanding of the importance of maintaining and nurturing one's culture and heritage. This will pave the way for opportunities to build relationships, bridge the gap between the communities, and engage in reconciliation in a positive way.

CULTURAL BRIDGING ACTIVITIES AS ENABLERS OF RECONCILIATION

In Saskatoon, we have been engaging newcomers in activities that facilitate education about the history of Indigenous Peoples, including treaties. We have partnerships with various Indigenous organizations, including the Office of the

Treaty Commissioner, which sends speakers to provide treaty education. We have programming for youth where both Indigenous and newcomer youth are provided with activities that respond to their needs and create opportunities for friendship and community building. We have been involved in Reconciliation Saskatoon, and we continue to partner with organizations in our community to further the conversation around reconciliation and build relationships for the betterment of our communities, society, and nation. We have hosted events specifically to promote reconciliation between newcomers to Canada and the Indigenous communities, for example, a blanket exercise to learn more about the nation-to-nation relationship between Indigenous and non-Indigenous Peoples in Canada. We organize many community events for the Indigenous and newcomer communities in Saskatoon that aim to build relationships and promote reconciliation and inclusion in our community. We invite Indigenous Elders, educators, and speakers to come and engage our clients, volunteers, and staff in reconciliation and conversations about Indigenous history, knowledge, and ways of doing things. We are in the process of partnering with one of the local Indigenous community organizations to create an educational program called Reconciliation through Multiculturalism, in which members of the Indigenous communities and newcomers to Canada would share, learn together, and build relationships. I believe that these cultural bridging activities are enablers of reconciliation and relationship building and therefore will facilitate community and nation building.

A lot has changed for Indigenous Peoples in the last few decades. The last federally supported residential school remained in operation until the late 1990s (TRC 2015), and the Survivors, their families, and their communities are still experiencing intergenerational trauma. More recently, the Indigenous communities' struggle for equal rights and equal access to services and resources has been gaining momentum through movements such as Idle No More. It is promising that the current government has made commitments to better the relationship with Indigenous Peoples, but these commitments must include nation-to-nation relations and the implementation of the recommendations of the Truth and Reconciliation Commission. I believe that to engage in truth and reconciliation is the responsibility of everyone living in Canada, both citizens and residents alike. I feel proud to live and work in a city like Saskatoon, which declared 2015–16 the Year of Reconciliation. Since then, the city has seen many community efforts to engage in reconciliation. This has not been achieved by the provincial or federal government, but through the efforts of many community organizations and support from the city of Saskatoon. Fifty-eight organizations, including non-profits, businesses, faith communities, and other partners, came together to initiate a city-wide conversation about reconciliation and provide opportunities for everyone to engage in the TRC's calls to action (Office of Treaty Commission 2018) at the grassroots level. From this, Reconciliation Saskatoon was born. This movement allowed the Saskatoon community to engage in a walk for reconciliation called Rock Your Roots, which has taken place for the past few years. In addition, conversations and other activities, including celebrations with music and food, are a part of the National Indigenous Peoples Day on June 21.

Indeed, it is not all negative. Our Indigenous sisters and brothers and their ancestors have welcomed many people from diverse backgrounds and shared their land with them. They have shown us all a great deal of generosity, settlers and newcomers alike. Although there are still ongoing injustices and inequities toward many Indigenous communities, we have come a long way, and we have an opportunity to work together through dialogue and relationship building. That is what reconciliation is all about. I find that there is a lot of engagement and education about reconciliation, as well as awareness of Indigenous Land Rights, cultures, and heritage. Still, the injustices and inequities against the Indigenous communities continue, whether it is access to services, involvement in decision-making on resource development, or self-determination and governance. Some scholars have argued that these injustices continue, in part, because of conflicting desires on the part of settlers. As Indigenous scholar Taiaiake Alfred said, "In relation to settler colonialism 'Canadians are in denial, in extremes' [meaning that] our denial can be inferred from our failure to reconcile our conflicting desires" (O'Donnell and Perley 2016: 480). Although many of us want Indigenous Peoples to have their full rights and have a say on how resources are developed on their land, we still want to enjoy cheap consumer goods and maintain our economy, and we may fear Indigenous sovereignty would mean the loss of land and our homes. These conflicting desires may be preventing us from dealing with the injustices and inequities some communities face. Indigenous scholar Glen Coulthard argues that "for Indigenous nations to survive, capitalism must die" (O'Donnell and Perley 2016: 480). I agree there may be conflicting desires within us; however, we need to find ways to examine our conscience regarding what is happening in our society. One important issue that resonates with me is how we can focus on a damage-centred narrative without thinking about how to effectively build bridges and relationships and facilitate healing that deals with the ongoing injustices together as a community and society while keeping our elected officials accountable. I believe in embracing reconciliation over and above all the conflicting desires and competing priorities for the betterment of our communities and society.

THE TRUTH AND RECONCILIATION COMMISSION OF CANADA'S CALLS TO ACTION (NEW CANADIANS)

There have been some concerns that immigrants and refugees coming to Canada do not know about Indigenous Peoples and the history of colonialism. The orientation materials provided to newcomers to Canada lack information on the history of Indigenous Peoples. In my own move to Canada, I was not given the opportunity to learn enough about the Indigenous Peoples, their history, and their positive contributions to Canadian society. I had a brief orientation that only covered topics like living in Canada, what to expect, and how to access available services. It was about preparing newcomers for life in Canada. What is not included is the history of the Indigenous Nations, their relationship with the Government of Canada, and the current realities in many Indigenous communities in this country. One of the Truth and Reconciliation Commission of Canada's (TRC) calls to action, number 93, addresses this specific situation, exhorting the federal government, in collaboration with national Indigenous organizations, to revise its information kit for newcomers and its citizenship test to reflect a more inclusive history of the diverse Indigenous Peoples, including information on treaties and the history of residential schools (TRC 2015). Further, the calls to action recommend that the citizenship oath include the obligation to faithfully respect Indigenous treaties (TRC 2015). Though promises were made to incorporate these calls to actions in the Canadian Orientation Abroad program for newcomers to Canada and the citizenship oath, they have not yet been implemented, partly because modifying the citizenship oath requires an amendment to the Citizenship Act.

Another concern about newcomers to Canada, both immigrants and refugees, is that they will learn negative stereotypes about Indigenous Peoples from the settlers or newcomers who have arrived before them. While this is certainly happening (as Datta argues in his chapter), it is not inevitable. In research conducted by Immigration Partnership Winnipeg in 2014, participants from both Indigenous and newcomer communities were found to hold negative perceptions of the other that they acknowledged were not accurate. However, they also expressed sympathy regarding the similar challenges the two communities face, and they agreed that they have a lot in common and many shared experiences (Circles for Reconciliation 2017).

CONCLUSION

I learned more about Indigenous Peoples in my first year of graduate studies after I moved to Canada. I was studying at a university on the Traditional Territory of the Neutral, Anishnawbe, and Haudenosaunee peoples in what is now known as Kitchener-Waterloo, Ontario. During my studies, I was exposed to the traditions of Indigenous Peoples in the specific areas of smudging, dancing, drumming, songs, and food (soup and bannock). These traditions were observed regularly throughout the year and more so at events. In addition, I learned about the land acknowledgement and honouring the Elders from the Indigenous community. All this was made possible thanks to the Indigenous Field of Study program at Wilfrid Laurier University. I believe I was lucky as a newcomer to Canada to have had these opportunities. They encouraged me to maintain a strong sense of social justice and to stand with all disadvantaged peoples in Canada. To be honest, I was quite shocked to learn of the living conditions of many disadvantaged people(s) in Canada — I did not expect that this country would fail to take care of its people.

Talking about the challenges many Indigenous Peoples face is not enough. Land acknowledgements are not enough. We need to build relationships and act on behalf of the Indigenous Peoples. The question is, what can we do beyond land acknowledgements to truly engage in reconciliation work, community building, and nation building?

- Learn — We should learn about oppression, privilege, and the history of colonization of the Indigenous Peoples and their cultures.
- Build relationships — Building relationships is a vital aspect of standing together with our Indigenous sisters and brothers against the injustices and inequities the Indigenous communities face.
- Act — Being accountable to Indigenous communities, supporting their causes, and standing up against unacceptable abuse, myths, and racism toward Indigenous Peoples. Furthermore, we need to align with their struggle and speak up when something problematic is said. (Smith, Puckett and Simon 2016)

As an organization in the settlement sector in Saskatchewan, we at the Saskatoon Open Door Society realize the importance of working with the Indigenous communities to build relationships and promote diversity and inclusion. We have been doing this for years now through co-programming and creating venues for dialogue, storytelling, and sharing experience between the newcomers to Canada and the Indigenous communities in Saskatchewan. As a community member and leader of a settlement organization whose values include respect, inclusion, empowerment, engagement, and equality, I am committed to continuing to promote reconciliation and relationship building in our community as we work toward a diverse, just, and more inclusive community and country.

REFERENCES

Byers, Michael. 2005. "Are You a 'Global Citizen'? Really, What Does That Mean?" *The Tyee.* October 5. <https://thetyee.ca/Views/2005/10/05/globalcitizen/>.

Canadian Council for Refugees. 2016. "Resolutions Adopted June 2016. Saskatoon. SK." <http://ccrweb.ca/en/resolutions-jun-2016>.

Circles for Reconciliation. 2017. "New Canadians and Indigenous Peoples." Winnipeg, MB. <http://circlesforreconciliation.ca/2017/01/22/new-canadians-and-Indigenous-peoples/>.

Griffith, Andrew. 2017. "Building a Mosaic: The Evolution of Canada's Approach to Immigrant Integration." Migration Policy Institute. <https://www.migrationpolicy.org/article/building-mosaic-evolution-canadas-approach-immigrant-integration>.

Harper, Stephen. 2008. "The Statement of Apology to Former Students of Indian Residential Schools." Indigenous and Northern Affairs Canada. <http://www.aadnc-aandc.gc.ca/eng/1100100015644/1100100015649>.

IDEAS for Global Citizenship. n.d. "What Is Global Citizenship?" <http://www.ideas-forum.org.uk/about-us/global-citizenship>.

Liberal Party of Canada. 2015. "A New Nation-to-Nation Process." <https://www.liberal.ca/realchange/a-new-nation-to-nation-process/>.

MacDonald, David. 2014. Reforming Multiculturalism in a Bi-National Society: Aboriginal Peoples and the Search for Truth and Reconciliation in Canada. *The Canadian Journal of Sociology / Cahiers Canadiens De Sociologie,* 39(1), 65-86. <http://www.jstor.org/stable/canajsocicahican.39.1.65>.

McIntyre, Catherine. 2017. "Read Justin Trudeau's Apology to Residential School Survivors in Newfoundland." *Maclean's,* November 24. <https://www.macleans.ca/news/canada/read-justin-trudeaus-apology-to-residential-school-survivors-in-newfoundland/>.

O'Brien, Matt. 2016. "The Important Difference between Assimilation and Integration." Immigration Reform. <https://immigrationreform.com/2016/09/29/the-important-difference-between-assimilation-and-integration/>.

O'Donnell, Susan, and David Perley. 2016. "Toward a Sociology of Reconciliation of Conflicting Desires." *Canadian Review of Sociology,* 53, 4 (Nov.): 474–481.

Office of the Treaty Commissioner. 2018. "Reconciliation, Saskatoon." <http://www.otc.ca/pages/reconciliation_saskatoon.html>.

RCAP (Royal Commission on Aboriginal Peoples). 1996. *The Report of the Royal Commission on Aboriginal Peoples.* Ottawa: Minister of Supply and Services Canada.

Smith, Jackson, Cassandra Puckett, and Wendy Simon. 2016. "Know the Land, Territories Campaign: Indigenous Allyship: An Overview." Laurier Students' Public Interest Research Group. <http://www.lspirg.org/knowtheland/>.

Sosinski, Chucky. 2014. "Colonization of Somalia." AFR 110: Intro to Contemporary Africa. October 8. <https://sites.psu.edu/afr110/2014/10/08/colonization-of-somalia/>.

TRC (Truth and Reconciliation Commission of Canada). 2015. *Truth and Reconciliation Commission: Call to Action Report.* Winnipeg, MB. <http://www.trc.ca>.

Chapter Eight

INTEGRATING INDIGENOUS KNOWLEDGE IN PRACTICE AND RESEARCH

A New Way Forward for the Immigrant Health Professionals

FARZANA ALI

One may ask why it is important that foreign health professionals understand the Canadian context of colonialism and the residential school legacy. How does this awareness (or lack thereof) impact the delivery of health care to Indigenous Peoples? To answer this, I reflected deeply on my own learning curve as a recently migrated health professional, thinking about how it shaped my perspectives and worldview to become the person I am today.

Grounded in the evidence-based literature, this chapter reflects my journey — as an immigrant researcher and aspiring health professional in Canada — of understanding the importance and true meaning of truth and reconciliation. Learning the history of colonization and the legacy of residential schools has helped me to connect the contemporary barriers that Indigenous Peoples face to the past and present colonial policies that created these barriers. Many other immigrant health professionals, however, have little or no awareness of systemic and epistemic racism in Canada, nor the unilateral imposition of social, economic, cultural, and political dominance over Indigenous lands and lives. This knowledge gap often leads these practitioners to repeat the same stereotyped assumptions and practices that they hear and see around them. Repeated exposure to these practices and assumptions adversely affects health care delivery for Indigenous Peoples.

Reflecting on my own experiences, learning from other educators, and reading about colonization among other peoples in Canada, I began to understand the importance of integrating Indigenous worldviews in the development and implementation of Indigenous-specific curricula and culturally competent training programs for internationally educated health professionals (IEHPs). According to calls to action 22 and 24 of the Truth and Reconciliation Commission of Canada (TRC), this understanding has two benefits — not only will this knowledge help IEHPs ensure that Indigenous health interests have been adequately served through culturally safe patient-centred care, but it will also help the IEHPs themselves as they struggle to integrate into the Canadian mainstream. This whole process requires dialogical engagement and effort at individual, organizational, and policy levels.

BACKGROUND

Canada, like many other developed nations, is affected by the shortages and uneven distribution of health professionals across the country (McIntosh, Torgerson, and Klassen 2007). This is more acute in rural, remote, and northern communities, where inadequate health systems are unable to address higher health needs (Jama 2013; McIntosh, Torgerson, and Klassen 2007). The insufficiency of health care personnel and services in Canada has led to the evolution of immigration policies around the recognition of foreign qualifications of migrant health workers (Dumont, Zurn, Church, and Le Thi 2008). While the aim of new policies is to increase the supply of health professionals in the Canadian health care system, it also expands opportunities for IEHPs to practise in Canada (Government of Canada 2018).

Since the launch of the Internationally Trained Workers Initiative in 2005 (Government of Canada 2018), significant numbers of IEHPs have been recruited into the Canadian health care system (McIntosh, Torgerson, and Klassen 2007). More than 22 percent of physicians in Canada are foreign-trained and 37 percent are foreign-born. Similarly, the corresponding figures for nurses are close to 7.7 percent and 20 percent, respectively (Dumont et al. 2008). Data on the international migration of health workers shows that the majority of the IEHPs are from United Kingdom, India, China, Pakistan, South Africa, Kenya, Nigeria, and the Philippines (Rutten 2009). In order for their qualifications to be recognized and for them to practise in Canada, immigrant health professionals must go through many different licensing requirements (such as language proficiency) and supervised clinical training and certification assessments (Dumont et al. 2008). Occasionally, IEHPs may be required to redo some or all of their postgraduate training, as well as participate in bridging programs aimed at integrating and upgrading their skills (Dumont et al. 2008; Neiterman and Bourgeault 2015). Although there are some differences in the licensure process between provinces, the training and programs for IEHPs, unfortunately, lack education on the residential school legacy and history of colonization in Canada.

Entering the workforce, IEHPs learn and adapt to the wider Canadian culture of professional practice and interpersonal communication (Neiterman and Bourgeault 2015). Indigenous perspectives, informed by historical, cultural, and epistemological standpoints, are absent in the dominant Westernized biomedical practice (Hill, Lau, and Sue 2010). As a result, many foreign practitioners lack an understanding of the systemic and epistemic racism in Canada, and the unilateral imposition of social, economic, cultural, and political dominance over Indigenous lands and lives (Matthews 2017). This lack of knowledge often leads these practitioners to make stereotyped assumptions and follow practices that adversely affect health care delivery for Indigenous Peoples.

Beyond health care practices, most clinical research is organized by disciplines and fields of knowledge that are profoundly grounded in Western "ways of knowing," which too often perpetuate the notion that Indigenous Peoples are "problems" to be solved, "at risk," and needing to be saved by external experts (Cochran, Marshall, Garcia-Downing, et al. 2008: 22). Foreign-born professionals with little or no knowledge of Indigenous healing and cultural traditions will fail to acknowledge, respect, and address the distinct health care needs of Indigenous Peoples. Therefore, it is critical for IEHPs to understand the Canadian context of ongoing colonialism and the effects of the residential school legacy as primary determinants of Indigenous health, and how the actions of health care professionals impact the delivery of health care to Indigenous populations. It has been argued that increasing one's basic understanding of the context and impact of colonialism is the first step toward respectful and meaningful engagement with patients from Indigenous backgrounds — a key part of reconciliation between Indigenous Peoples and non-Indigenous IEHPs (Northwest Territories Health and Social Services Authority 2016). At the same time, reconciliation efforts help IEHPs to integrate into Canadian society by developing a shared understanding of the common history of colonialism, racism, and socioeconomic challenges that may confront both Indigenous Peoples and newcomers. These shared perspectives and cross-cultural learning break down stereotypes and enable them to develop friendships and work together to address the common challenges faced in integrating into the mainstream society (Gyepi-Garbrah 2010). As mentioned previously, this process requires not only individual-level effort, but also requires multilateral engagement and endeavours at organizational and policy levels.

GOING BACK TO THE ROOT: HISTORY OF COLONIZATION AND BEGINNING OF HEALTH ISSUES

> Recognition of human and cultural identity is mandated by respect for persons; and beneficence and nonmaleficence, interpreted through the lens of cultural safety, promote the best health outcomes.
>
> — Dr. Richard Matthews, "The Cultural Erosion of Indigenous People in Health Care"

Intentional or not, the organization, governance, curricula, and assessment of compulsory learning in Canada is very much shaped by the invisibilized dynamics of settler colonialism where settler perspectives and worldviews dominate knowledge and research (Tuck and Yang 2012). Efforts to assimilate Indigenous communities into mainstream Canada, and the ignorance and/or reinterpretation of Indigenous knowledge to make it fit within the "West knows best" paradigm, continue to this day (Durie 2004; Matthews 2017). The exclusion of Indigenous worldviews contributes to the power imbalance between groups that own and have access to the technology of knowledge dissemination and leaves the colonization of knowledge and cultures unchallenged (Dei 2000). The word settler here denotes the non-Indigenous privileged majority, representing groups within the power structures that are defined by such things as race, culture, gender, sexuality, and socioeconomic status (Hardwick 2015).

The health system is not any different. Indigenous knowledge of well-being, harmony, and ways of addressing illness, whether physical, spiritual, or otherwise, have historically been ignored, denied, or eroded (Hill, Lau, and Sue 2010). In both clinical settings and health research, Indigenous Peoples are routinely compared unfavourably with their non-Indigenous counterparts, without taking into consideration the history of colonization that resulted in the "loss of culture, loss of land, loss of voice, loss of population, loss of dignity, loss of health, and wellbeing" (Durie 2004: 1138). Consequently, Indigenous Peoples have fared worse than non-Indigenous Peoples on almost all indicators of health determination and social well-being, in terms of epidemiological patterns of disease and life expectancy (Durie 2004: 1138). These indicators further label Indigenous Peoples as "asterisk peoples," represented by an asterisk in large and crucial data sets, where they are described as being on the verge of extinction, culturally and economically bereft, and engaged or soon-to-be engaged in self-destructive behaviours (Tuck and Yang 2012).

In order to understand and address the alarming health disparities and barriers to health care experienced by Indigenous Peoples, the IEHPs must expand their knowledge beyond the mainstream paradigms and the large dataset, and "dig down" to the origin of it. The origin lies at the colonial foundations of Canada — where the effect of colonization was, and remains, profound (Gracey and King 2009; Matthews 2017). It is of great importance for IEHPs to realize that Indigenous health cannot be understood outside of the context of colonial policies and practices — both ongoing and historical.

Colonization suppressed the traditional lives of Indigenous Peoples by imposing foreign regulations and socioe-conomic and political marginalization, as well as through racial prejudice. The systemic imposition of these regulations and efforts at marginalization negatively affected Indigenous Peoples' well-established traditional laws, languages, dress, religions, sacred ceremonies, healers, and remedies (Gracey and King 2009). The oppressions were further entrenched and institutionalized through forced dispossession of traditional lands, wherein many Indigenous Peoples were forced to live on infertile lands contaminated by heavy metals and industrial waste. The imposed relocation resulted in increased poverty, undereducation, unemployment, and subsequent dependence on social welfare (Gracey and King 2009; Matthews 2017), which are some of the important determinants of health and well-being. Indigenous Peoples' health was worsened by the exposure to environmentally degraded health hazards, including contamination from heavy metals, industrial gases, effluent wastes, and microorganisms introduced by the settlers (Gracey and King 2009).

Many scholars have argued that settlers engaged in a cultural genocide of Indigenous Peoples. One egregious example of this is residential schools, which were institutions where Indigenous children could become "civilized." Based on the assumption that Indigenous culture was "savage" (Truth and

Reconciliation Commission of Canada 2015: 3) and that European culture, civilization, and Christian religions were superior, children were forcibly separated from parents and sent to residential schools. Parents who refused were labelled unfit. Spiritual practices and Indigenous languages were banned. Any individuals who refused to abandon their Indigenous identity were denied the right to participate fully in Canadian political, economic, and social life. Cultural genocide endangered the health and well-being of residential school children, and the trauma from physical, mental, and sexual abuse was often passed on to their own children and for several generations thereafter (Truth and Reconciliation Commission of Canada 2015). Damage to individual and cultural Indigenous identities and the assertion of inferiority toward Indigenous Peoples continues to this day and negatively impacts mental health, individually and collectively (Truth and Reconciliation Commission of Canada 2015; Matthews 2017).

IGNORANCE IS BLISS NO MORE: RACISM IN THE HEALTH CARE SYSTEM

Janet Smyli, a Métis physician at St. Michael's Hospital in Toronto, suggested that "the Canadian healthcare system is a loose extension of colonialism," founded on the racist ideologies and belief that one set of people is superior to another (Puxley 2014: n.p.). Systemic racism, the "unjust distribution of power that is built into law, policy and economic practice," and epistemic racism, "the imposition of one world view over another," are embedded within the system (Matthews 2017: E78–E79). These ensure that only mainstream biomedical knowledge is taken seriously and that Indigenous healing practices and traditions have no value; they determine how resources are distributed and to whom. This also influences medical training by defining what counts as a medicine, a medical intervention, or a treatment. In short, these are the modern forces of colonialism (Matthews 2017). Institutionalized racism and marginalization are intertwined and, in turn, profoundly contribute to the uneven distribution of health funding, resources, and services, and affect the quantity and quality of the care (Allan and Smylie 2015; Gracey and King 2009). For instance, only those who are classified by the Canadian government as registered First Nations and recognized Inuit are eligible for the Non-Insured Health Benefits Program, which is provided through the federal government. At the same time, having this state-constructed Indigenous identity does not always ensure access, since some services require that people live on reserve.

Further, the roster of approved services and medical products for coverage is changing constantly (Allan and Smylie 2015).

In addition to the inequity in resource availability, Indigenous Peoples in Canada often feel stigmatized in the delivery of their care (Cochran et al. 2008). Many, if not most, Indigenous Peoples experience racism and discrimination, which have lasting and deleterious effects on their health (Allan and Smylie 2015). Frequent and unpredictable racial discrimination has a direct link with psychological distress and depressive symptoms, such as increased feelings of insecurity about personal worth and competence and a sense of inferiority (Currie, Wild, Schopflocher, Laing, and Veugelers 2012). In fact, discriminatory treatment by health care providers is so pervasive that people actively strategize around anticipated racism or, in some cases, avoid care altogether (Allan and Smylie 2015).

As an example, Michelle Labrecque, an Indigenous woman who presented at the Royal Jubilee Hospital in Victoria, British Columbia, with severe stomach pain in 2008, described her experience: While she discussed her pain with a doctor, she also shared her struggles with alcohol and finding a home. Once discharged, she discovered that all the doctor had scribbled on her prescription form was a drawing of a beer bottle, circled with a slash through it (McCue 2015).

Racism in the Canadian health care system can also be fatal. In 2008, Brian Sinclair, a forty-five-year-old Indigenous man, presented at the emergency room (ER) of the Winnipeg Health Sciences Centre in Manitoba (Allan and Smylie 2015). He was referred to the emergency department for a bladder infection. He vomited on himself several times while he waited in the ER for thirty-four hours. Other people waiting in the ER begged the nurses and security guards to attend to him, but to no avail. The entire time he waited, Mr. Sinclair was never formally entered into the hospital triage system and was never asked if he was waiting for medical treatment. He was discovered dead only after rigor mortis had set in. During an internal investigation, several hospital staff admitted that they did not think Mr. Sinclair was waiting for treatment, but rather was a "drunk Aboriginal man" waiting for a ride or just needed a warm place to rest (Puxley 2014).

These are just two examples of many discriminatory experiences that Indigenous Peoples face. In response to racism toward Indigenous communities, a participant in a study by Currie et al. (2012: 10) stated, "We are all not drunks and addicts and gamblers and we don't go through life on welfare and

educationless. We are people. I sometimes feel so stereotyped by this." It is of
no surprise, then, that these colonial, stigmatized, and stereotyped views toward
Indigenous Peoples are transferred from mainstream society to newcomers
who do not have the proper knowledge of history. Consequently, "layers or
separation" exist between marginalized and mainstream society (Chung 2012:
29), between groups, and between Indigenous patients and IEHPs. A literature
review conducted by Chung in 2012 revealed that racism, misinformation,
isolation, and lack of interconnectedness between immigrants and Indigenous
groups mostly stemmed from lack of knowledge, ignorance, and over-simplified
beliefs (Madariaga-Vignudo and Ghorayshi 2009).

International providers are often uninformed about Indigenous Peoples
before arriving in Canada and mostly learn about them anecdotally from mainstream Canadians (Chung 2012; Madariaga-Vignudo and Ghorayshi 2009).
A qualitative study conducted by Madariaga-Vignudo and Ghorayshi in 2009
to explore African-Indigenous relationships in Winnipeg found that mainstream society often labels Indigenous Peoples with demoralizing adjectives
and characterizes them by problematic traits (such as substance abusing, not
working hard enough, not paying taxes, and depending on social assistance).
A public service provider in Manitoba, speaking to newcomers, said, "Why
would you go to Winnipeg? There's all the Indians there," and "this Indian; they
don't do anything, they are on welfare" (Madariaga-Vignudo and Ghorayshi
2009: 24–28). These negative accounts of Indigenous Peoples, coupled with
impersonal random encounters with intoxicated individuals from Indigenous
backgrounds, lead IEHPs to form misperceptions about Indigenous patients
without having a concrete understanding of underlying oppressive historical
relations. Soon enough, the newcomers start associating negative behaviours
(such as alcohol and/or drug use) with Indigenous Peoples and quickly adopt
the stereotypes held by mainstream populations (Madariaga-Vignudo and
Ghorayshi 2009).

INCORPORATING INDIGENOUS WORLDVIEW: UNLEARN TO LEARN BETTER

Public health care is important to Canadians because this makes the health
care system seem fair. Health care is assumed to be fair when everyone has
equal access to resources in society, irrespective of their category of social
membership. Health care providers are expected to uphold these values of
"equality and fairness" of their patients with the presumption that patients'

social or ethnocultural backgrounds have no bearing on how they would be treated (Tang and Browne 2008: 117). This perspective negates the historical processes and structural constraints that exist among Indigenous groups to exercise their rights and makes their access to health and health care inequitable (Tang and Browne 2008: 117).

Daniel Elliot, residential school Survivor, stated that:

> I think all Canadians need to stop and take a look and not look away. Yeah, it's embarrassing, yeah, it's an ugly part of our history. We don't want to know about it. What I want to see from the Commission is to rewrite the history books so that other generations will understand and not go through the same thing that we're going through now, like it never happened. (Truth and Reconciliation Commission of Canada 2015: 13)

The inherent tension between the perceived experience of racialization and the ideal of equality cannot be addressed without learning the truth. And the truth is that poor health and social status among Indigenous Peoples are not necessarily reflective of their "personal choices" or poor lifestyle patterns; rather, they are the "symptoms" of longstanding discriminatory practices and policies (Tang and Browne 2008: 118). The notion of whole patient care requires all health care professionals, whether locally trained or internationally, to understand the history of colonization in the context of Indigenous health issues and the effects exerted from this process at the personal, interpersonal, and systemic levels (Duncan and Gilbey 2007; Tang and Browne 2008). To do so, more educational opportunities and cultural competence training are needed for IEHPs at both micro and macro levels. Health care providers who recognize the effects of history on Indigenous Peoples are more likely to adapt how they provide care in a way that is responsive to the distinct needs of their patients and free of stereotypes (Ward, Smylie, and Firestone 2017).

With a focus on patient-centred care, there has been a shift in the Canadian health care system. There is effort within the system to provide culturally relevant and meaningful health care. In turn, Canadian medical school curricula have placed a greater focus on social accountability, advocacy, and social determinants of health (Arkle et al. 2015). As suggested in the calls to action by the Truth and Reconciliation Commission (TRC), students in medical and nursing schools in Canada are now required to take a course on Indigenous health issues, including "the history and legacy of residential schools, the UN

Declaration on the Rights of Indigenous Peoples, Treaties and Aboriginal rights, and Indigenous teachings and practices" (Truth and Reconciliation Commission of Canada 2015: TRC 22 and 24). In response to the TRC calls to action, the number of Indigenous cultural safety (ICS) training programs and the number of organizations committed to mandating ICS training have significantly increased in recent years (Ward, Smylie, and Firestone 2017). While this heightened interest and investment in Indigenous cultural safety training and cultural competence curricula is promising, it alone is not enough.

As much as curricula have tried to respond to the TRC calls to action and integrate Indigenous health topics into clinical education, it is still not a standard of accreditation for Canadian medical institutions (Arkle et al. 2015). The opportunity to learn Indigenous knowledge is almost nonexistent for students in other health professional programs apart from medicine and nursing. This indicates limited institutional support and/or understanding of the critical importance of Indigenous health curricula to support clinical training (Huria, Palmer, Beckert, Lacey, and Pitama 2017). There are epistemic barriers as well. Scholars argued that, much of the time, Indigenous history and knowledge included in the curricula are the "neutralized ahistorical, guilt-free, pain-free, romanticized version of Indigenous knowledge" that non-Indigenous settlers find acceptable to receive and are often incorporated by non-indigenous scholars (Korteweg and Russell 2012: 8). There is also a lack of opportunity for Indigenous faculty leadership to develop and evaluate curricula (Huria et al. 2017), which results in inadequate resourcing of Indigenous content within health education. Additionally, there is still variability in both uptake of Indigenous knowledge and emphasis on Indigenous health within this training by health professionals (Arkle et al. 2015). This existing gap, in fact, is exacerbated for IEHPs who are trained and educated overseas.

Indigenous health education is an emerging pedagogy (Dei 2000) and there have been concerns about the quality of cultural safety training and assessment of Indigenous health for IEHPs. The complexity and richness of Indigenous knowledge are very much embedded in its culture, passed down from generation to generation through traditional ceremonies and oral teachings (Vinkle 2012). It is imperative to shape and mandate the curricula, licensing procedure, and training for IEHPs such that they obtain an in-depth cultural, social, and economic understanding of this knowledge to competently apply to their practice. It is necessary within the profession to raise awareness about "recognizing, centring, validating, and honouring Indigenous rights, values, epistemologies or worldviews, knowledge, language, and the stories of the people of the Land" (Korteweg and Russell 2012: 7). These must be implemented by making stronger connections with Indigenous Elders, culture, language, and through robust experiential learning (Korteweg and Russell 2012).

Exposing IEHPs to a wide spectrum of rewards and challenges of Indigenous health care in a practical setting will help them to understand the diversity of cultures within the broad category of Indigenous Peoples (Arkle et al. 2015). Integrating traditional and holistic approaches to healing is equally important, not only to respect patients' choices but also to ascertain whether patients are taking any traditional medicines to address their ailment. Indigenous Peoples may also practice diverse spiritual traditions that are customary among them. IEHPs should be trained properly to accommodate Indigenous Peoples' spiritual beliefs and practices — including ceremonies and sacred customs (Ontario Human Rights Commission n.d.). These traditional approaches for healing have been used by Indigenous Peoples for centuries (Arkle et al. 2015). The efficacy of these approaches should be evaluated as a crucial part of teaching and practice. This evaluation must be ongoing and done in a culturally safe and participatory manner in order to protect Traditional Knowledge (Arkle et al. 2015; Gair, Miles, and Thomson 2005). Adequate funding is also needed, in addition to ideological support, for IEHPs to be engaged in Indigenous health-focused community activities, for instance, funding to support participation in Indigenous conferences and/or sharing circles.

Marie Battiste, an Indigenous scholar, states that "the pedagogical challenge of [Canadian] education is not just reducing the distance between Eurocentric thinking and Aboriginal ways of knowing but engaging decolonized minds and hearts" (Korteweg and Russell 2012: 7). Indigenizing knowledge and pedagogies is an inclusive way of thinking and designing education, training, research, and practice (Korteweg and Russell 2012). There are multi-faceted benefits for IEHPs to incorporate this immense knowledge base into their mainstream practice. Evidence shows that professionals who understand how colonial history has affected Indigenous Peoples are far more culturally competent than those who do not have this understanding (Arkle et al. 2015; Vinkle 2012). Collaborating with Elders and Indigenous scholars to build allies within health care systems and to understand the issues together creates spaces for acknowledging the two worlds of Indigenous knowledge and the Euro-Western worldview, known as Two-Eyed Seeing models of teaching and learning (Korteweg and Russell 2012). Acknowledging Treaty and Traditional

Rights of Indigenous Peoples also initiates the decolonization of the relationship between Indigenous and immigrant health professionals (Korteweg and Russell 2012), reducing personal biases and stereotypes and enhancing community engagement. Although decolonization can be uncomfortable or even painful to re-educate or relearn from the beginning, sometimes one must unlearn stereotypes to learn better ways to deliver health care (Gair, Miles, and Thomson 2005).

IEHPS INTEGRATION: DECOLONIZING THE MIND

Despite immigrating to the Global North to improve their own quality of life, access advanced technology, and increase their opportunities for career advancement, many IEHPS face their own struggles integrating into the Canadian mainstream (Jama 2013). Many IEHPS from the Global South find it difficult to obtain certification and secure desired positions of employment, mostly due to challenges with language proficiency and educational background (Neiterman and Bourgeault 2015). The existing gaps also stem from socio-economic positions where newcomers' incomes are below those of health professionals born in Canada. Consequently, many newcomers experience a devaluation of their skills and eventual deskilling in the Canadian labour market (Jama 2013).

Cultural backgrounds and professional norms of the country of origin also play a vital role in the integration of IEHPS into the Canadian social structure. IEHPS who were trained in the health care systems of professional hierarchy in the workplace experience difficulties in the presentation of their professional selves (Neiterman and Bourgeault 2015). Immersed in a new professional environment, IEHPS often must learn the "Canadian style" of communicating with their patients and other health care professionals. Adjusting to these cultural differences becomes even more overwhelming with institutional racism. As expressed by many IEHPS, their professional readiness and skills are often questioned and/or harshly critiqued by their colleagues in order to uphold the perceived inferiority of the IEHPS in professional practice (Jama 2013; Neiterman and Bourgeault 2015).

Literature focusing on the topic of immigrant integration barely addresses the ways newcomers relate to other racialized minorities in Canada, such as Indigenous groups. Indigenous Peoples have official "distinct nation" (Madariaga-Vignudo and Ghorayshi 2009: 7) status in Canada, where they became a minority through centuries of colonization and oppression. Immigrant groups in Canada, on the other hand, comprise a different type of minority. They migrate from other countries and seek to adapt to the larger Canadian society to fit in, to be regarded with respect, and to prove their competencies. Despite many differences between these inter-minority groups, there are some similarities, too. Both newcomer IEHPs and Indigenous Peoples face profound difficulties in having a sense of community belonging in the mainstream society (Gyepi-Garbrah 2010; Madariaga-Vignudo and Ghorayshi 2009). Being ethnically and culturally different from the mainstream society means that members of both groups experience racism and discrimination in different aspects of their lives (Madariaga-Vignudo and Ghorayshi 2009).

Decolonization could be a useful tool for IEHPs, not only to appreciate and respect the history, culture, and inherent rights of Indigenous Peoples, but also to value cultural differences and the similar history of colonialism where they exist (Gyepi-Garbrah 2010; Korteweg and Russell 2012). Decolonization recognizes the isolation that colonialism fosters and advocates bringing people together by rejecting Western individualism and replacing it with respectful and peaceful coexistence among Indigenous and non-Indigenous Peoples. Contrary to individualism, it emphasizes community engagement by connecting Indigenous and non-Indigenous Peoples cooperatively rather than competitively (Dmytriw 2016; Korteweg and Russell 2012).

While decolonization nurtures connections between people, this concept equally emphasizes reconnecting with the land we live upon. In the Indigenous paradigm, integration into the community comes from a connection to the land through cultural membership (Scully 2012: 148). It demands that, like Indigenous Peoples, it is also newcomers' responsibility to treat the land with respect and as a place that sustains them (Dmytriw 2016). Learning to decolonize the mind helps newcomers to re-connect with the land they have no historical spiritual connection to, by recognizing their responsibility to one another as members of a community. Intercultural relationships encourage dialogical engagement between groups, break down various epistemic barriers, enrich and diversify cultural exchange, bring harmony and belongingness, and create more compassion within the communities (Korteweg and Russell 2012).

CONCLUSION

The process of bringing Indigenous knowledge and experience to medical practice requires policy-level change and the establishment of a national body to address licensure and minimum standards issues, to examine training capacity and support mechanisms, and to facilitate effective integration of IEHPs into the Canadian health care workforce. However, education toward reconciliation is an important responsibility of the IEHPs and one worth taking up as it will help them ensure that Indigenous health interests are served adequately through culturally safe, patient-centred care and will also help them face their own struggles with integrating into the Canadian mainstream. Moreover, reconciliation education contributes to a systemic shift toward safer, more equitable experiences and optimized outcomes for both IEHPs and Indigenous Peoples.

ACKNOWLEDGEMENT

I acknowledge all the residential school Survivors, Indigenous Elders, and Knowledge Keepers for sharing their sacred stories and life experiences for us to learn from. A sincere thank you to Ms. Sugandhi del Canto for her diligent support of this chapter and for providing insightful feedback.

REFERENCES

Allan, Billie, and Janet Smylie. 2015. *First Peoples, Second Class Treatment: The Role of Racism in the Health and Well-Being of Indigenous Peoples in Canada.* Wellesley Institute.

Arkle, Madeline, Max Deschner, Ryan Giroux, Reed Morrison, et al. 2015. "Indigenous Peoples and Health in Canadian Medical Education: CFMS Position Paper." <cfms.org/files/position-papers/2015_indigenous_people_in_canadian_med_ed.pdf>.

Chung, Melissa May Ling. 2012. "The Relationships Between Racialized Immigrants and Indigenous Peoples in Canada: A Literature Review." Unpublished master's thesis, Ryerson University, Toronto, ON.

Cochran, Patricia, Catherine Marshall, Carmen Garcia-Downing, Elizabeth Kendall, et al. 2008. "Indigenous Ways of Knowing: Implications for Participatory Research and Community." *American Journal of Public Health,* 98, 1: 22–27. DOI: 10.2105/AJPH.2006.093641.

Currie, Cheryl, Cameron Wild, Donald Schopflocher, Lory Laing, et al. 2012. "Racial Discrimination Experienced by Aboriginal University Students in Canada." *Canadian Journal of Psychiatry,* 57, 10: 617–625. DOI: 10.1177/070674371205701006.

Dei, George J Sefa. 2000. "Rethinking the Role of Indigenous Knowledges in the Academy." *International Journal of Inclusive Education,* 4, 2: 111–132. DOI:

10.1080/136031100284849.

Dmytriw, Anne. 2016. "Decolonizing Immigration: Addressing Missing Indigenous Perspectives in Canadian Immigration Policies." Unpublished master's thesis, Ryerson University, Toronto.

Dumont, Jean-Christophe, Pascal Zurn, Jody Church, and Christine Le Thi. 2008. *International Mobility of Health Professionals and Health Workforce Management in Canada: Myths and Realities.* OECD Health Working Papers, no.40. <who.int/hrh/migration/Case_study_Canada_2008.pdf>.

Duncan, Geraldine F., and David Gilbey. 2007. "Cultural and Communication Awareness for General Practice Registrars who Are International Medical Graduates: A Project of CoastCityCountry Training." *Australian Journal of Rural Health,* 15, 1: 52-58. DOI: 10.1111/j.1440-1584.2007.00850.x.

Durie, Mason. 2004. "Understanding Health and Illness: Research at the Interface Between Science and Indigenous Knowledge." *International Journal of Epidemiology,* 33, 5: 1138–1143. DOI: 10.1093/ije/dyh250.

Gair, Susan, Debra Miles, and Jane Thomson. 2005. "Reconciling Indigenous and Non-Indigenous Knowledges in Social Work Education: Action and Legitimacy." *Journal of Social Work Education,* 41, 2: 179–190. DOI: 10.5175/JSWE.2005.200300358.

Government of Canada. 2018. "Internationally Educated Health Care Professionals." March 07. <canada.ca/en/health-canada/services/health-care-system/health-human-resources/strategy/internationally-educated-health-care-professionals.html>.

Gracey, Michael, and Malcolm King. 2009. "Indigenous Health Part 1: Determinants and Disease Patterns." *The Lancet,* 374, 9683: 65–75. DOI: 10.1016/S0140-6736(09)60914-4.

Gyepi-Garbrah, John Victor. 2010. "Understanding Diversity and Interculturalism between Aboriginal Peoples and Newcomers in Winnipeg." Unpublished master's thesis, University of Saskatchewan, Saskatoon.

Hardwick, Jennifer. 2015. "Dismantling Narratives: Settler Ignorance, Indigenous Literature and the Development of a Decolonizing Discourse." TOPIA: *Canadian Journal of Cultural Studies,* 33. DOI: 10.3138/topia.33.99.

Hill, Jill S., Michael Y. Lau, and Derald Wing Sue. 2010. "Integrating Trauma Psychology and Cultural Psychology: Indigenous Perspectives on Theory, Research, and Practice." *Traumatology,* 16, 4: 39. DOI: 10.1177/1534765610388303.

Huria, Tania, Suetonia, Palmer, Lutz Beckert, Cameron Lacey, and Suzanne Pitama. 2017. "Indigenous Health: Designing a Clinical Orientation Program Valued by Learners." BMC *Medical Education,* 17, 1: 180. DOI: 10.1186/s12909-017-1019-8.

Jama, Sadia. 2013. "In the Pursuit of the Canadian Dream: Equity and the Canadian Certification of Internationally Educated Midwives." Doctoral dissertation, University of Saskatchewan, Saskatoon.

Korteweg, Lisa, and Connie Russell. 2012. "Decolonizing+ Indigenizing= Moving Environmental Education Towards Reconciliation." Editorial. *Canadian Journal of Environmental Education,* 17: 5–14. <cjee.lakeheadu.ca/article/view/1226/642>.

Madariaga-Vignudo, Lucia, and Parvin Ghorayshi. 2009. *"More Strangers Than Neighbours": Aboriginal-African Refugee Relations in Winnipeg's Inner City.* Manitoba Research Alliance. <mbresearchalliance.files.wordpress.

com/2012/11/26-lucia_madariaga-vignudorevised.pdf>.

Matthews, Richard. 2017. "The Cultural Erosion of Indigenous People in Health Care." *Canadian Medical Association Journal,* 189, 2: E78. DOI: 10.1503/cmaj.160167.

McCue, Duncan. 2015. "Racism Against Aboriginal People in Health-Care System 'Pervasive': Study." *CBC News,* Feb 03. <cbc.ca/news/indigenous/racism-against-aboriginal-people-in-health-care-system-pervasive-study-1.2942644>.

McIntosh, Thomas Allan, Renée Torgerson, and Nathan Klassen. 2007. *The Ethical Recruitment of Internationally Educated Health Professionals: Lessons from Abroad and Options for Canada.* Ottawa: Canadian Policy Research Networks. <assets.aspeninstitute.org/content/uploads/files/content/images/options%20for%20canada.pdf>.

Neiterman, Elena, and Ivy Lynn Bourgeault. 2015. "Professional Integration as a Process of Professional Resocialization: Internationally Educated Health Professionals in Canada." *Social Science & Medicine,* 131: 74-81. DOI: 10.1016/j.socscimed.2015.02.043.

Northwest Territories Health and Social Services Authority. 2016. "Building a Culturally Respectful Health and Social Services System." <hss.gov.nt.ca/sites/hss/files/resources/building-culturally-respectful-hss-system.pdf>.

Ontario Human Rights Commision. n.d. "Indigenous Spiritual Practices." <ohrc.on.ca/en/policy-preventing-discrimination-based-creed/11-indigenous-spiritual-practices>.

Puxley, Chinta. 2014. "Brian Sinclair Inquest Told Aboriginals Face Racism in ERs." *Canadian Press,* June 10. <cbc.ca/news/canada/manitoba/brian-sinclair-inquest-told-aboriginals-face-racism-in-ers-1.2670990>.

Rutten, Martine. 2009. "The Economic Impact of Medical Migration: An Overview of the Literature." *The World Economy,* 32, 2: 291–325. DOI: 10.1111/j.1467-9701.2008.01147.x.

Scully, Alexa. 2012. "Decolonization, Reinhabitation and Reconciliation: Aboriginal and Place-Based Education." *Canadian Journal of Environmental Education,* 17: 148–158. <cjee.lakeheadu.ca/article/viewFile/1113/660>.

Tang, Sannie Y., and Annette J. Browne. 2008. "'Race' Matters: Racialization and Egalitarian Discourses Involving Aboriginal People in the Canadian Health Care Context." *Ethnicity and Health,* 13, 2: 109–127. DOI: 10.1080/13557850701830307.

Truth and Reconciliation Commission of Canada. 2015. *Honouring the Truth, Reconciling for the Future: Summary of the Final Report of the Truth and Reconciliation Commission of Canada* (0660020777). <trc.ca/websites/trcinstitution/File/2015/Findings/Exec_Summary_2015_05_31_web_o.pdf>.

Tuck, Eve., and K. Wayne Yang. 2012. "Decolonization Is Not a Metaphor." *Decolonization: Indigeneity, Education & Society,* 1, 1.

Vinkle, Erin. 2012. "Cultural Competency — Working with Aboriginal Peoples: A Non-Native Perspective." *Indigenous Social Work Practices and Theories,* 8. <zone.biblio.laurentian.ca/dspace/handle/10219/1986>.

Ward, Alycia Fridkin, Diane Smylie, and Michelle Firestone. 2017. "Evidence Brief: Wise Practices for Indigenous-Specific Cultural Safety Training." <soahac.on.ca/wp-content/uploads/2015/01/CS_WisePractices_FINAL_11.02.17.pdf>.

Chapter Nine

RECONCILIATION VIA BUILDING RESPECTFUL RELATIONSHIPS IN INDIGENOUS RESEARCH

VALERIE ONYINYECHI UMAEFULAM

This chapter provides an overview of operationalizing reconciliation during research with Indigenous Peoples by leveraging community engagement and relationship building. Indigenous Peoples have always been objects of research and have learned to be suspicious of research done *on* them, rather than *with* them, and so transparency in research practices, community engagement, and relationship building is vital to the efforts toward reconciliation. Non-Indigenous researchers can promote reconciliation in practice by respecting Indigenous research values and principles and Indigenous epistemology throughout the entire research continuum and by carrying out research that establishes rapport through interaction and relationship building with Indigenous Peoples in both qualitative and quantitative studies. Researchers can practice reconciliation by encouraging harmonious relationships through their own actions.

REFLECTIVE BACKGROUND

Growing up in a large African family, where family in its true sense comprises not only the nuclear unit but the entire extended family, is similar to being born into a community where we are guided by the principle of mutual support, where we celebrate life, share sorrows, applaud accomplishments, and offer comfort when needed. I grew up in an environment where everyone was treated with dignity and opinions were freely expressed. It was here that I developed an appreciation for the different perspectives every individual brings. These opinions, and the space of respectful debate from which they emerged, formed the norms, principles, and values of my life. I also obtained a formal education in health care, which enabled me to look at life, health, and research as a systematic process with clearly defined conclusions, where an action or cause results in an effect. As such, my way of knowing and my assumptions are rooted in formal training and education and are reinforced by the community I grew up in.

These assumptions have evolved over time, especially as my career focus moved away from clinical practice to community practice, where I found my niche. I was astonished by the numerous traditional health care practices and beliefs I encountered that complement and, in some cases, are more effective than modern medicine but are disregarded by health professionals. In addition, I have come to understand that providing culturally competent care will encourage the use of health services.

When I arrived in Canada, I found the diversity intriguing; although I had read about the Indigenous Peoples of Canada, I was not fully aware of their history and way of life. Since making Canada my home, I have come to understand that I am not merely an immigrant here, I am also a settler and a treaty person since I benefit from the treaties made with Indigenous Peoples. Thus, I am responsible for upholding the rights of Indigenous Peoples and ensuring that I reflect reconciliation in my work, research, and every aspect of my life. But, how do I operationalize reconciliation in practice? It is one thing to talk about reconciliation, but are we truly reflecting the principles of reconciliation?

As a health care professional, I worked within the Western perspective in addressing health conditions and issues. In many cases, I leveraged the "fear factor" in motivating patients to make health and behavioural changes. But, upon reflection, I have come to realize that this often does more harm than good. Individuals need to have the autonomy to make health decisions based on their needs, cultural norms, and beliefs without fear of "finger-pointing and blame" from health care professionals. I know now that open dialogue, deep listening, and reflective action are necessary if we are to bring about sustainable change, and that these things emerge from respectful and trusting relationships.

I understand the relevance of research in society and its potential impact on individuals and the community. However, it is important to initiate activities that proactively react to identified community health needs and the strength of individual and community empowerment in achieving a set goal. Developing and maintaining relationships are crucial in every aspect of life. For instance, to carry out research with people in my home country, I must know their customs and traditions and in many instances learn a bit of the local language, particularly greetings; since food is a big part of many tribes in Nigeria, I must be willing to sample various local delicacies. The term *tribe(s)* is used to refer to Indigenous Peoples in Nigeria and in other parts of the world. Researchers always, or should always, design protocols in consultation with the local agencies and organizations, and when working with a specific community, design research with the participation of the community leadership. This process of carrying out research and engaging with communities in my home country is the process of doing research the proper way and for the proper reasons when working with peoples of other cultures, including Indigenous Peoples.

Thus, the emphasis in this chapter is on carrying out Indigenous health research from a perspective that reflects the key facets of who I am, including an immigrant, health professional, health researcher, and settler in Canada. These personas shape who I am, my epistemology, and they influence my role in reconciliation. The views contained herein are mine alone, emerging from my own unique perspective, but I hope they may help you on your own journey toward reconciliation.

RECONCILIATION AND HEALTH RESEARCH

Reconciliation is a desire to journey into a better place (Patten and Ryan 2001) and is crucial for societies after periods of conflict. Reconciliation looks different depending on the specific context: in the Canadian context, it generally refers to the relationship between Indigenous Peoples and settler Canadians. But what does this mean to individuals? Although people often imagine that reconciliation is something Indigenous Peoples need to do, it is about healing relationships and is everyone's responsibility. This means that non-Indigenous people must also consider what it means to them as individuals and how they can support the healing process by building positive relationships with the Indigenous communities. As treaty people, we must individually and collectively take strides to reconcile with Indigenous Peoples so that every person in Canada can live side-by-side peacefully. We must engage in joint activities on individual and community levels that are characterized by respectful, pragmatic interactions and daily cooperation between peoples (Strupinskienė 2017).

For researchers, as for all of us, understanding Indigenous Peoples means understanding and acknowledging the history and ongoing reality of colonialism and the reconciliation process — confronting the histories of the colonial encounter. Researchers must consciously engage in this confrontation throughout the research continuum (Johnstone 2007). This unlearning and relearning provide knowledge and information that enable health researchers to better carry out their work in Indigenous communities and to have a clearer picture of the factors that influence the way of life of the research participants. It is through this knowledge that researchers come to know the factors, shaped by history, politics, the environment, and economics, that create the research context.

The word *research* often generates negative feelings, suspicion, and a defensive reaction for marginalized communities due to shared memories of negative experiences with "helicopter research," wherein researchers enter Indigenous communities and undertake research on rather than with communities, imposing values and results without regard for the perspectives of the community. As a result of this, Indigenous communities are profoundly distrustful of non-Indigenous health researchers. Indigenous Peoples feel over-studied by health and academic researchers, who often undertake research that focuses on obtaining knowledge from the community without reciprocity, rather than community-driven research, thereby marginalizing Indigenous knowledge, with little community input, involvement, and benefit to the community.

There has been a surfeit of research describing and analyzing Indigenous Peoples' lives from a Eurocentric perspective (Getty 2010). The comparison made between the culture of the researcher and that of Indigenous Peoples, which is often reflected in the language, tone, and focus of the research, is also problematic. In many instances, the focus of the research is on the negative aspects of life, such as illness rather than health (Wilson 2008). The focus of non-Indigenous researchers often results in stereotyping and blaming Indigenous Peoples for their illnesses, without any acknowledgement of the source of the problems, which traces back to the colonial regime (Getty 2010).

But non-Indigenous researchers can undertake Indigenous research if structures are present for equal partnership in the research. Non-Indigenous researchers need to be aware of Indigenous values, beliefs, and epistemology when researching with Indigenous Peoples. They can improve their research practices by reflecting on and being critical of their own culture, values, assumptions, and beliefs, and by recognizing that these are not the norm but be open to different worldviews and ways of knowing. In undertaking Indigenous research, it is imperative that researchers locate themselves and their culture within the research, use decolonizing methods, and adopt Indigenous Protocol and ethics.

Researchers should recognize Indigenous epistemology if Indigenous methods, such as storytelling, are being used rather than assuming that it is appropriate to contain Indigenous methods under a Western epistemology (Kovach 2009).

ETHICAL GUIDELINES

In an attempt to resolve and strengthen the research relationship in Indigenous health, various research ethics guidelines and frameworks have been developed (Johnstone 2007). For example, the OCAP principles (i.e., ownership, control, access, and possession), developed by Canadian Indigenous leaders, and the Tri-Council Policy Statement 2 (TCPS 2) were designed to counter exploitative practices in Indigenous research and maintain self-determination among Indigenous Peoples over the research process. The TCPS 2 and OCAP expect researchers to be responsible for meeting specific ethical standards, fundamentally shifting the design and approach of research projects (Morton Ninomiya and Pollock 2017).

Although ethical guidelines are necessary steps toward re-orienting research practices, to improve the research relationship with Indigenous Peoples, researchers need to also understand the intertwined relationship between Indigenous health research and the history of colonialism (Johnstone 2007). Researchers need to make a commitment to ensuring that they understand and acknowledge the colonial history of research in order to ensure they do not repeat the harmful errors of the past (Johnstone 2007). Communication, engagement, listening, paying attention to the community, taking note of what is important to the community, and being consistent and open are essential to the relationship building process. Thus, transparency in research practices is vital to improving the guiding principles in research (Morton Ninomiya and Pollock 2017) and promoting reconciliation with Indigenous Peoples. This can be done by being clear about the objectives, methods, and procedures used.

The future of Indigenous research must be a decolonized research process in which genuinely positive relationships exist between Indigenous and non-Indigenous Peoples. Respectful relationships and community engagement are integral and intertwined aspects of a decolonized research practice. They are both essential facets of Indigenous research that can serve as a framework for operationalizing reconciliation. Indigenous research should move toward harmony with an emphasis on direction, movement, and transformational change.

Community Engagement

In research, community engagement is a process whereby individuals within an identified geographical area are respectfully included as partners in addressing issues within the community (Ahmed and Palermo 2010). Community engagement essentially translates into having good relations with a group of people who share similar interests. Respect must be earned, and this works both ways. This process creates an intercultural space for social interactions and empowerment for both the researcher and participants.

Community engagement should be explicit in the entire research continuum, from the development of research objectives to implementation, evaluation, and knowledge translation. It is challenging to change policies without appropriate community engagement and collaboration with organizations, community leaders, and researchers who can collectively influence health politics.

Building Relationships

Healing is at the centre of reconciliation; the first stage of healing comes with acknowledging the history of colonization and the harm experienced by communities and working to dismantle the relational structures of inequality and inequity. Researchers need to debunk stereotypes and recognize the direct historical relationship between settler privileges and the deprivations observed among Indigenous Peoples that result in inequalities (Nagy 2013). This also means acknowledging the harm caused by the research itself. This can form the foundation for relationships based on open and honest communication, inclusion, and community involvement (Riddell, Salamanca, Pepler, Cardinal, and McIvor 2017). Implementing research values, such as respect, open communication, responsibility, and accountability with the intended community, show a desire to have an ethical, decolonized relationship with the community (Riddell et al. 2017). This relationship also allows the community to hold the researchers accountable.

The goals of health research with Indigenous Peoples should be self-determination and a holistic balance of health and harmony with the land and all other living beings. Non-Indigenous researchers can receive education on Indigenous culture and traditions and on the connection between Indigenous arts, culture, heritage, land, and sea. But, they need to be culturally humble and listen to Indigenous Peoples with their hearts, or they may fail to fully understand these connections (Patten and Ryan 2001). Thus, respectful relationships evolve from an open-minded engagement with Indigenous Peoples' extensive knowledge systems; systems that have often been ignored or dismissed as folklore and as lacking any scientific basis (Getty 2010). This means contesting the dominance of Western research in Indigenous communities and changing the research dynamics so that Indigenous Peoples control their own knowledge systems and identities.

Reconciling the two cultures and learning styles may be a challenge for non-Indigenous researchers, but relationship building through listening and dialogue enables researchers to discover what really informs their thinking and behaviour (Patten and Ryan 2001). Dialogue redresses non-Indigenous presumptions and unexamined prejudices while listening deeply accelerates learning and provides personal enrichment (Patten and Ryan 2001).

INDIGENOUS EPISTEMOLOGY AND RESEARCH METHODS

Indigenous philosophy indicates that all entities are interrelated and life/existence consists of energy that is animate, filled with spirit, and in constant motion (Little Bear 2000). Indigenous approaches holistically embrace every part of an individual as integral to the whole, including the artistic, the spiritual, the sensual, and the intuitive. This is in contrast to Western knowledge, which is characterized by linear and hierarchical thinking (LaFrance, Nichols, and Kirkhart 2012) that seeks to isolate and compartmentalize (Wilson 2008).

Despite these differences, both knowledge systems can work together for the common good. This idea can be seen in the Métis infinity symbol, which signifies a bridge between two worldviews — a middle ground and blend between Indigenous and Western practices with the centre of the infinity symbol representing a connection and an endless relationship between nations and research paradigms (Lavallee 2014). Considering the fluidity of Indigenous knowledge, it is vital that strategies of inquiry allow for change and adaptation along the way, i.e., it needs to be fluid.

Grounded in practising reconciliation via Indigenous research, research methods must include the following components: contextual reflection of the researcher and participants in the research process; the inclusion of Indigenous Peoples in the research process in a way that is respectful and preserves self-determination; and the acknowledgement of Indigenous ways of knowing (Drawson, Toombs, and Mushquash 2017). These aspects are experiential in various approaches, including community-based participatory research, mixed/multi-methods, and qualitative research.

Community-Based Participatory Research

Community-based participatory research (CBPR) is a collaborative, inclusive, non-directive, mutually beneficial, and respectful approach to research in which community members are active in defining and analyzing their own solutions, thereby bringing about empowerment in the community (Maar et al. 2011). This approach is well suited for diverse populations and facilitates reciprocity and relationship building. It's also ideal for researching disparities between communities (Ritchie et al. 2013).

CBPR has become a precondition for Indigenous health research and is an approach that develops culturally centred research designs and integrates Indigenous research methods (Simonds and Christopher 2013). Features such as equal contribution, shared decision making, ownership, and credibility of the findings guide Indigenous health research. CBPR recognizes the community as a unit of identity, builds on the strengths and resources of the community, facilitates equal partnership in research via a power-sharing process, fosters co-learning and capacity building, creates a balance between data generation and intervention so that both parties equally benefit, and enhances sustainability (Braun, Browne, Ka'Opua, Kim, and Mokuau 2014).

At the core of CBPR is the belief that research that incorporates community cultural values and ways of knowing is critical for improving quality of life and reducing health disparities. CBPR endorses community partners as knowledge co-creators, sees Indigenous insight as invaluable to developing trusting relationships, balancing power relations, and producing appropriate and sustainable efforts to promote social justice and improve population health (Mertens 2012). CBPR and other forms of community-engaged and collaborative research often employ mixed and multi-method research designs to generate outcomes that are meaningful to communities (Lucero et al. 2016).

Mixed /Multi-Methods Designs and Indigenous Research

Indigenous Peoples use different methods to tell stories and share knowledge, such as visual symbols or metaphors, song, dance, and prayer (LaFrance et al. 2012). A mixed methods approach uses both qualitative and quantitative research — words, pictures, and narratives, as well as statistics and numbers — to gain a deeper understanding of issues (Hesse-Biber 2010). Researchers should be willing to be flexible and modify their methodological and personal choices and behaviour to address the phenomenon under study and the issues raised; this will lead to results that are of greater value to the community (Maar et al. 2011).

Researchers often use a variety of methods to study the same phenomenon in order to triangulate findings and obtain a broader understanding of research problems. In Indigenous research, mixed methods are a means to invite different voices to participate in a dialogue that embraces all cultures and promotes the social validity of the research, since community participation is important to every phase of the research (Mertens 2007). This can build relationships by promoting collective action and social change that is driven by population needs, integrating knowledge systems, and engaging in a decolonized research process (Chilisa and Tsheko 2014).

A mixed method approach to research with Indigenous Peoples is known as Two-Eyed Seeing. Two-Eyed Seeing is the gift of multiple perspectives in which we are tasked with "learning to see from one eye with the strengths of Indigenous knowledge and ways of knowing, and from the other eye with the strengths of Western knowledge and ways of knowing, ... using both eyes together, for the benefit of all" (Bartlett, Marshall, and Marshall 2012: 5). Two-Eyed Seeing shows that both Indigenous and non-Indigenous worldviews and knowledge can coexist to inform solutions (Blackstock 2011). Additionally, it is a way to decolonize research as it demands that a researcher pay careful attention to the research approach and understand the phenomenon from different perspectives. When both eyes are used together, the researcher views the world with a new lens and respects the strengths and differences within the multiple perspectives, which can lead to novel ways of obtaining knowledge and understanding and can begin to reconcile disparate worldviews.

However, it is not enough to simply add Indigenous methods, such as sharing circles, to a research design. It is imperative that the researcher applies Indigenous research protocols and epistemology throughout the research. Two-Eyed Seeing is about incorporating other ways of knowing into the research design. Combining Indigenous and Western approaches is not a failsafe against the oppression of Indigenous Peoples and knowledge. If the research does not respectfully include the values, practices, and beliefs of Indigenous Peoples, then it can perpetuate inequality. It's important, for example, not to make statistical generalizations that ignore the diversity of Indigenous Peoples and cultures.

Qualitative Research Designs and Indigenous Research

Since Indigenous Peoples have traditionally had an oral culture — emphasizing storytelling as a means of sharing knowledge — they are often supportive of qualitative approaches to health research and data collection. This is not to say that Western qualitative methodologies are the same as Indigenous methodologies, but there are intersections in Indigenous and qualitative research (Kovach 2009). Qualitative research is a design that is exploratory and allows for a rounded look at phenomena and experience and provides depth and detailed understanding of attitudes, feelings, and behaviours (Watkins 2012). As such, qualitative research methods can be useful when attempting to understand the experiences of Indigenous Peoples.

Respecting Indigenous Research Values and Principles

Indigenous epistemology views knowledge as holistic, animate, and derived from the interconnectivity (relationships) with one another, nature, and spirit (Kovach 2016). Therefore, Indigenous philosophy originates from values of respect, reciprocity, and responsibility toward all of creation. Researchers should adhere to the four Rs: respect, relevance, reciprocity, and responsibility, which are requirements for transforming research in Indigenous communities (Lavallee 2014) and are key features of any healthy research relationship (Wilson 2008).

Researchers have to respect the customs, codes, ethics, and practices of the participating Indigenous community, adopt research protocols, such as giving tobacco, which signifies respect and reciprocity (Kovach 2009), and respecting the narratives, knowledge, and stories shared by participants. Researchers must build into the research culturally appropriate methods for feedback and dissemination of the research findings to the community. This reciprocity shows respect (Singe and Jae 2017).

Reciprocity in Indigenous research involves sharing between the researcher and participants in order to connect them together in the acts of giving and receiving, listening and talking, and teaching and learning. This relationship is a sacred ceremony (Wilson 2008), and the researcher is responsible and accountable for the impact of the research on the lives of the participants and community members. Relationships with the community, protocols and ethics in Indigenous research design, and relational methods for hearing stories are key when utilizing Indigenous methodologies (Kovach 2016). Therefore, research should seek not only knowledge creation, but also healing and community building while ensuring that values are respected and beliefs are adhered to, including Indigenous laws on collective rights, personal responsibilities, and stewardship, as well as ethical responsibilities and community accountability.

Responsibility involves the assurance that the researcher will uphold the integrity involved in carrying out research in the community and of individuals that choose to partake in the research (Lavallee 2014). Researchers must ensure that the research is culturally safe by recognizing Indigenous worldviews and being respectful and accountable. Thus, it is not research about Indigenous Peoples, but research for and with Indigenous Peoples (Singe and Jae 2017). Also, the researcher must honour the Indigenous laws of love, respect, kindness, honesty, generosity, reciprocity, and caring in the research (Kovach 2016).

Indigenous research should make a difference in people's lives and must be incorporated in the entire research process and not as an afterthought (Wilson 2008). Indigenous research should benefit the community by providing information on the health and well-being of its people. The research must also be relevant and based on what really matters to the community, which will be enhanced by developing relationships and partnerships with individuals and community members (Lavallee 2014).

Researchers must address relationality by taking into account the impact of their own values and beliefs on the collection, interpretation, and analysis of data. The researcher needs to embed reflexive and collaborative practices in the entire research process and report how this process occurred in the findings (Singe and Jae 2017). They must also be accountable to Indigenous participants and the wider community in how they communicate findings.

Respectful Recruitment and Research Objectives

Essentially, researchers need to accept and initiate their responsibility for reconciliation via respectful recruitment. The respectful recruitment of study participants starts with the development of the study itself: do the community and organizations involved see the value in the research? Does the research use culturally appropriate methods? The researchers must also make a commitment to communicating the results of the study in a way that is useful and meaningful to the community (Maar et al. 2011). Researchers must maintain good research practice throughout their study. For example, they should have clear communication about ownership and appropriate use of information, uphold commitments to return draft reports and share information, and check in about findings to ensure they accurately reflect the understanding of the community. If researchers do not ensure that they are building trusting relationships with the research community then trust is eroded and this will lead to wariness and restraint toward research (Lynch 2017).

Researchers should carry out research that closes the health disparity gap and avoids unequal power relationships by conducting themselves aptly with and in communities. Overall, researchers must reflectively examine their own moral stance, reasons, and motivations for undertaking the research in the first place.

Respecting Diversity in Indigenous Peoples

Indigenous Peoples worldwide differ, and so it is important to note that there is no one set of cultural protocols (Roman 2016). A specific group's research protocol is localized to their place, language, and worldview; thus, researchers must tweak the protocols used depending on the population, area of study, and community needs. For example, dreams are an important source of information for some Indigenous groups, such as the Cree and Mi'kmaq in Canada and Indigenous Australians, but may not be equally important for other Indigenous groups (Braun et al. 2014). Therefore, it is important that the researchers understand how to alter every necessary element of the research design in order to ensure that the research is respectful within the dynamics of the particular context (Thesnaar 2014).

In this respect, it is essential that researchers understand not only the ethical principles of research but also the cultural norms and values held by the community and adopt ethical principles for different communities (Riddell et al. 2017). Since there is so much diversity in Indigenous Peoples in Canada, with different groups having different languages, cultures, and identities, including this diversity in the design and writing up of research documents provide rich meaning to data (Roman 2016). For example, it could be that there are specific issues experienced by non-status Indigenous Peoples that differ from those affecting Status Indians under the Indian Act. In addition, experiences may differ among Indigenous Peoples from one group to the other, such as among Inuit, Métis, or First Nations peoples.

It is also vital that researchers understand how cultural protocols may impact the nature of relationships. For example, in many traditional Inuit communities, a young person would never speak after an Elder has spoken, even if the young person disagrees with him or her or has something to add, as this will be disrespectful (Riddell et al. 2017). This may influence the manner of discourse, the ability to ask follow-up questions during interviews, and data collection guides. Awareness and understanding of cultural norms are essential in every stage of the research process to maintain respect.

MY RESPONSIBILITIES FOR RECONCILIATION

Having explored the various evolving features of carrying out Indigenous research, it is clear what my responsibility or role is in reconciliation as a non-Indigenous health researcher. How do I operationalize reconciliation via research practice while engaging with communities and building relationships? It is my responsibility to ensure that I am asking the right questions, in the right way, and for the right reasons. This is because inconsistency between the social and cultural assumptions of the researcher and the community may compromise the inquiry.

I must utilize methods that will encourage community engagement so that dialogue with community members can highlight areas of interests and concern, as well as possible culturally appropriate solutions. The approaches I utilize must be culturally congruent, collaborative, and resonate with tradition to enhance mutual understanding and learning, equal partnership, and contribution, as well as shared decision making. In addition, the methods and approaches I utilize must explore the complexity of interactions among social and cultural determinants and examine pathways linking determinants to health outcomes. Understanding the relationships between immigrants, settlers, and Indigenous Peoples is central to understanding existing power dynamics (Blair and Wong 2017).

It is essential that I work to overcome the negative image of research by respecting and understanding cultural diversity, such as the differences between Indigenous groups and the differences between the various communities within groups (Prior 2007). I must recognize the implications of these differences in my research, understand traditional sovereignty, recognize the role of Elders and Knowledge Keepers, use Indigenous methods when and where possible, and interpret the data within the cultural context (Ritchie et al. 2013).

Solidarity and ally relationships are complex and, moving forward, will require a collective effort to disrupt discrimination and oppression in research practice (Blair and Wong 2017). I must overcome stereotypes and develop lasting friendships that will influence the formation of genuine relationships based on mutual respect, solidarity, cooperation, and trust. It is important that I approach research encounters with Indigenous Peoples not just with ethical rigour, but in a sincere manner that would bring about reconciliation in research contexts (Patten and Ryan 2001). Researchers should reflect on research values and what we are doing; in addition, we should search for ways of doing research that take time to establish rapport, which will foster engagement and empowerment that develop from interaction and relationship building with Indigenous Peoples.

CONCLUSION

In the context of immigrant-settler-Indigenous relationships, the same structures that oppress Indigenous Peoples may also adversely affect immigrants and settlers as well, especially people of colour (Blair and Wong 2017). As such, immigrants and settlers of colour might feel a resonance with Indigenous Peoples on the impact of colonialism, power dynamics, and the preservation of cultural identity and empowerment. However, as Ranjan Datta points out in Chapter 1 in this book, some immigrants and settlers of colour prefer to distance themselves from the colonial experience of Indigenous Peoples rather than exploring this resonance.

The way that I relate to the world, my perception of problems, ways of conceptualizing, and decision making are influenced by my experiences; thus, culture and traditions shape my beliefs, values, and principles. I believe that in research, knowledge is co-constructed between the researcher and the research participant and is shaped by both experiences. Relationships, interactions, and experiences are vital in reconciling peoples worldwide.

In addition, it is paramount that researchers who are new to Indigenous research in Canada obtain education about the history of colonialism and its continued impact on the lives of Indigenous Peoples today, its impact on research, the relevance and appropriateness of community engagement, and acknowledgement of Indigenous cultures (Maar et al. 2011). This ensures that reconciliation education includes information on relationships, communications, and consultations is upheld and implemented among researchers.

There is no neutral and static researcher since researchers can either help or hinder reconciliation by either encouraging or discouraging harmonious relationships by their actions (MacDonald 2013). Our actions as researchers will reflect on how we take up our responsibility in the long-term process of restoring relationships in research.

REFERENCES

Ahmed, Syed M., and Ann-gel S. Palermo. 2010. "Community Engagement in Research: Frameworks for Education and Peer Review." *American Journal of Public Health,* 100, 8: 1380–1387. <https://doi.org/10.2105/AJPH.2009.178137>.

Bartlett, Cheryl, Murdena Marshall, and Albert Marshall. 2012. "Two-Eyed Seeing and Other Lessons Learned within a Co-Learning Journey of Bringing Together Indigenous and Mainstream Knowledges and Ways of Knowing." *Journal of Environmental Studies and Sciences,* 2, 4: 331–340. <https://doi.org/10.1007/s13412-012-0086-8>.

Blackstock, Cindy. 2011. "The Emergence of the Breath of Life Theory." *Journal of Social Work Values and Ethics,* 8, 1.

Blair, Julie, and Desmond Wong. 2017. "Moving in the Circle: Indigenous Solidarity for Canadian Libraries Settler-Indigenous Relationships." *Canadian Journal of Library and Information Practice and Research,* 12, 2: 1–8.

Braun, Kathryn L., Collete V. Browne, Lana S. Ka'Opua, Bum J. Kim, and Noreen Mokuau. 2014. "Research on Indigenous Elders: From Positivistic to Decolonizing Methodologies." *Gerontologist,* 54, 1: 117–126. <https://doi.org/10.1093/geront/gnt067>.

Chilisa, Bagele, and Gaelebale N. Tsheko. 2014. "Mixed Methods in Indigenous Research: Building Relationships for Sustainable Intervention Outcomes." *Journal of Mixed Methods Research,* 8, 3: 222–233. <https://doi.org/10.1177/1558689814527878>.

Drawson, Alexandra S., Elaine Toombs, and Christopher J. Mushquash. 2017. "Indigenous Research Methods: A Systematic Review." *The International Indigenous Policy Journal,* 8, 2. <https://doi.org/10.18584/iipj.2017.8.2.5>.

Getty, Grace A. 2010. "The Journey Between Western and Indigenous Research Paradigms." *Journal of Transcultural Nursing,* 21, 1: 5–14. <https://doi.org/10.1177/1043659609349062>.

Hesse-Biber, Sharlene N. 2010. *Mixed Methods Research: Merging Theory with Practice.* New York: Guilford Press.

Johnstone, Megan J. 2007. "Research Ethics, Reconciliation, and Strengthening the Research Relationship in Indigenous Health Domains: An Australian Perspective." *International Journal of Intercultural Relations,* 31, 3: 391–406. <https://doi.org/10.1016/j.ijintrel.2006.09.003>.

Kovach, Margaret. 2009. *Indigenous Methodologies: Characteristics, Conversations, and Contexts.* Toronto, ON: University of Toronto Press.

___. 2016. "Doing Indigenous Methodologies — A Letter to a Research Class." In Norman K. Denzin and Yvonna S. Lincoln (eds.), *Sage Handbook of Qualitative Research,* 5th edition. Thousand Oaks, CA: Sage Publications.

LaFrance, Joan, Richard Nichols, and Karen E. Kirkhart. 2012. "Culture Writes the Script: On the Centrality of Context in Indigenous Evaluation." In D.J. Rog, J.L. Fitzpatrick, and R.F. Conner (eds.), *Context: A Framework for Its Influence on Evaluation Practice. New Directions for Evaluation,* Vol. 135. Wiley Periodicals Inc. <https://doi.org/10.1002/ev>.

Lavallee, Amanda M. 2014. *Converging Methods and Tools: A Métis Group Model Building Project on Tuberculosis.* University of Saskatchewan.

Little Bear, Leroy. 2000. "Jagged Worldviews Colliding." In M. Battiste (ed.), *Reclaiming Indigenous Voice and Vision*. Vancouver: University of British Columbia Press.

Lucero, Julie, Nina Wallerstein, Bonnie Duran, Margarita Alegria, et al. 2016. "Development of a Mixed Methods Investigation of Process and Outcomes of Community-Based Participatory Research." *Journal of Mixed Methods Research*, 1–20. <https://doi.org/10.1177/1558689816633309>.

Lynch, A. Jasmyn J. 2017. "Respect, Reflect, and Engage — Enhancing Biophysical Research Practices with Indigenous People, Their Land, and Culture." *Australasian Journal of Environmental Management*, 24, 3: 319–331. <https://doi.org/10.1080/14486563.2017.1349694>.

Maar, Marion A., Nancy E. Lightfoot, Mariette E. Sutherland, Roger P. Strasser, et al. 2011. "Thinking Outside the Box: Aboriginal People's Suggestions for Conducting Health Studies with Aboriginal Communities." Public Health, 125, 11: 747–753. <https://doi.org/10.1016/j.puhe.2011.08.006>.

MacDonald, David B. 2013. "Reconciliation after Genocide in Canada: Towards a Syncretic Model of Democracy." *AlterNative: An International Journal of Indigenous Peoples*, 9, 1: 60–73. <https://doi.org/10.1177/117718011300900105>.

Mertens, Donna M. 2007. "Transformative Paradigm." *Journal of Mixed Methods Research*, 1, 3: 212–225. <https://doi.org/10.1177/1558689807302811>.

___. 2012. "Transformative Mixed Methods." *American Behavioral Scientist,* 56, 6: 802–813. <https://doi.org/10.1177/0002764211433797>.

Morton, Ninomiya M.E., and Nathaniel J. Pollock. 2017. "Reconciling Community-Based Indigenous Research and Academic Practices: Knowing Principles Is Not Always Enough." *Social Science and Medicine,* 172: 28–36. <https://doi.org/10.1016/j.socscimed.2016.11.007>.

Nagy, Rosemary L. 2013. "The Scope and Bounds of Transitional Justice and the Canadian Truth and Reconciliation Commission." *International Journal of Transitional Justice*, 7, 1: 52–73. <https://doi.org/10.1093/ijtj/ijs034>.

Patten, Herb, and Robin Ryan. 2001. "Research and Reconciliation." *Australian Journal of Indigenous Education*, 29, 1: 36–42. <https://acces.bibl.ulaval.ca/login?url=https://search.ebscohost.com/login.aspx?direct=trueanddb=eric&AN=EJ666837&site=ehost-live>.

Prior, Deborah. 2007. "Decolonising Research: A Shift Toward Reconciliation." *Nursing Inquiry*, 14, 2: 162–168. <https://doi.org/10.1111/j.1440-1800.2007.00361.x>.

Riddell, Julia K., Angela Salamanca, Debra J. Pepler, Shelly Cardinal, and Onowa McIvor. 2017. "Laying the Groundwork: A Practical Guide for Ethical Research with Indigenous Communities." *International Indigenous Policy Journal*, 8, 2. <https://doi.org/10.18584/iipj.2017.8.2.6>.

Ritchie, Stephen.D., Mary Jo Wabano, Jackson Beardy, Jeffery Curran, et al. 2013. "Community-Based Participatory Research with Indigenous Communities: The Proximity Paradox." *Health and Place*, 24: 183–189. <https://doi.org/10.1016/j.healthplace.2013.09.008>.

Roman, Curtis. 2016. "Indigenous People and Qualitative Research — Making it Work." *Aboriginal and Islander Health Worker Journal*, 40 (January/December): 11–16.

Simonds, Venessa W., and Suzanne Christopher. 2013. "Adapting Western Research

Methods to Indigenous Ways of Knowing." *American Journal of Public Health*, 103, 12: 2185–2192. <https://doi.org/10.2105/AJPH.2012.301157>.

Singe, Myra, and Major Jae. 2017. "Conducting Indigenous Research in Western Knowledge Spaces: Aligning Theory and Methodology." *Australian Educational Researcher*, 44, 1: 5–19. <https://doi.org/10.1007/s13384-017-0233-z>.

Strupinskienė, Lina. 2017. "'What Is Reconciliation and Are We There Yet?' Different Types and Levels of Reconciliation: A Case Study of Bosnia and Herzegovina." *Journal of Human Rights*, 16, 4: 452–472. <https://doi.org/10.1080/14754835.2016.1197771>.

Thesnaar, Christoffel H. 2014. "Seeking Feasible Reconciliation: A Transdisciplinary Contextual Approach to Reconciliation." *HTS Theological Studies*, 70, 2: 01–08. <https://doi.org/10.4102/hts.v70i2.1364>.

Watkins, Daphne C. 2012. "Qualitative Research: The Importance of Conducting Research That Doesn't 'Count.'" *Health Promotion Practice*, 13, 2: 153–158. <https://doi.org/10.1177/1524839912437370>.

Wilson, Shawn. 2008. *Research Is Ceremony: Indigenous Research Methodologies*. Black Point, NS: Fernwood Publishing.

Chapter Ten

RECONCILIATION

A White Settler Learning from the Land

JANET MCVITTIE

In this chapter, I present some of the lessons that I have learned in my work developing a garden near my home department, the College of Education at the University of Saskatchewan. As a white settler, I am working to understand reconciliation and to promote greater understanding among my (mostly) white settler teacher candidates. My work in the garden involves researching what plants were indigenous to the prairies, how Indigenous Peoples lived here, which plants they used and how, and how all this was informed by their epistemology. It is hard intellectual labour, as well as physical labour, digging out invasive species to create homes for indigenous plants. It is also hard emotional labour as I struggle to understand my ongoing privilege as a white person in Canada. The work in the Prairie Habitat Garden provides a place for me to attempt to make myself someone that an Indigenous person might want to reconcile with.

RECONCILIATION

The Truth and Reconciliation Commission of Canada noted that reconciliation is an ongoing process whereby past injustices against Indigenous Peoples are recognized, and the hard work of making up for those injustices, of "maintaining respectful relationships," takes place (Truth and Reconciliation Final Report 2015: 11). Through examples from the creation and ongoing work in a garden, where I am attempting to recreate a small slice of native prairie, I explore some of the lessons that I have learned in Treaty Six Territory, Traditional Homeland of the Neyinowak Inniwak (Cree), Saulteaux, Dakota,

Nakota, Lakota, and Métis peoples, in the country now known as Canada. I would like to create and maintain respectful relationships with Indigenous Peoples. My family's history in Canada, through the male lines, reveals wilful ignorance and reifies the portrait Europeans painted of themselves: relative wealth due to the white man's hard work; property rights duly earned through the domestication of wild unoccupied land; survival due to wily intelligence. But as James Daschuk (2013) documented, British, American, and Canadian governments enacted policies intended to starve, slaughter, steal children, and destroy the culture and language of the Indigenous Peoples of the great plains of North America. Settlers, despite finding artifacts on their so-called empty land, despite living near residential schools, managed to maintain their narratives of being more deserving than those who were here, while also denying that there was anyone here. My ancestral history is filled with half-truths and overt lies, all designed to create and reinforce white supremacy. The systems that have always, to this day, shaped our relationships with Indigenous Peoples are colonial, racist, and patriarchal. These systems remain in place because we allow them to, so it is up to us to see the problems inherent to these systems and challenge ourselves to build something better.

I, personally, want to work toward reconciliation, but what does, or can, that look like? I have taken on one small project in my attempt to learn and to teach other white settlers that Indigenous Peoples were here, that they are still here, that they knew the land, worked with the land, had complex understandings of this land, that this land was healthy and biodiverse, and that Indigenous Peoples had methods to maintain its, and their, health. The Prairie Habitat Garden is a project that I believe can support my work toward reconciliation. The Prairie Habitat Garden is a small slice of native prairie, nestled up against the College of Education at the University of Saskatchewan. My work is oriented toward changing myself and other individuals, primarily teacher candidates and teachers.

LOCATING MYSELF

My ancestors came to North America, some as early as the 1700s, from a variety of European countries, forced out of their original homes by poverty. They settled here, taking land that they had been told was empty. My father searched his ancestral roots, looking to understand what caused the roots to bend in certain directions and what their experiences were along the way. What

I have learned from my father's searching is that person after person believed that if he (women are rarely featured) worked hard, he was entitled to land, and that the land was empty — that there were no other people here prior to their arrival. My family history reveals a wilful ignorance of the people and other beings that lived on and with the land. My father, a hard-working, kind man and a good father, grew up in a white supremacist and patriarchal society, and benefited thereby; a few years ago, I would not have understood what this meant. And I would not have recognized that I also grew up in the same white supremacist and patriarchal society.

One story my father found of an ancestor was of a "pioneer" woman who answered a knock on the door one winter evening while home alone with her small children. She opened the door to find three Indigenous women and their children standing in the cold. Despite the lack of common language, the three women managed to communicate that they wished to trade some beaded leather clothing for food. My ancestor "courageously" (as written up in a feature story in the local newspaper) served them tea and then sent them back into the winter night. The tone of the article suggested that the Indigenous women and their children were a threat, and the white woman had been brave and generous. She had met the danger head-on, and she had given these people tea and a warm place for a short time. This is white supremacy in action. It is only a white supremacist who could feel generous while sending three non-white women and their children out into a Canadian winter night.

I, having been given a more critical education about Canadian history and having some understanding of my own white privilege, have begun to dissect this kind of story and to dissect my own memories. I remember a unit of learning focused on prejudice at my elementary school in a small northern community. We learned about how cruel Americans from the southern United States were to black people. After the unit was completed, one child proclaimed that there were just two kinds of people she hated: prejudiced people and Indians. I was not very old at the time, perhaps in Grade 4, but I noticed the paradox. I wondered, at that moment, why we were learning about prejudice and racism so far away and not learning about the prejudice closer to home. Somehow, my understanding of another child's racism supported my belief that I was not racist. Nonetheless, about ten years later (in the early 1970s), on a walk in England, I met a young Englishman who wanted to go to Canada, "to work with the Indians." Imagining this naïve Englishman attempting to save the people, I told him he did not know "what they were like" — I had seen, in my home city of Saskatoon, poverty, alcoholism, damaged people. Shortly afterwards, I was watching an English television news show, with an English reporter interviewing a white South African who said, in support of apartheid, that the reporter did not know "what they were like." I recognized, suddenly, that I had to either identify myself as racist, or I had to change how I viewed Indigenous Peoples. Changing identity is hard work, but I did not want to think of myself nor be known as racist. Thus, I knew it was time for me to learn more about Indigenous Peoples living in Canada.

What followed for me was life. I had a living to earn, children to raise, family to spend time with, mind and body to keep healthy. Ultimately, life took me through a PhD in education and a faculty position in the College of Education at the University of Saskatchewan.

I had been open to thinking about the world differently, attempting to unlearn what I thought "they were like," and challenging the anecdotal stories white people often tell of Indigenous Peoples. When I participated in a study by one of my colleagues (Margaret Kovach), she helped me realize that anti-racism was something I did "off the side of my desk." Unlearning and relearning about racism had not yet been a focus for me. I was living and working alongside Indigenous colleagues, and all I was doing was supporting their work off the side of my desk! Clearly, it was time to step up. I took a course on anti-oppression from Verna St. Denis. Since then, I have been fortunate to serve on the committees of graduate students who research race, racism, systemic racism, anti-racist theory, and critical race theory. I have read books; I have put myself into situations led by Indigenous Peoples; I have left myself open to hearing what Indigenous Peoples have to say. All that I have learned is still filtered through how I was raised, which includes the historical distortions that have created this "great" country of Canada and which often lead me to say stupid things. Fortunately, my Indigenous colleagues are here to give me gentle intellectual adjustments, helping me to see my ignorance. Racism is not just an individual thing, although there are individuals who support this terror. Racism is systemic; it permeates our institutions — legal, medical, and educational. These come from the historical distortions.

An example of a historical distortion is the concept of land. When my ancestors arrived in North America, they were met and helped by people who had lived here from time immemorial, and yet the story of an empty land persists. The idea of land and the related concepts of place and space are central to reconciliation because settlers and Indigenous Peoples have very divergent conceptions of land emerging from very different worldviews or epistemologies. Epistemology is shaped over generations and then informs our perceptions:

> An epistemic genealogy — the ethics, logics, and ideologies foundational to a knowledge system that have been passed down across generations, a knowledge framework that establishes what is known (the socially constructed commonsense of a culture), how things come to be known (the process of attaining new knowledge), how the world is to be interpreted according to what is known (the social construction of reality), and how the self is known in relation to perceived reality (the politics of self). (Seawright 2014: 557)

White settlers derive from a particular epistemic genealogy and, because of colonialism, Indigenous Peoples have this same epistemology thrust upon them. White children grow up believing that they are entitled to the land and its resources and that they have earned this entitlement through their hard work and intelligence. Indigenous children also learn that white children are entitled to land and resources and are good. Indigenous children learn that the colour of their skin makes them inferior — that they are lazy, stupid, undeserving. Over the generations, my ancestors and I have been encouraged to feel confident, even arrogant, in our rights. We are entitled. My Indigenous friends and colleagues, on the other hand, have spent their lives being convinced of their unworthiness. Just as it has taken generations to construct this epistemology, it takes time to deconstruct it. Time, thoughtfulness, research, conversation — all are necessary for unlearning. My work in the Prairie Habitat Garden has provided me with the time to think, to research, and to converse.

I am attempting to make myself someone worth reconciling with (Cappello 2018). I will describe the garden, the original intent, and how three different concepts of land ownership and different ways of relating to place have challenged my thinking about and work in the Prairie Habitat Garden. I consider how the garden might perhaps support reconciliation. Why only "perhaps reconciliation"? Reconciliation involves at least two parties. It is a relational act. I must make myself worthy, such that the other party will be willing to reconcile. The burden for reconciliation must not be on those who have been wronged. Rather, as Michael Cappello (2018: n.p.) noted about the teacher candidates he will work with:

> How will these things help students move from voyeurs, from

sympathy (at best), move from an arm's length, content only understanding of residential schools and the invitation to reconcile... toward
bearing witness, toward feeling the weight of their own implications
in these stories and systems, to becoming the kinds of people, that
might be worth reconciling with?

Thus, I see that my role in reconciliation is to re-make myself into someone
worth reconciling with.

LOCATING THE PRAIRIE HABITAT GARDEN: UNLEARNING AND RELEARNING

I put my hands into the soil, dig deep around a blade of crabgrass, find the
rhizome, and gently tug on it. About fifteen centimetres away, a blade of
grass disappears under the loosened soil. There is satisfaction in this work, of
removing invasive grasses from a piece of land we are trying to reclaim as native
prairie. After an afternoon of this work, my back is sore from bending over;
my skin exudes a pleasant odour caused by the sun, fresh air, and wind. This is
good work, though. This is a project I have invested time and energy into. It
is penance, in some way, for being a white settler on this land. But as penance,
it fails. I am not suffering. I enjoy the materiality of gardening.

The Prairie Habitat Garden is a project originally designed by a group of
teacher candidates and is on the University of Saskatchewan campus, which
is on Treaty Six Territory, the Traditional Homeland of the Neyinowak
Inniwak (Cree), Saulteaux, Dakota, Nakota, Lakota, and Métis peoples. The
purpose of the garden was to show off the beauty of the prairies. There are far
too many city and farm yards with non-native, invasive, high-maintenance
grasses, tidily clipped, and neatly fringed with exotic flowers. On the other
hand, the random proliferation of subtle hues and brilliant colours of the
native prairie, or the cold hard snow crystals on ice ridges in winter — this is
true beauty for those who consider the prairie to be home. But, many white
people on the prairies remain unconvinced that this stolen land is worthy
in and of itself. This was the original purpose of the garden — to support
attitudinal change to the land and to demonstrate a way to re-wild the city,
one yard, one park at a time.

The purpose immediately metamorphosed to also recognize the people who
lived here from time immemorial. This land — the prairies, Saskatchewan, the
whole of Canada — was not empty space that was waiting to be developed
when Europeans arrived. Rather it was a place occupied by stories, emotions,

and beings (see Resor 2010 for defining place as storied and space as real estate to be developed). The puzzle for the Prairie Habitat Garden illustrates this. The students and I chose an area that was "empty" — it comprised a few elm trees but was mostly lawn grass, which is a mix of very similar grass species, some which thrive in the sun, some in the shade, and all requiring a lot of water and fertilizers to grow. The grasses are not native to this part of the world, but the elms are. The elms were occasionally occupied by birds, surveilling the people who walked by. There were no animal beings that we noticed on the surface of the grass. But we did not look closely. We, the teacher candidates and I, deemed this space empty, devoid of stories, emotions, and, other than the grass and elms, devoid also of living beings. We, fallible humans that we are, determined that this was a good space to enrich with native prairie plants, to enrich with flowers, which we thought would bring insects, birds, and who knows what else. We judged this to be empty space and wanted to develop it, to turn this space into a place.

Our original goals have been met: a plethora of other beings have come to the garden, making it their home, their place. People walk along the trails and speculate about the flowers and the replicas of Indigenous artifacts. They rest here on their breaks; they eat their lunches here. One of my colleagues has taken up encouraging a variety of bird species to eat from her hand.

Initially, however, we took a white settler attitude, judging this place to be empty, needing development. Was our judgment a good one, because we were returning this "empty" (but colonized) space to a much more biodiverse area, reclaiming the space/place for those prairie plants that had been here, some of which are now on provincial endangered species lists? Were we, indeed, enriching this place with stories and feelings? European settlers deemed the biodiverse places of North America to need domestication. They wanted to tame the wilderness, eliminate unnecessary or dangerous animals, and plant crops that they knew how to use. I think that we are doing something better in the garden, and I take enriching biodiversity in a colonized place as my rationale. Given the current state of humanity's relationship with the planet, I did not feel that doing nothing was an option. Nonetheless, our taking up the space/place illustrated the value judgments that humans make and supported my understanding of what white settlers decided to see and believe when they arrived here on the Indigenous Land of Turtle Island. Although Turtle Island is an English expression and represents the creation story of only some First Nations, it is a term that acknowledges the first inhabitants of the land. Thus,

I have chosen the term Turtle Island to represent this land, when writing from my (versus my ancestor's) perspective.

In the ongoing work in the Prairie Habitat Garden, I struggle to eliminate invasive species. An invasive species is one that takes over, crowds out other species, and limits biodiversity. There are non-native yet non-invasive species, such as the dandelion. Dandelions, brought to North America from Europe, squeeze themselves in between native plants, innocuous, adapting well, and contributing to this geography. At first, in my need to control, to ensure that only native plants lived here, I weeded out all the dandelions. Dandelions flower early (and continue to flower throughout the summer), often taking up the niche of early flowering endangered native plants by providing pollen for spring bees. Dandelions are not a problem for biodiversity; they have settled in, provide essential ecosystem services, and do not crowd out native species. Indeed, Indigenous Peoples quickly adopted dandelions, including this plant in their food and pharmacopeia (Karst 2010: 9). The crabgrass, on the other hand, is a problem. It is persistent, grows fast and tall, has tough cell walls making it difficult for animals to digest, and spreads both vegetatively by rhizomes and with seeds. Is there a metaphor here? Are some white settlers like crabgrass and others like dandelions? Or are all settlers thieves, taking land from the rightful occupants? This brought me to research settler colonialism to learn how it affects places.

LOCATING SETTLER COLONIALISM AND CONCEPTS OF LAND OWNERSHIP

Colonialism is about taking the resources of another place, also often taking the bodies of the people of that place (Wolfe 2006). Colonialism will result in the destruction of Indigenous cultures, including the loss of language and spiritual practices. Scholars have differentiated between colonialism, in which colonizers steal the resources and leave, and settler colonialism, in which colonizers steal the resources but also stay and occupy the land. Settler colonialism involves removing the Indigenous Peoples from the land so that the land can be stolen (Calderon 2014; Tuck, McKenzie, and McCoy 2014; Wolfe 2006). Patrick Wolfe noted that settler colonialism was genocide: it involved the destruction of Indigenous Peoples to legitimate the new occupants. Part of the legitimation included storying Indigenous Peoples as less than, as inferior to, the settlers.

Gardner Seawright (2014) argues that anthropocentrism, the belief that humans are superior to all other entities, enabled the creation of hierarchies within humans (men over women, white men over people of colour, etc.), which then led to ideas about the right to own the bodies of others and the land. Seawright cites John Locke, an influential seventeenth-century English philosopher and the "Father of Liberalism," who argued that land has no value in and of itself; rather it is a man's labour on the land that gives the land value, and creating that value gives the man property rights over that land. It is for this reason, among others, that Europeans determined the Americas to be empty, populated only by "savages." Indigenous Peoples did not labour on the land in the proper European fashion, and so they were low on the hierarchy. Instead of being the master of the land and bending it to their will, Indigenous Peoples lived with the land. Believing in the superiority of certain humans over others leads to the exploitation and "development" of the land in the interest of those certain humans.

Europeans brought with them to Turtle Island two different concepts of land ownership. The first concept is that of the commons: land that belongs to the community and is used communally. Raj Patel (2009) described how, prior to the lords enclosing common land (privatizing it) for their own use, the commons ensured the survival of the communities. Peasants worked out grazing rights among themselves, and they could hunt and fish on communal land. But, with the widespread acceptance of Locke's political philosophy and as European societies transitioned from feudalism to capitalism, the commons were enclosed. The peasants were forcibly removed from lands and forced into property relationships with the elites. Once the people who had shared the land could no longer graze their animals or hunt and gather on the lord's private property, they began to starve.

This new system was the second concept of land ownership that was taken to the Americas: the idea of private property or personal ownership of land. This idea is still sacred to us today. White immigrants, arriving to settle in North America, were not interested in communal ownership of land. Most of them were poor and facing starvation if they remained in their homelands because of the privatization of previously common land. Thus, they wanted to own property, and they had come to this so-called empty land to gain it. That this land was occupied was an inconvenience to them, but one they could get past. They took up the official proscribed government rhetoric: this was empty land; it was space awaiting development.

Indigenous epistemology and concepts of ownership are not commensurate with Western epistemology. Indigenous attitudes toward land were neither about communal ownership nor about private ownership. Rather, humans were one species among many, sharing the land, water, and air. As Annie Peaches said, "The land is always stalking people. The land makes people live right. The land looks after us. The land looks after people" (cited in Basso 1995: 38). The land is not a "place" because of human stories — it exists regardless of humans, and their attachments to that space/place. Within Turtle Island epistemologies, the land is not able to be bought, sold, or stolen; rather, we humans and all other beings are part of it. As we consider how we will live on and with the land, we must consider all the other beings that are here.

North America was not empty and awaiting development. The humans who were here engaged in practices that meant that the land would be healthy for all species. For example, the Indigenous Peoples of the great plains regularly burned the overburden of grass on the prairies, the leaf litter that could, over several years, become tinder-dry fuel for fast-moving, intensely hot grass fires. The regular controlled burning, done in early spring, prevented dangerous uncontrolled grass fires in later summer. These fires were lit before the arrival of ground-nesting birds, thus ensuring their nests were not destroyed. The fires would have released carbon and nitrogen back to the soil for other plants to use. Prairie grasses and forbs, with their deep water-seeking roots, would come back quickly after an early spring fire.

I seek to understand an Indigenous epistemology, one rooted in notions of humans as living with the land. I have learned and continue to learn how we might have to fundamentally change to have a healthier future. My work, having my hands in the earth, supporting plant life, getting to know the plants that grew here on this land on the campus of the University of Saskatchewan, supports my developing understanding of land-based practices and reciprocal and ethical social relations. I am learning that no individual species exists outside of relationships. As I struggle to introduce a new species to the garden, I am learning that the soil will have organisms in it (or not) that support that species. For example, the plant known as paintbrush will only live with other native plant species, such as June grass. A research project currently taking place in the Prairie Habitat Garden examines an introduced species of beetle; in its country of origin this beetle eats earthworms. Now that earthworms live on Turtle Island, there is food for this beetle. But, will the beetle also eat other organisms? Will it, perhaps, outcompete some of its Indigenous cousins, as it tries out other potential food sources? All organisms live in relationship.

As biodiversity increases in the garden, there is less and less bare ground, thus providing rich locations for humus to build up. In the meantime, the soil does not yet have the rich smell that an ecosystem should have, the smell that comes from healthy fungus and microbe-rich soil. When mushrooms begin to erupt, when the trees begin to have bracket fungi, when I suspect the trees are communicating through their rootlets and fungal friends (Wohlleben 2015), and when I can put my nose close to the earth and smell the rich biodiversity, I will rest more easily with the work. I am trying to live in humility, supporting the ecosystem in developing in healthy and biodiverse ways, encouraging all those species that need support, and controlling those that are overly aggressive in ways that I am allowed to (i.e., no fires, no large grazers such as bison).

LOCATING INDIGENOUS BELIEFS ABOUT RELATIONSHIPS

Indigenous epistemology centres on relationships: the idea that we all live in relation to each other and the world around us, that we are all interconnected (Bowers 2001, 2010; Cajete 2005; Deloria 2001; Ritchie 2015; Wildcat 2001). As Vine Deloria (2001: 2) argued: "The best description of Indian metaphysics was the realization that the world, and all its possible experience, contributed a social reality, a fabric of life in which everything had the possibility of intimate knowing relationships because, ultimately, everything was related." Gregory Cajete (2005: 70) agreed, noting that: "*Mitakuye Oyasin* (we are all related) is a Lakota phrase that captures an essence of tribal education because it reflects the understanding that our lives are truly and profoundly connected to other people and the physical world."

The hare takes up a place in the garden because of its relationship to the plants, the soil, and the sun. The crab spider takes on the colour of the flower it hides in; the flowers use colour or scent to draw pollinators to ensure their reproduction, but inadvertently provide homes for crab spiders. The pollinators carry the pollen to fertilize other flowers and use their collection of pollen for making food for their young, who can inadvertently become food for crab spiders. All the organisms use this web of life for food and reproduction. It is the webs, the delicate lines that connect us all, that are important, not so much the individual nodes. In Western science, the focus is on the nodes, on the objects; relationships are studied as side effects. The focus on relationships, rather than on individual entities, means that Indigenous epistemology expands its focus outward; the Western focus on individual entities narrows to smaller and smaller particles that make up the entities.

As an example, a summer student and I shifted our perspective from enti-ties to relationships as she related her observations (and relationship with) four baby warblers. The student worked daily in the garden, hands in the soil, pulling out invasive species, and noticing other organisms around her. After finding a nest with four eggs in it, she made checking the nest her first act in the morning. The parents hovered nearby as she peeked into the nest, returning to their eggs the moment she left. The eggs hatched into four tiny naked bodies with huge beaks. When the student approached the nest, the babies would sense her presence and open their beaks, awaiting food. The student felt she had developed a relationship with these little ones. Her focus on the entities, the individuals, allowed her to care about them and to develop a relationship with them. This went on for about a week. Then one day, the baby birds, who were not nearly ready to fledge, were gone. We were forced to recognize that there were other relationships going on in the garden. Some baby birds will grow up to be adults, and others will be food for crows. Thus, our interactions in the garden expanded beyond the narrow focus on the birds as entities, in relation with ourselves, to the inter-relationships among the different species in the garden. It is not that entities do not exist in Indigenous ontologies, nor that relationships do not exist in Western ontologies; rather, relationships are foregrounded in Indigenous ontologies, and entities in Western ontologies.

I want to represent these inter-species relationships in the garden, but I am also learning about Indigenous Peoples and thinking about how their stories and perspectives can be represented. My Indigenous colleagues at the University of Saskatchewan have provoked, lobbied for, and demanded change in teacher education, and as a result, all teacher candidates are taught how they have been socialized into roles in a patriarchal, heteronormative, white supremacist society. The hope is that they will come to understand this and take this knowledge into classrooms to challenge stereotypes and discrimination. This is hard emotional work. I have been working on it much longer than the teacher candidates, and I am often "schooled" by my Indigenous colleagues. One of my colleagues explained to me: "This university was built on the bones of my people." The garden is not a place devoid of people, just as the prairies were not devoid of people. There is a human history that took place on this land, and we become increasingly aware of it despite attempts at erasure. The Prairie Habitat Garden has its own (recent) history, but the history of this piece of land stretches back long before teacher candidates suggested we re-inhabit this place with native plants. It was land where Indigenous Peoples would have spent their summers, high on the riverbank, near creeks that flowed down to the river, down past and through saskatoon berries, choke cherries, wolf willow, and buffalo berries. There would have been a plethora of building materials, foods, and medicines. Deer would have been present in all seasons; fish would have swum in the river. These people were killed, and their culture was destroyed by various means — mostly by disease and starvation — to make room for white people to build their glorious buildings for "higher learning."

There is an irony in my taking up this work. I am not Indigenous. I have read Indigenous scholars, I have worked with Indigenous Elders, and I am able to ask my Indigenous colleagues about the generalizations I am making. It is a bit frightening to me how often I talk to Indigenous teacher candidates about attitudes toward land, or perhaps about one particular artifact in the garden, the celestial circle, and see them shift their perspectives on what the land is. Who am I to teach this?

And yet, I must ensure the garden includes the people who were here, what they believed, and what they did. To ignore it is to continue the narrative of an empty land. The garden must include the richness of Indigenous cultures prior to the arrival of settlers. The land and its biodiversity are integral to the lives and values of Indigenous Peoples, and the garden is meant to honour that. With support from Indigenous Elders, replicas of Indigenous artifacts have been built into the garden to support teaching and learning about Indigenous Peoples. There is, for example, a replica of an Earth turtle in the garden. With the assistance of an Indigenous Elder, a group of daycare children and Grade 4 students carried and smudged soil and stones; under the direction of the Elder, the shape of the turtle emerged. We planted sage, strawberries, dotted blazing star, and blue grama grass on it. It is now obscured in mid-summer by the blaze of colour from surrounding sunflowers, bergamot, giant hyssop, and raspberries. The story of Turtle Island, as told by Robin Wall Kimmerer (2014), illustrates the concept of cooperation among all the animals. Kimmerer described how the woman who fell from the sky was caught by geese, and how the turtle offered its back for her to rest on, and how the other animals worked to increase the size of the turtle so that all could live together on the land. As Kimmerer notes, this contrasts sharply with the biblical story of the Garden of Eden, where God gave man dominion over nature and all of the animals. It is interesting to consider how these very different stories have guided our understanding of and relationship with nature.

A recent addition to the garden has been a celestial circle (King 2017).

There are many forms of circles found on the prairies, most of them named as medicine wheels. However, there are many different kinds of circles of stones on the great plains with different interior partitions. Some are tipi rings, the stones left from those placed to hold down the outer edge of the tipi. These might also have a small central circle for the hearth or heart of the family home. Some circles, not tipi rings, are sectioned into quadrants. Natasha King noted:

> The medicine wheel symbol, of two equal length lines crossed inside a circle dividing the space equally into quarters, is used in many Indigenous and non-Indigenous teachings but the origins of the symbol are not that clear. It has been found in art and the archaeological record from almost every continent. In Europe, it is often referred to as the Celtic cross, Odin's cross, Gnostic cross or solar cross. (2017: 43–44)

Judie Bopp, Michael Bopp, Lee Brown, Phil Lane, and Patricia Lucas (1984) developed the symbol into a medicine wheel, with the four quadrants representing the whole person with each quadrant representing one interrelated aspect of a healthy person. To remain healthy, one must care for all four aspects — the spirit, the physical body, the emotions, and the intellect.

Other circles on the prairies, however, are much more complex than the quadrants and tipi ring circles. Some have more lines and circles, and some have been found to track the sun and the stars. A celestial circle (King 2017) might mark sunrise and sunset for both the solstices, and some celestial circles also track major stars. As well, celestial circles often have a line of stones indicating the direction of travel to reach the next celestial circle. How was this done, considering how far apart these circles often are? What is especially interesting is that some of these circles are about 5,300 years old (King 2017: 39), which makes these ones as old or older than Stonehenge, which also tracks the solstices. Indigenous Peoples of the North American Great Plains had a sophisticated knowledge of the skies at the same time or before the Europeans were tracking the sun so systematically.

The celestial circle in the Prairie Habitat Garden is a miniaturized replica of one that is in the Moose Mountain area in Saskatchewan. The original circle has a central cairn that is nine metres in diameter and one and a half metres high, holding eighty tonnes of rock. Rays extend 150 metres to the north, 450 metres to the southwest, and more than 600 metres to the south (King 2017: 43). These are the current dimensions. Reports suggest it was originally much larger. The cairn would have stood out; it would have been obvious that it had been erected intentionally. Yet, stones have been stolen from it. There is an arrogance to someone who takes a souvenir from what must be another people's sacred site.

Working with graduate student Natasha King as she researched and built the replica of the celestial circle in the garden, I have learned of the complexity of the understandings that Indigenous Peoples had of the skies. When I describe the replica to teacher candidates, I always hear surprise, I sometimes learn of ignorance of basic astronomy (what is a solstice?), and I almost always hear excitement from the Indigenous students. Many of the Indigenous students are proud of their heritage, which has not been represented in the curriculum. Indigenous Peoples have been absent from the curriculum, appearing occasionally only as dangerous or sad characters. To hear of their own history, to read it on the land, is exciting. And it serves to school the white students as it has schooled me.

I am learning through this work. I am sharing this learning with teacher candidates. I am hoping to be a person worth reconciling with. The hard emotional and intellectual work will be ongoing, but will, I hope, always be moving toward increasingly respectful relationships among all peoples.

CONCLUSION

As noted, I am occasionally schooled by my Indigenous colleagues. I am grateful that they are gentle in their approach. As I teach teacher candidates that they must act, that they cannot passively accept the ongoing damage that systemic racism does to Indigenous Peoples, I can assure them that they will stumble and will make mistakes, and I can tell them of my latest mistakes. For example, last summer, in my ramblings in the native prairies around the province, I found bones and brought them back to the garden. I thought of how these would provoke young children's imagination and stories. An Indigenous colleague asked me about them, noting that some Indigenous friends of hers thought this was disrespectful to the animals. Whoops. I am learning; I am learning that this is a complex task to negotiate. However, as I learn of this complexity, I am also learning that different people have different ideas. I asked my colleague what I should do to treat the bones more respectfully. She said that she, herself, did not think having the bones there to provoke children's thinking about the land was disrespectful. She thought of it as an ongoing sign of respect, ensuring the animal continued to serve a role in the ecosystem. This difference in understandings has been described by Deloria (2001: 3), who noted "the metaphysics possessed by *most* American Indian tribes"; I have added the emphasis on "most" to show that not everyone, and not every group, has a common understanding. Deloria (2001: 6) also speaks of the Indigenous concept of suspended judgement, in which conclusions about the world are not thought to be "correct," but are, rather, known to be tentative, potentially wrong, open to modification, or to be held in parallel to another potential "conclusion." I take this concept up regarding my own conclusions, beliefs, and ideas. Not only *could* I be wrong, but I *am* often wrong. The world is complex, and the people in it are complex. It is in relationships that we learn and continue to learn. We must not ever arrogantly assume that we know, or that there is only one knowable truth.

And thus, my work to make myself someone that Indigenous Peoples would be willing to reconcile with is ongoing and humbling. It is hard work, both physically in the garden and emotionally in my thinking. Every day I learn. I am fortunate to have a place in which to labour to learn. The Prairie Habitat Garden is becoming richer in biodiversity, and it is also becoming a richer resource for teaching about Indigenous values and perspectives. It is one act that I engage in toward making myself someone worth reconciling with. And, I use it in my teaching of teachers, inviting them to consider how they might become people worth reconciling with.

REFERENCES

Basso, Keith H. 1995. *Wisdom Sits in Places: Landscape and Language Among the Western Apache.* Albuquerque, NM: University of New Mexico Press.

Bopp, Judie, Michael Bopp, Lee Brown, Phil Lane, and Patricia Lucas. 1984. *The Sacred Tree.* Lethbridge, AB: Four Worlds International Institute for Human and Community Development.

Bowers, Chet A. 2001. "Addressing the Double Binds in Educating for an Ecologically Sustainable Future." *International Journal of Leadership in Education,* 4, 1: 87–96.

Cajete, Gregory. 2005. "American Indian Epistemologies." *New Directions for Student Services,* 109: 69–78.

Calderon, Dolores. 2014. "Speaking Back to Manifest Destinies: A Land Education-Based Approach to Critical Curriculum Inquiry." *Environmental Education Research,* 20, 1: 24–36.

Cappello, Michael. 2018. *Panel on Reconciliation.* Panel presented at annual conference of the Canadian Society for the Studies of Education. Regina, SK: May 27–30, 2018.

Daschuk, James. 2013. *Clearing the Plains: Disease, the Politics of Starvation, and the Loss of Aboriginal Life.* Regina, SK: University of Regina Press.

Deloria, Vine Jr. 2001. "American Indian Metaphysics." In V. Deloria, Jr., and D. Wildcat (eds.), *Power and Place: Indian Education in America.* Boulder, CO: Golden Press.

Karst, Amanda. 2010. *Conservation Value of the North American Boreal Forest from an Ethnobotanical Perspective.* Vancouver, BC: Canadian Boreal Initiative, David Suzuki Foundation, and Boreal Songbird Initiative.

Kimmerer, Robin Wall. 2014. *Braiding Sweet Grass: Indigenous Wisdom, Scientific Knowledge and the Teaching of Plants.* Minneapolis, MN: Milkweed Editions.

King, Natasha. 2017. "Medicine Wheels and Celestial Circles: History, Symbolism and Teachings." Unpublished master's thesis, School of Environment and Sustainability, University of Saskatchewan.

Patel, Raj. 2009. *The Value of Nothing: Why Everything Costs So Much More Than We Think.* Toronto: HarperCollins Publishers.

Resor, Cynthia. 2010. "Place-Based Education: What Is Its Place in the Social Studies Classroom." *The Social Studies,* 101: 185–188.

Ritchie, Jenny. 2015. "Food Reciprocity and Sustainability in Early Childhood Care and Education in Aotearoa New Zealand." *Australian Journal of Environmental Education,* 31, 1: 74–85.

Seawright, Gardner. 2014. "Settler Traditions of Place: Making Explicit the Epistemological Legacy of White Supremacy and Settler Colonialism for Place-Based Education." *Educational Studies,* 50, 6: 554–572. DOI: 10.1080/00131946.2014.965938.

Truth and Reconciliation Commission Final Report. 2015. *Honouring the Truth, Reconciling for the Future, Volume 6, Reconciliation.* Montreal and Kingston: McGill/Queen's University Press. <http://www.trc.ca/websites/trcinstitution/index.php?p=890>.

Tuck, Eve, Marcia McKenzie, and Kate McCoy. 2014. "Land Education: Indigenous, Postcolonial, and Decolonizing Perspectives on Place and Environmental Education Research." *Environmental Education Research,* 20, 1: 1–23.

Wildcat, Daniel. 2001. "Indigenizing Education: Playing to Our Strengths." In V. Deloria, Jr., and D. Wildcat (eds.), *Power and Place: Indian Education in America.* Golden, CO: Fulcrum Publishing.

Wohlleben, Peter. 2015. *The Hidden Life of Trees: What They Feel, How They Communicate.* Vancouver, BC: Greystone Books.

Wolfe, Patrick. 2006. "Settler Colonialism and the Elimination of the Native." *Journal of Genocide Research,* 8, 4: 387–409. DOI: 10.1080/14623520601056240.

Chapter Eleven

HOLES AND GREY

KHODI DILL

The poems presented here focus on my identity as an immigrant of colour and on the importance of reconciliation to my connection to the land on which I live. I have always felt a sense of empathy toward Indigenous Peoples, whose land was appropriated by settlers. My own people were brought to this part of the world forcibly by the very same settler stock. Our connections to the land are different, but our relationships to the settler community are similarly complicated, strained, and tied up in the colonization of lands and bodies here and abroad. As a Bahamian-Canadian, I certainly feel a responsibility to uphold both truth and reconciliation as the main tenets of my art and practice. I consciously choose to focus on truth, the element of this work that is often left by the wayside, as I incorporate counter-narratives in my poetry and attempt to promote solidarity between Indigenous Peoples and non-Indigenous Canadians of all backgrounds. As of now, we are living on the land together. I believe that immigrants of colour are specially positioned to promote the work of reconciliation through new or revised settler perspectives regarding the land, as our connections to the land are more recently formed and con-textualized differently than the historical white settler perspective. This is the type of contextualized perspective that I try to put forth in my social justice poetry, particularly in my poems "Grey" and "Holes."

HOLES

So Mike Holmes is rebuilding First Nations housing; he's makin' a pledge to "make it right."
Ain't that your job, Mr. Harper?
Please, excuse my spite, but do the rules not apply to the "red-skinned" masses

cuz they tote eagle feathers and burn sweet grasses?
It took you two days to hit flooded white communities and been two years since Nicky lost his immunity
To the mould in his basement that grows where it's dim
Cuz each year in his basement you could go for a swim
And his mama stopped tryin'; she just lets it in
And embraces her boy in the dry spot

Mr. Harper, this is real. This is real; I didn't write it
I'm just tellin' the story of the very undelighted and the very blindsided by this tragedy
It's tragic, but they go unprovided for; it's the last thing they was hopin' for
If it was you I wouldn't ask what you was dopin' for; maybe now you understand what
I'm mopin' for, and if you're not gonna help, just say so
Cuz right now, they don't know what they're copin' for
And why bother? I mean, your inaction speaks louder than your residential school
apology
See, Mama is weepy and the kids are sleepy, but awake cuz their house is so damn creaky
that it's almost creepy; you promised 'em a house but they'd rather a tipi
Maybe then they'd stay dry and outta the cold
At least then the roof would only have one hole
Mr. Harper, when the holes in your promise become the holes in the dyke
It's your job to plug 'em — thanks anyways, Mike
Now somebody tell me — how is it that our 1st Nations people live like 2nd class citizens in 3rd world conditions in the UN's 4th best country in the world to live? Somebody ask that question on W-5 cuz out in Treaty number 6, they just tryin' to survive. Hungry for 7th heaven but they already 8 — a belly full o' lies; little Nicky almost died many times. Who says only a cat has 9 lives? So he breathes, but he cries — no surprise. Dry his eyes. That's ten reasons why we should try!
I mean, you said these rights would last just as long as the river. If not, it turns out you are the "Indian giver."
But whatever you decide behind closed doors, if you take their rights, then they oughta have yours.

Oh you forgot that your rights were Treaty Rights, too?
Forgot that native peoples weren't lesser than you?
Forgot that this land is still on loan and you default but reserve the right to
cast the first stone?
Excuse my tone
Mr. Harper, you can take my house but not my home, and my pride is still alive
We traded land for rights, and if you wanna trade back,
Start with Sussex Drive.

GREY

I am made from black and white so my essence is grey — how flattering
Though all things considered, there is at least a smattering
Of blond hair and blue eyes, though by a look you'd never guess
Cuz I am brown-skinned, therefore, my essence is "less"

They call me mulatto, from mule; well that's at least half-crass
It makes one parent a thoroughbred and the other an ass
So I am hoping these words become a thing of yesterday
But they mixed brown and white ice cream and called it moo-latte

When I was twelve, I won a contest at a Christian youth centre. Turns out the
winner got a free CD. I was thrilled, man. So the pastor took me into the back
room and took one look at me and he said, "You look like you like rap music."
I swallowed hard and thought to myself, *you're lucky you're right!*

They try to pinhole my future so I'm tryin' to make plans
That don't involve b-ball, beat-box or break-dance
I'm tired of Sandra Bullock movies, with clichés of white saviours
Savin' poor black kids from poor black behaviours

It reminds me of back when they used blackface.
Thought the straight-haired blacks musta been a new race
And you'd think that new producers would be more creative
But the *Twilight* movies had a white play a native

When I was in Grade 4, the class bully called me and my best friend niggers.

It was sad, but strange cuz my best friend was Indian. But anyway, we told the
teacher and she made everything better, God bless her. She slapped the bully
on the wrist and said, "The word is Negro!"
My Indian friend thought he was black for three years.
If we're buildin' a nation, then pain is in the mortar
I'm watchin' grasses get greener even south of the border
They got a black man in office; the paradox means we equal
But my life hasn't changed, so I am waiting for the sequel

I don't wanna be the same, I'm just tryin' to be a peer
But whether black, brown, Muslim, disabled or queer
Although we are citizens, we're still second-class
We're still outside the circle, just others in the mass

They say Jim Crow's dead — that we're free from separation. But if you come
to my town and you wanna find the First Nations just look on the west side.
See, when they wrote segregation out of policy, they left it in economy and
wrote it into geography.

Beneath 22nd, between the alphabets
Where eastside visits are eastside regrets
I never cease to be amazed how soon we forget
Racism's still alive, we haven't beat it yet.

I'm still watched at the store, still my freedom's rescinding
— Still the police call me bro, condescending
I prayed that this poem could have a good ending
But as it turns out, we're broken, not blending
And breaking, not mending

I'm still a little less than kin, though my heart is more than kind
And now that I'm finally proud to be black, the world is colourblind.

Chapter Twelve

CONCLUSION

RANJAN DATTA

All Canadians must take responsibility for reconciliation.

—Erica Lee (Cree First Nation and one of the Idle No More
founders)

Reconciliation requires engaging in an ongoing, complex, and dynamic process grounded in a lifetime commitment, which occurs at the levels of the individual, family, community, and nation. As many Indigenous scholars, Elders, and Knowledge Keepers have suggested, our responsibility and actions for reconciliation can empower all of us (Indigenous, settlers, and newcomers/immigrants), and it is our hope that the stories and experiences shared in this book will inspire and empower all of us to evoke visions and actions of reconciliation in our everyday practice. Through these stories of cross-cultural activities, the contributors begin to answer the questions raised here: *How can I learn the meaning of reconciliation? Why does reconciliation matter to me? Is reconciliation an end goal to be achieved, or is it a process? Why am I responsible for the meaningful implementation of reconciliation? How am I benefiting from Indigenous perspectives on reconciliation?*

How can I learn the meaning of reconciliation? Reconciliation must be defined by Indigenous Peoples, and they are the ones who should lead the way. As non-Indigenous people (i.e., settlers, newcomers/immigrants, and refugees) we have a responsibility to learn and to follow Indigenous Peoples' guidance in our practice. This begins with decolonizing ourselves and our institutions, learning about Indigenous ways of being, and reflecting on how we need to treat and how we have treated those who have been our friends, neighbours, and hosts for centuries. It also means heeding the TRC calls for actions for the meaningful implementation of reconciliation. Perhaps most importantly, it means focusing on advancing Indigenous sovereignty, rather than blithely continuing to assert settler-colonial control over land and natural resource management. Reconciliation is capacity building for all of us.

Learning from Indigenous Elders and Knowledge Keepers can build our capacity as individuals and as communities. Building capacity means accepting individual responsibility for reconciliation and belongingness. For instance, Warda Rusheeye, who is originally from Somalia and has been in Canada for twelve years working with Syrian youth as a recreation coordinator, says reconciliation means "that I need to learn about the history of Canada, and what happened to Indigenous Peoples" (CBC 2016: 1). She defines responsibility by saying, "I hold a responsibility of two ways — to educate myself and my community, and do the work of standing next to Indigenous Peoples to make sure that reconciliation happens, according to their rights" (CBC 2016: 1). She explains her responsibility for reconciliation:

> I need to continuously learn from the people rather than learn from books and institutions. I need to make sure that my people, from my ancestral country, as well as other Muslim community newcomers, would learn about it along the way. I need to make sure that the message goes across correctly. And then I need to make sure that we are standing next to Indigenous Peoples while they're doing this work to make sure reconciliation is happening properly. (CBC 2016: 1)

Another new refugee, Ahmad Moussa, from Saskatoon, Saskatchewan, Canada, describes his responsibility for reconciliation as follows:

> I have a responsibility as an individual and as an outsider of this territory. My role is that I stand beside the Indigenous people of this territory. Their struggle is to restore and recover their right to self-determination. It starts with respect. Respect has not been the essence of the relationship between Indigenous peoples and the state. (CBC 2016: 2)

Moussa further explains his understanding of taking responsibility for reconciliation as "what we need to do as individuals is to respect Indigenous Peoples of this territory — respect their beliefs, their cultures, their way of life, and to stand behind them as they recover that right. That to me is reconciliation"

(CBC 2016: 2). Warda Rusheeye and Ahmad Moussa clearly articulated that we need to learn the meanings of reconciliation from Indigenous Peoples in Canada. Their interest in learning can inspire all of us to rethink and take our responsibilities seriously, which creates hope for new possibilities for building a cross-cultural bridge among Indigenous Peoples, settlers, immigrants, and refugees in Canada.

Why does reconciliation matter to me? Reconciliation is a lifelong unlearning and relearning process. It is a space that empowers and in which to make claims, and so is always open to revision. For this to happen, however, it is critical that the question of Indigenous Land Rights, Indigenous justice, and Indigenous sovereignty be broached. It is not necessarily the case that reconciliation has replaced Indigenous claims for sovereignty and land restitution, as Dirk Moses (2011: 157) has suggested; nor is it the case that the politics of reconciliation are counter to the politics of self-determination and sovereignty, as many critics have put forward. Rather, as Paul Muldoon and Andrew Schaap (2011: 196) argue, the politics of reconciliation and sovereignty are not only complementary but are necessarily invoked together if we are to be guided by the ideal of mutual recognition. As we have learned from Indigenous Peoples and the TRC, reconciliation is a significant learning process for all of us, and it has to be led by Indigenous Peoples. For instance, Alexa Potashnik, a founder of Black Space Winnipeg, thinks that reconciliation is the notion of self-determination: "If you're going to try to address such a damaging effect on what you did to people for generations, then you have to start with raw dialogue and make people feel uncomfortable" (CBC 2016: 2). Another youth, Ahmad Moussa, originally from Palestine, says, "As a Palestinian, we are Indigenous people, but my presence on this territory means I'm still part of the system that is colonizing Indigenous people" (CBC 2016: 2). Senator Sinclair (2016: n.p.) questions "what is the role of adult newcomers to Canada in the ongoing work of reconciliation if they are not connected to this history?" He suggests that "if you feel connected to the future of this country, and if you feel responsible for the future, then you need to care about reconciliation, for the sake of the future of this country." He further explained that reconciliation learning is applicable to all Canadians, regardless of whether they are newcomers or not. We all need to learn and act for meaningful reconciliation.

Is reconciliation an end goal to be achieved, or is it a process? As Indigenous scholars, Elders, and Knowledge Keepers have explained, reconciliation is not a concept or a tool; it is a lifelong process. It does not have fixed meanings — its meanings vary from community to community, generation to generation, and time to time. Ongoing learning and respect require that we recognize and appreciate that individuals and communities are at different places in their journeys of healing and reconciliation. In our (non-Indigenous) efforts and actions, we must continue to create spaces for discussion, and face issues of racism and privilege openly — even though these conversations are challenging, difficult, emotional, and uncomfortable for some, requiring inner and outer work.

Reconciliation is more than a single event. To be fully realized, everyone will need to engage in genuine forms of learning, relationship building, and advocacy. We have all been called upon — by the TRC, residential school Survivors, and legacy holders — to live well, together. As education for reconciliation becomes more commonplace, perhaps we will see a reconceptualizing of our education system — reconciling the structures — toward reconciliation for education. In these ways, we would want our children, all children, and future generations to be educated in love and in community, with and on the land. Taking responsibility for reconciliation requires action, and it is through these actions that all of us, regardless of our colour, race, or creed can make a difference that affects the future. For me as an Indigenous educator, reconciliation is a continuous learning process about the colonial past and present, stories involving Indigenous lands (colonization), Indigenous children (Sixties Scoop, residential schools, etc.), and so on. Re-education will not only help us to understand Indigenous struggles but will also contribute to rebuilding relationships among Indigenous and non-Indigenous Peoples and is a much-needed part of meaningful reconciliation. Rebuilding relationships with the land is an integral part of reconciliation for settlers, immigrants, and refugees.

Why am I responsible for meaningful implementation of reconciliation? How am I benefiting from Indigenous perspectives on reconciliation? Indigenous scholars, Elders, and Knowledge Keepers suggest that for reconciliation to succeed, non-Indigenous (i.e., settlers and newcomers/immigrants) peoples must recognize their roles and responsibilities and actively support Indigenous Peoples' Land Rights and sovereignty. In reconciliation, we as settlers and immigrants have the responsibility to learn about Canadian colonial history, critical anti-racist education, decolonization, and Indigenous Land Rights in Canada. As the contributions to this book demonstrate, our responsible learning of reconciliation will not only educate us but also create our becomingness and empowerment.

The TRC has given us ninety-four calls to action to advance the process of reconciliation between Indigenous and non-Indigenous Peoples in Canada. Now is the time for all of us to get involved in re-educating ourselves, learning from Indigenous Peoples, and following their guidance on how we may better contribute to reconciliation through our work and research. The final report of the TRC suggests that:

> Together, Canadians must do more than just talk about reconcili-
> ation; we must learn how to *practise* reconciliation in our everyday
> lives — within ourselves and our families, and in our communities,
> governments, places of worship, schools, and workplaces. To do so
> constructively, Canadians must remain committed to the ongoing
> work of establishing and maintaining respectful relationships. (Truth
> and Reconciliation Commission of Canada 2015: 17)

Every person, organization, community, and institution in Canada has a responsibility to learn, support, and practise reconciliation according to the TRC's calls to action. The contributors to this volume have taken the call seriously and challenge everyone else in Canada to do the same; to make the call a priority and not a choice. This will require that all of us be open to conflict, to reflecting upon our identities, and perhaps most importantly, to building meaningful relationships. This also means engaging in cross-cultural practices and embracing diverse voices. As the TRC suggests, reconciliation is everyone's responsibility and coming together as a community allows us to build stronger relationships, build solidarity, recognize the accomplishments of the Indigenous community, educate ourselves about the history of Indigenous Peoples, and start the journey toward healing as a community.

REFERENCES

CBC. 2016. "What Does Reconciliation Mean to You?" Oct. 19. <https://www.cbc.ca/news/indigenous/what-does-reconciliation-mean-mb-1.3803617>.

Moses, Dirk. 2011. "Official Apologies, Reconciliation, and Settler Colonialism: Australian Indigenous Alterity and Political Agency." *Citizenship Studies*, 15, 2: 145–159.

Muldoon, Paul, and Andrew Schaap. 2011. "Confounded by Recognition: The Apology, the High Court and the Aboriginal Embassy in Australia." In A. Hirsch (ed.), *Theorising Post-Conflict Reconciliation: Agonism, Restitution and Repair*. New York and London: Routledge.

Sinclair, Murray. 2016. "Education Is Key to Reconciliation." Kairos. <https://www.kairoscanada.org/murray-sinclair-education-key-reconciliation>.

Truth and Reconciliation Commission of Canada. 2015. "Canada's Residential Schools: Reconciliation." The Final Report of the Truth and Reconciliation Commission of Canada, Volume 6. Montreal & Kingston: McGill-Queen's University Press.

INDEX